AMATEUR MEDIA AND PARTICIPATORY CULTURES

Amateur Media and Participatory Cultures aims to delineate the boundary line between today's amateur media practice and the canons of professional media and film practice. Identifying various feasible interpretative frameworks, from historical to anthropological perspectives, the volume proposes a critical language able to cope with amateur and new media's rapid technological and interpretative developments.

Conscious of the fact that amateur media continue to be seen as the benchmark of visual records of authentic rather than mass-media-derived events, Annamaria Motrescu-Mayes and Susan Aasman pay particular attention to the ways in which diverse sets of concepts of amateur media have now merged across global visual narratives and everyday communication protocols. Building on key research questions and content analysis in media and communication studies, they have assessed differences between professional and amateur media productions based on the ways in which the 'originators' of an image have been influenced by, or have challenged, their context of production. This proposes that technical skills, degrees of staging and/or censoring visual information, and patterns in media socialisation define central differences between professional and amateur media production, distribution and consumption.

The book's methodical and interdisciplinary approach provides valuable insights into the ways in which visual priming, cultural experiences and memory-building are currently shaped, stored and redistributed across new media technologies and visual channels.

Annamaria Motrescu-Mayes is an Affiliated Lecturer in new and digital media at the Department of Social Anthropology, University of Cambridge; Fellow and Tutor at Clare Hall; and a member of the Cambridge Digital Humanities Network and the Centre for the Study of Global Human Movement. She is the author of *Visual Histories of South Asia* (co-edited with Marcus Banks, 2017) and of *British Women Amateur Filmmakers: National Memories and Global Identities* (with Heather Norris Nicholson, 2018), and has written extensively on the theme of colonial amateur film practice and imperial studies. Motrescu-Mayes is also the founder of the Amateur Cinema Studies Network.

Susan Aasman is Associate Professor at the Media Studies Department and Director of the Centre for Digital Humanities at the University of Groningen. Her field of expertise is in media history, with a particular interest in amateur film and documentaries, digital culture and digital archives, web history and digital history. She was a senior researcher in the research project 'Changing Platforms of Ritualised Memory Practices: The Cultural Dynamics of Home Movie Making' (2012–2016). Together with Andreas Fickers and Jo Wachelder, Susan has co-edited *Materializing Memories: Dispositifs, Generations, Amateurs* (2018).

AMATEUR MEDIA AND PARTICIPATORY CULTURES

Film, Video, and Digital Media

Annamaria Motrescu-Mayes and Susan Aasman

Routledge
Taylor & Francis Group
LONDON AND NEW YORK

First published 2019
by Routledge
2 Park Square, Milton Park, Abingdon, Oxon OX14 4RN

and by Routledge
52 Vanderbilt Avenue, New York, NY 10017

Routledge is an imprint of the Taylor & Francis Group, an informa business

British Library Cataloguing in Publication Data
A catalogue record for this book is available from the British Library

Library of Congress Cataloging-in-Publication Data
Names: Motrescu-Mayes, Annamaria, author. | Aasman, Susan, author.
Title: Amateur media and participatory cultures : film, video, and digital media / Annamaria Motrescu-Mayes and Susan Aasman.
Description: London ; New York : Routledge, 2019. | Includes bibliographical references and index.
Identifiers: LCCN 2018029789 (print) | LCCN 2018047758 (ebook) | ISBN 9781315396149 (ebook) | ISBN 9781138226142 | ISBN 9781138226142 (hardback :alk. paper) | ISBN 9781138226159 (paperback :alk. paper) | ISBN 9781315396149(ebk)
Subjects: LCSH: Amateur films--Social aspects. | Video recordings--Social aspects. | Digital media--Social aspects.
Classification: LCC PN1995.9.S6 (ebook) | LCC PN1995.9.S6 M677 2019 (print) | DDC 384.55/8--dc23
LC record available at https://lccn.loc.gov/2018029789

ISBN: 978-1-138-22614-2 (hbk)
ISBN: 978-1-138-22615-9 (pbk)
ISBN: 978-1-315-39614-9 (ebk)

Typeset in Bembo
by Taylor & Francis Books

To Lisbon

CONTENTS

LIST OF FIGURES

FOREWORD

The word 'amateur' entered the English language with duelling definitions. Its first documented appearance in the late eighteenth-century harked back to the term's Latin roots, referring to 'one who loves … or has a fondness or taste for something'. But within two years it had acquired an additional meaning: 'one who cultivates anything as a pastime, as distinguished from one who prosecutes it professionally'. Two related but quite different definitions: one categorical, describing a mode of engagement; the other relative, marking out the terms of distinction.

This definitional instability would persist and intensify, with 'amateur' in the relative sense acquiring a disparaging connotation thanks to the steady growth of the professional classes in the nineteenth and twentieth centuries. This relativistic status was given a further twist by twenty-first-century challenges to hierarchies of expertise, with the 'wisdom of the crowd' destabilizing the professional and, by implication, its reciprocal 'amateur' … while not necessarily relieving it of its negative connotations.

Categorical uses of amateur as 'one who has a fondness for something' also experienced a shift in meaning. In this case, at least for some critics, environmental reconfigurations in the form of widespread distribution (especially the Internet, with its platforms and aggregators) have recast labours of love into inadvertent sites of exploitation. We upload our content and others make the profits. 'Amateur' has grown to include naiveté along with affection among its conditions, and in so doing, provoked an ongoing debate about the nature of pleasure and everyday agency.

The point is that 'amateur' is a slippery term that is bound up in fast-changing cultural practices – precisely why this book is so important. We can use the term 'amateur' to describe the scientists who developed photography in the early nineteenth century; the masses who simply pressed the button and let Kodak do the rest; and contributors to digital platforms such as Flickr and Shutterstock, whose images may generate income for others or earn income for themselves. Amateurs, all … but the meanings of the term differ significantly.

The digital turn has lowered the barrier to production across media forms, of course. Perhaps more profoundly, it has enabled global distribution and access. But these aren't the only factors reshaping the media landscape and our inherited notions of 'amateur'. Consider the ubiquity of smartphones and, with them, our production of still and moving images, sound and word … How should we frame the media expressions that ensue? As basic assertions of existence, like the hand prints adorning prehistoric caves? As elements in our identity construction and assertions of group membership? As encounters with the world, as familiar as speech was in the past? Or, indeed, as related to the 'love of something' at the root of amateur's definition?

The pervasiveness of surveillance cameras and sensors of various kinds, together their increasing autonomy, have combined further to unsettle familiar categories. How can the notion of amateur help us with the various streams of video that might document an event (police body cameras, car- and street-mounted surveillance cameras, bystander footage …)? What does it contribute to our understanding of the increasingly hybrid media texts that surround us and the quite different notions of agency behind them? And how, in light of all of these sources of production and recycling, might we reimagine the needs of cultural memory, the uses of the archive, and the nature of ephemerality?

As used in the pages that follow, the amateur takes on these and many more questions as a way of exploring the borders between the private and public, the personal and professional, as these binaries shapeshift and dissolve in a fast-changing cultural ecosystem. It offers a way to interrogate media practices epistemologically as symptom, expression, and evidence. And the work of the amateur is considered from a stance of methodological and disciplinary diversity, permitting deep and nuanced insights. The historical contingencies of the term 'amateur' may render it an elusive term, but as a heuristic through which to investigate the operations of everyday media Cultures, it offers a precise and well-calibrated instrument.

Professor William Uricchio
The Massachusetts Institute of Technology (Cambridge, USA)
and Utrecht University (The Netherlands)
May 2018

ACKNOWLEDGMENTS

Strange circumstances often prompt surprising outcomes. A few years ago, while sharing a quick lunch in a Lisboan bodega and fending off an eerie conversation with a colleague attending the same conference, we explored for the first time the idea of writing a book together on the theme of amateur media. Since then we have written other books, chapters and articles, have given several conference papers and taught new courses on this theme – all the time trying to identity feasible research questions and methodologies relevant to the study of amateur media. By the time we had completed our book project, it became clear that our research remains a work in progress, one that often combines perplexing theoretical perspectives and several open-ended analyses. Therefore, we would like to present our book as an invitation to other scholars as well as our future students to consider new and better ways of exploring this field of study.

Collaborating on this book was made possible by the invaluable help and advice we received from our colleagues, friends and families. We would like to thank James Laidlaw and Rupert Stasch from the University of Cambridge, Tom Slootweg from the University of Groningen, Tim van der Heijden and Andreas Fickers from the University of Luxembourg, and Joseph Wachelder from Maastricht University for having contributed in numerous and instrumental ways to our book project. It is also a great pleasure to gratefully acknowledge Natalie Foster, Jennifer Vennall and Katherine Laidler from Routledge for their vote of confidence, encouragement and unfaltering support, which allowed us to submit the manuscript in a timely manner. Our heartfelt thanks to William Uricchio, Patricia Zimmermann, Gustave Deutsch and Ali Hyde for their vital suggestions and pertinent critiques. Also, our thanks go to Eye Filmmuseum, the Netherlands Institute for Sound and Vision, the Groninger Archieven, and to Kevin Greenbank from the Centre of South Asian Studies (Cambridge, UK) for supplying us with crucial archival footage and photographs.

As always, Eric Mayes and Jan Swart have our deepest gratitude for their patience and encouragement, and for proposing some of the central case studies discussed in our book. Our families' love, support, patience and strong sense of humour have allowed us to develop and enjoy a rewarding research collaboration and a durable friendship too.

INTRODUCTION

> It's hard to define the concept of perfection. Philosophers have debated the meaning of perfection for centuries, wondering aloud whether it can ever truly be achieved. But we here at Gizmodo believe that we have finally found it. This video, posted to Twitter on 20 May 2018 AD, is perfect.
>
> *(Novak 2018)*

McDonald's digital self-order kiosks have been en vogue across the world since 2015, with their tall touch-screens meant to put 'more choice and control in the hands of customers', as if they were smartphones or iPads (Kowitt 2016). On 19 May 2018, a short amateur video filmed with a mobile phone was tweeted, then retweeted in less than 24 hours, and almost instantaneously reached over 8 million viewers.[1] It is a mixture of an amateur instructional film – how to use the McDonald's self-order kiosk when choosing a burger menu – and a 'fly-on-the-wall' recording of an altercation between several customers and the security guards. The images are a series of panoramic shots recorded with a pendulum-like movement and show in a continuous, linear narrative: the touch-screen with its various menu options, a security guard having immobilised a male customer in a headlock grab (Figure 0.1), the vegetable and fish burgers icon, a young couple shouting at the man being held by the security guard, the Mayo Chicken burger icon then, again, the couple shouting belligerently while being restrained by another security guard and, finally – while the price menu is loading on the touch-screen – a member of the public addressing the man immobilised by the security guard's jujitsu manoeuvre. The comic effect of the scene, heightened by a cheerful soundtrack, is overwritten by several questions about media and social ethics, amateur media practices and social media behaviour patterns. For instance, the weblog Gizmodo adjudicated half-ironically, and on behalf of non-academic audiences, that this example of amateur media has existential implications:

> Where did it come from? What are these innocent pixels trying to tell us? Who are the frail human forms that bookend the high-tech screens that divide them? What does it all mean? What does it mean to be a human? Philosophers will no doubt debate the meaning of this video for centuries to come. But all that they'll be able to agree upon is that this video, in all its glory, is perfect.
>
> *(Novak 2018)*

This book, prompted by lesser philosophical doubts, aims to map the boundary line between today's amateur media practice and the canons of professional media and film practice. What used to be a niche and expensive pastime in the early twentieth century, amateur audio-visual media production has become a hundred years later a crucial and defining feature of twenty-first-century everyday lives.

Amateur media technologies have been widely developed and adapted by users across generations, gender and nationalities, making it a rich research source for

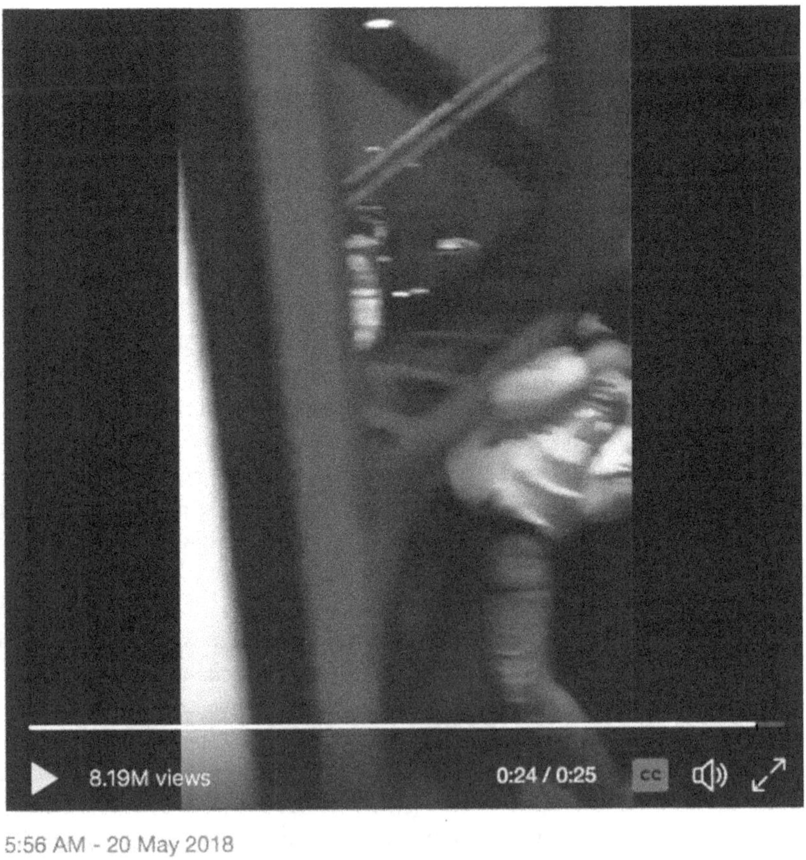

FIGURE 0.1 *IsThisThePerfectVideo*. 20 May 2018. Screengrab via Twitter.

media scholars, historians, anthropologists, sociologists and researchers of new media communication networks. The current amateur media culture is defined by the adjustments in practice styles from home-movie making to new forms of first-person and self-referential (selfies) visual narratives. Also, the hobbyist media practice of the last century has recently escaped the periphery of theoretical approaches and thus gained a much-deserved centre stage in visual and media studies as the foundation of today's 'amateurized media universe' (Zimmermann 1995, 2013; Norris Nicholson 2012; Tepperman 2015; Motrescu-Mayes and Norris Nicholson 2018; Aasman et al. 2018). Moreover, the primary production contexts and the emotional and social ambitions that defined twentieth century pater familias' amateur film practice – mostly men took up amateur filmmaking – also inform the twenty-first-century amateur media makers: they all attempt to record life across images that are simultaneously subsequent and antecedent to the very act of filming (Aasman, 2004; Schneider and Foot 2004; Shand and Craven 2013; Motrescu-Mayes 2017; Motrescu-Mayes and Norris Nicholson 2018).

More recently, the contemporary 'amateurized media universe' raised new questions about media ethics, which became critical to the understanding of moral frameworks defined by the global dynamics of mediation such as the use of amateur footage in TV news (Kember and Zylinska 2012). Importantly, whether the result of experimentation within canonical technologies or the keystone of hobbyist practices, amateur visual records allow us to constantly explore new orders of historical visibility (Grau 2011). Furthermore, since the emergence of the digital era, the study of amateur media has prompted new methodologies enabling reinterpretations of alternative accounts, from 'it could have been otherwise' to a ubiquitous media environment of multiple, simultaneous histories (Elsaesser 2004). As a result, we are now able to explore in greater depth the historical changes that chart the gradual transformation of a traditional (analogue) memory practice into a digital (often ephemeral) activity.

This book considers several key stages of this development, from early amateur film formats such as 9.5mm, 8mm and Super 8mm, and 16mm to VHS videotapes and recent mobile phone digital formats. It also discusses the extent to which such technologies have influenced the development of the analogue-self, from its family-centred persona, to the new digital-selfie culture. Alongside considerations on amateur media technological developments and cultural conventions, the book also identifies and discusses new challenges at the level of interpretation, archiving and preservation. In this theoretical context, *Amateur Media and Participatory Cultures* presents a survey of important scholarship and academic and public networks that define contemporary amateur and new media studies (Zimmermann 1995; Horak 1998; Odin 2000, 2014, 2016; Koltay 2011; Hunter et al. 2013; Andén-Papadopoulos 2014; et al. 2014; Slootweg 2018). Alongside recent trends in film studies and pedagogical practices inspired by the use of amateur media, the volume also maps the impact that this new and fast-developing visual literacy has on conventional historical and cultural approaches. It considers developments in technologies of recording alongside theories of perception and visual priming. On several occasions, the authors have experimented with different modes of historicising new media and with pertinent ways of re-contextualising amateur moving images as primary resources for social and historical studies, while scheduling a similar overview of amateur feature films, amateur animation, amateur porn and YouTube tutorials for a future research project.

The main purpose of *Amateur Media and Participatory Cultures* is to offer scholars, researchers, and students of new media studies and digital humanities several novel perspectives on current theoretical and practice-based projects dedicated to amateur media, as well as the opportunity to examine the concept of 'amateur' across new media and anthropological journalism studies.

Ever since digital media and Web 2.0 became the globally dominant, almost ubiquitous mode of communication and representation, everyday amateur media production has also become the centre of today's media and news culture. Mindful of the fact that amateur media (both still and moving images) continue to be seen as the benchmark of visual records of 'genuine event[s], rather than [images] of mediatised or staged one[s]' (Margolis and Pauwels 2011, 278), the authors have paid particular attention to the ways in which diverse sets of concepts defining amateur media have gradually merged across global visual narratives and communication protocols. Moreover, building on central research questions and content analysis from across media and communication studies, they have assessed differences between professional and amateur media productions based on the ways in which the 'originators' of an image have been either influenced by or have challenged their immediate visual context. It is from this perspective that issues of technical affordance and technological affordability, as well as of staging or censoring visual information and patterns in media socialisation, define key differences between professional and amateur media production, distribution and consumption. However, this perspective often fails to assess the wider impact of amateur media on the central cultural histories of the twentieth and twenty-first centuries. For instance, when social scientists and scholars of cultural and media studies examine early twentieth century silent home movies made on 9.5mm or 16mm film (usually viewed among the filmmaker's family and friends) or vlogs of the mid-2010s uploaded and shared daily by a global audience, amateur media continues to be assessed against professional media-making standards and conventions rather than within its specific means of production and distribution. Moreover, media scholars exploring the development of the amateur media maker–audience relationships since late 1890s face a challenging albeit often rewarding task. The present volume identifies several pertinent and valuable methodologies by comparing, for example, early twentieth-century home movies, colonial amateur films, video movies distributed by activist groups advocating racial and gender equality in the 1960s–70s, and personal visual narratives in the digital space of the free-access World Wide Web. In this context, specific narrative forms and practices recurrent across uploaded old home movies or recent user-generated personal content such as Instagram posts, vlogs, Snapchats, and Vines demand a consolidated study of how social memory travels across various and almost simultaneous visual constructions of meaning. Furthermore, there is an urgency to circumscribe, redefine and develop a critical language able to cope with the rapid shift between what was conventionally categorised as private and personal – i.e. home movies watched and distributed as 'home entertainment' – and what has become in the digital global space an issue of aesthetic undercurrents where the image-maker adopts the amateur's innovatively liberating status. It is at the confluence of such clashing and yet co-dependent moving-image production and distribution practices that a new and vibrant interdisciplinary scholarship is currently being developed – several features of this emerging scholarship form the core research agenda for this volume too.

Also considered are central research questions about the use of amateur media in producing online insurgent visual narratives, as well as current theoretical issues such as the 'notion of the social [that] is at stake in understanding digital media's consequences for new politics' (Couldry 2012, 131). For instance, user-generated media content is being used daily by major international news organisations with over 72 per cent of this source remaining unacknowledged in the final version of the broadcast.[2] Similarly, numerous examples of amateur media can help assess the ways in which non-professional, first-person visual narratives have become the stylistic badge of honour of professional, commercial and advertising programmes as well as the visual arsenal for political activism and anti-war rhetoric. Case studies discussed in this theoretical framework include, for instance, amateur video recordings of US police brutality, smartphone amateur films of rape scenes uploaded live by teenagers on Periscope, and vlogs posted on Facebook and YouTube by children (young citizen journalists) showing their daily suffering during the civil war in Syria.

Amateur Media and Participatory Cultures's contribution to current media studies is anchored in a clear and varied set of theoretical and methodological perspectives on global amateur media practices and studies, and supported by a wide-ranging collection of case studies selected from all genres of amateur media. This framework encourages a coherent and careful investigation of the relationship between amateur media, significant chronological changes in its technological, distribution and reception patterns, and the resulting development of a global visual literacy. The co-authors – a visual anthropologist and a media historian – address these topics while considering feasible cross-disciplinary theoretical and historical approaches. While Motrescu-Mayes explores several theoretical perspectives on issues of ephemerality (Chapter 3), ethics (Chapter 4) and memory of trauma and war (Chapter 5), Aasman considers the historical dimensions of media innovation (Chapter 1), global online communication (Chapter 2) and archival practices (Chapter 6). This approach supports the rationale for selecting particular theories and methodologies, and the ways in which they operate in a reliable regime of interdisciplinarity. Correspondingly, the review of the main theoretical trends and practices relevant to current studies of amateur and new media is accompanied by the detailed discussion of the term 'amateur media' and its theoretical applicability when discussing 'old' media, i.e. early twentieth century home movies, and 'new' media such as Snapchats or Finstas. This particular survey brings into focus the problematic of the 'archivability of presence' experienced by the film/media makers' intrinsic (automatic) archival aspirations while recording and representing the ephemeral (Doane 2002). Finally, the authors' research for a book like *Amateur Media and Participatory Cultures* contributes to the rapidly growing academic and general interest in amateur media practice and reception studies. This is particularly relevant in the context of the ongoing transformations across interdisciplinary programmes in cultural studies and digital humanities, from film studies to media archaeological approaches highlighting how 'transdisciplinary regimes of knowledge' inform or demand new perspectives on media and digital cultures (Parikka 2012, 13).

The first chapter, *From marginal to mainstream: a history of amateur media*, presents a historical perspective on the ways in which amateur media has been defining new means of cultural production from the early twentieth century until the current digital era. The survey starts from the premise that amateur media transformed a rather modest and mostly private hobbyist practice into a prominent and visible feature of new media culture. Aasman explores here the changing traditions and connotations of 'amateur' film – conceptually and as a practice – across more than hundred years. For most of the twentieth century, home-movie making was integral to everyday life as a new cultural practice in which the film camera became a technology of memory-building, of archiving representations of family life, and the core apparatus for community-based amateur filmmakers' network. Eventually, new media technologies brought fresh representational possibilities explored by diverse groups of users, each attracted by distinctive modes of amateur media usages. For instance, political and social activists embraced analogue video as a political *weapon*; avant-garde filmmakers explored the ideal of amateur film as a personal medium enabling a more intimate and genuine approach, while ethnic minorities, LGBT communities and the Women's Movement adapted amateur media technologies to document their lives in greater detail. More recently, the emergence of the Web 2.0 challenged media amateurship in entirely new ways, moving beyond small social circles of production and reception. YouTube's initial call to 'broadcast yourself' individualised the opportunity to present oneself in front of a potentially worldwide audience. The diverse ways in which amateur media technologies have been employed over the last century, including emerging amateur media practices within diverse social and cultural contexts, poses serious methodological challenges to most media historians. Consequently, there is a plurality of theoretical perspectives that explore the ways in which amateur media have been closely connected to specific local and national film cultures, television histories and, more recently, to global web histories. This intermingling of established media traditions and practices such as cinema, video, television and digital media has led to an increased hybridisation of home movie/amateur filmmaking (Van der Heijden 2018). This is particularly evident in the contemporary digital era in which, by profiting from the 'rapid circulation across a range of social networks' (Jenkins et al. 2013, 39), amateur media has acquired a central place across mainstream media platforms. The ability to circulate amateur content across global online networks can be thus assessed as a movement toward a more participatory model of cultural production. In this context, the amateur media makers and users shape, share and remix media content in a way that was previously inconceivable and technically unmanageable (Jenkins et al. 2013).

In the second chapter, *Everyday complexities and contradictions in contemporary amateur media*, Aasman discusses further the impact of the ongoing, rapidly developing production and circulations of amateur media. She assesses how these changes prompt transformations of formerly conventional genres of home movies and home videos into a ubiquitous practice which has become deeply embedded in contemporary everyday life. Several examples of amateur media have been selected for a comparative analysis and to highlight their intrinsic and highly complicated social arrangements, as well as the crucial, constructive role played by direct access to and the availability of media technologies and social media platforms. By analysing lesser-known online home videos, as well as popular (family) vlogs it could help identify the proliferation of overlapping communication and recording technologies, changing conventions on how to use those new media technologies, and broader issues related to the overall infrastructure that affected contemporary amateur media, especially the home mode. They also help address the question of what happens once the home mode transgresses the living room and starts circulating on social media platforms such as YouTube. The chapter introduces new critical approaches that help to emphasise how current amateur media technologies encourage a wide variety of new social and cultural practices and protocols (Uricchio 2009), and so support interpretative complexities and contradictions dictated by how people today 'incorporate digital media into their routine practices of relating' (Baym 2010, 5). For instance, one of the several applicable analytical perspectives is the *dispositif* – a concept that can help explore the variety of social, economic, cultural and material relationships. It allows the researcher to understand complex interrelations between the material dimensions of production and sharing technologies, the textual dimension of specific aesthetics or genres, and the perceptual dimensions of viewing and responding to the amateur media (as text) within particular socio-technical screening contexts (Aasman et al. 2018). Relying on the use of the *dispositif* (Figure 0.2) also allows a thorough examination of the new spatial and temporal dimensions of social family gatherings across contemporary digital home/amateur video practices. This exploratory strand considers the use of non-traditional recording devices such as webcams, computer applications (video-calling technologies) and smartphones, and also how the use of such technology has changed people's notion of connectivity and simultaneously challenged one's archival desire to record and store certain instances of social intimacy. Moreover, once amateur media makers and users turn to non-traditional ways of sharing and screening home videos, they enter a communication space that is no longer private. From this perspective, it then becomes imperative to re-evaluate the term 'amateur media' since the amateur filmmaker/media maker's identity and political economies have now entered a highly public and commercialised space.

Motrescu-Mayes proposes in the third chapter, *The non-ephemeral amateur media and constructions of self*, several theoretical approaches that classify ephemeral (new

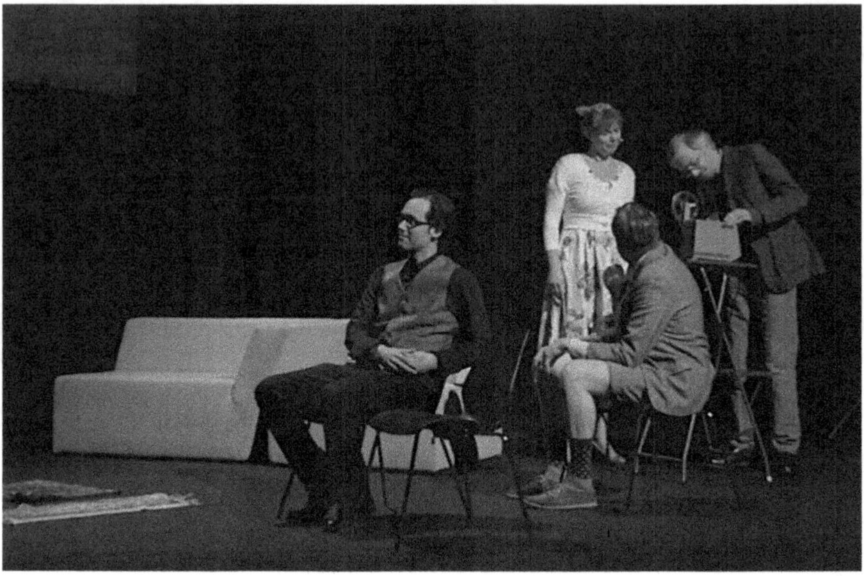

FIGURE 0.2 *Staging the amateur dispositif* at the Orphans Film Festival in Eye Filmmuseum, Amsterdam. 2014. Screengrab from Vimeo.[3]

and amateur) media as a functional social tool as well as a deceptive theoretical and technological construct. Issues of amateur media makers opting for anonymity and the ephemerality or time-restricted distribution of their records indicate a choice for a renewable, non-punishable freedom of expression. This leads to cases of political, sexual and racial abuse, to name just a few strands, often reaching high levels of (involuntary) online archivability. Most often, this is due either to active legal frameworks or to pervasive cultural and visual priming processes that preserve the original media records – from selfies translating impudence and narcissism, to scenes documenting acts of terrorism or domestic abuse. The chapter is less concerned with a review of the developments in recording technologies that, at some point or another, relegated a 'new media' equipment as obsolete and impractical, and its feasibility as just another ephemeral recording mode. Instead, it explores how several pervasive cognitive and cultural frameworks allow the current amateur new media-*periscoping* behaviour. This is a behaviour in which media makers find shelter behind their online persona, whether through in-character performance, distribution channel-specific digital avatars, or ad hoc and in situ journalism. This new amateur media-making modus operandi allows the amateur media producers to self-(obsess)observe, to mirror trope identities across meteoric cultural trends, and to identify and expose crucial social and political requests. The comparative analysis of the cases selected for this chapter is introduced by a brief discussion of the visual priming processes at work across most cultural networks, and of visual literacy's role in preserving means of expression that overwrite, by default, new features offered by the latest recording technologies. For instance, questions about selfies' panopticism – a digital, online identity construction that uses new media self-surveillance protocols to document one's visual and behavioural memes – are considered across a number of amateur and new media examples such as Sobrr, Snapchat uploads, Instagram and Finstas, and some seemingly ephemeral media recordings and orphan films. Also explored are issues of access to media technology and distribution in relation to modes of perception that determine both the subsequent historic merit of amateur images and their ephemerality as a common interpretative ground. In this context, it is argued that old or new media can function as para-texts, which are highly *recyclable* across specific geopolitical visual priming process and the respective ensuing visual literacies. This framework leads to renewed acts of self-referential memory-building processes and to ongoing reinterpretations of a private and/or collective past identities. The chapter concludes with an exploration of amateur new media records made by children and teenagers – the type of media experience and expertise that is bound to define the research framework for future media scholars.

The fourth chapter, *The politics of ethical representation in amateur media*, has been structured by Motrescu-Mayes around several case studies that facilitate a detailed analysis of the ways in which cultural and social networks of amateur media redefine core concepts of surveillance and media ethics. Examples selected from different amateur media genres, i.e. home movies, web dramas, vlogs, Snapchats, are central to the argument around issues of authenticity and of global, national and gender identities. This perspective proves particularly relevant when considering amateur media as an ever-changing vernacular text within the global visual (new media) literacy and its efficacy in modelling new perspectives on media ethics and semantics. The current visual culture and its by-product literacy are constantly shared and shaped by a synchronous global network of producers-cum-audience. While studies of the rapid alterations in popular visual and digital culture have already been published (Hunter et al. 2013), and scholarship addressing home movies and/or amateur film culture is gaining momentum (Motrescu-Mayes and Norris Nicholson 2018; Kmec and Thill 2012; Rascaroli et al. 2014), the study of amateur media as a text able to challenge conventional critical methodologies is still uncharted territory for most media scholars. Several examples of amateur media are compared in this chapter to help identify how specific visual identities, memories and histories have been negotiated within private networks of distribution (i.e. family and friends, social clubs, etc.) and/or continue to be interpreted across online, free-access global media networks. When appropriate, the analysis borrows from theories of perception and visual anthropology to assess the ways in which amateur media functions as a psychological and emotional *prompter* as well as a feasible ethnographic record text within a theoretical framework. This methodology highlights the framework in which common conventions of reality-construction patterns are most often challenged or cancelled by the intrinsic (non-)logic of fortuitous and urgent visual narratives found in, for instance, colonial home movies, amateur military films, VHS video recordings, early YouTube videos, vines, online video memes, Skype recordings and Snapchats. Question of media ethics are extended to the use of amateur media as *illustrations* in mainstream documentaries such as *The British Empire in Colour* (Carlton Television, TWI, 2002) or *5 Broken Cameras* (dir. Guy Davidi and Emad Burnat, 2012). In the case of *5 Broken Cameras*, it is argued that *recycling* the allegedly unmediated testimonial authority of amateur media as a primary source-text for constructing and confirming particular identities and events challenges dominant understandings of private and national memory and of traditional histories of gender and racial identities. Other examples draw on participatory amateur 'phone media' and children's citizen journalism made in Palestine and Syria respectively. In this context, the discourse centres on issues of interpersonal social media surveillance as the cornerstone of the netizens' global culture (Hauben et al. 1997). The chapter concludes by proposing a methodology capable to adapt theories of cine- and media ethics and semiotics in support of a new visual literacy defined by the developing amateur media cultures and their various texts, from analogue to digital first-person narratives.

In the fifth chapter, *Memory and new media's visual counter-histories*, Motrescu-Mayes charts the extent to which amateur media challenges private and national memories while simultaneously promoting visual counter-histories within global cultural engagements. Concepts such as national memory, visual counter-histories and global networks of social and ephemeral media are defined in relation to technological developments relevant to the recent changes in visual/media literacy. The discussion is supported by a cross-disciplinary analysis of several examples of amateur media (all genres) with the aim to assess how they might challenge representations of collective memories within global cultural engagements and across visual counter-histories. Among the research questions considered in this chapter is whether amateur media constructions of private, collective, gendered, racial and national histories demand new theories in memory studies. Relying on theories of perception and digital forensic guidelines, it is explored how amateur media productions can often redefine memory studies through issues of ubiquitous visual immediacy, re-imagined collective memory, and instant online access to representations of gender, religious affiliations and specific socio-political identities. Additionally, the chapter addresses questions of memory authenticity across several in-depth analyses of first-person visual narratives, from mid-twentieth-century soldiers' amateur films to twenty-first-century guerrilla fighters' videos of civil war casualties. Examples of amateur media (mis)constructed global identities and events are discussed in relation to theories of memory studies pertinent to emerging cultural frameworks of recording technologies, and to recent interpretative perspectives within digital cultures. In this context are addressed renewed explorations of mainstream histories by employing counteractive perspectives in the analysis of several case studies of amateur media. For instance, a detailed media forensic approach is employed when analysing the use of amateur (video) media in making *Sri Lanka's Killing Fields* (dir. Callum Macrae, UK, 2011) – the award-winning documentary about the last months of the Sri Lankan civil war (1983–2009). Whereas the study of amateur media making presents new orders of historical, national and ethnic visibility, particular new media recordings reveal agonising instances of a mutable, open-ended collective memory – the new social media grand narrative of a plural storytelling defining most recent historical developments. This theoretical framework also helps explore the open-ended collective memory that is simultaneously lived *in* – the present tense of viewing the material online, and lived by proxy – the construction and appropriation of the visual memory created by the amateur media. Building on several critical perspectives proposed throughout the book, this chapter also emphasises a key analytical framework – the ubiquitous online network of shared visual documentations – from allegedly monotonous scenes of domestic life, to early twenty-first-century vlogs uploaded by victims of ongoing wars. This framework ultimately requires a thorough enquiry into existing hierarchies of private and official access to acts of remembrance about globally relevant historic events and repurposed national identities.

In the final chapter, *Lost and found: amateur media in the archive*, Aasman focuses on the relation between memory-recording practices and memory-archiving practices. Although home-movie making flourished during the twentieth century as a new cultural memory practice, it has only recently been recognised as a source of valuable archival and historical documentation. By the mid-1980s home movies started being assessed as reliable and popular historical resource. Consequently, regional and national audio-visual archives started gradually to collect home movies and amateur films in earnest. This change in archival appreciation immediately raised legal issues of ownership and copyright as well as ethical questions relating to the re-use of archival footage. In addition, with the arrival of digital audio-visual material have emerged serious issues about the sustainability of digital formats and devices. Furthermore, the development of new digital memory practices reflected in the daily production of YouTube videos on a mass scale also prompted new archival questions about the status of such digital records as historical documents. This chapter explores a few possible ways in which future scholars will revisit today's digital videos, particularly since many media archivists are concerned that born-digital data might become lost, unreadable and untraceable, as backwards technological compatibility cannot always be guaranteed. Digital material such as Snapchats and Tweets have a closer resemblance to oral cultures than to the more stable regimes of print and film cultures (Uricchio 2009), and therefore online materials can be subjected to processes of updating and synchronisation that are paradoxically 'making the ephemeral endure' (Chun 2016, 78). Nevertheless, there remains the risk that contemporary generations might lose access to their 'cultural reference memory' (Assman 2008). In addition, the new amateur media productions can be interconnected, remixed or fragmented, hence acting as pieces that lack a clear authorial and contextual origin. These developments have destabilised conventional archival protocols as well as the concept of the classical archive per se, and everyday conceptions of institutional archives (Prelinger 2009). Some of the research (open) questions proposed in this chapter consider whether and to what extent current institutional, technical, commercial, political and social opportunities and constraints influence memory-building and archival schedules. Currently, many amateur and new media makers and users prefer social media platforms as their 'default archive', a new archival practice that disrupts the exclusiveness of scholarly access to niche research sources. In lieu of conclusion, the chapter evaluates the challenges currently faced by some of the institutional archives, popular archives (YouTube), amateur archives (fan-based archives) and personal archives (family archives).

The case studies selected for discussion in *Amateur Media and Participatory Cultures* are meant to demonstrate in a clear and coherent manner why it has become imperative to identify new theories and methodologies for current amateur media studies. While new media technologies call for new visual and digital literacies, the visual priming and emotional contagion effects experienced by online audiences remain anchored in traditional scholarship of perception and social psychology (Aronson 2012; Vohs and Baumeister 2012). Such theoretical premises are matched by recent research of new media, which highlights the ways in which both old and new user-generated content produces tensions between stasis and mobility, stability and impermanence, substantial and evanescent and monumental and momentary (Straw 2010). As a complementing methodology, the authors have employed theories of visual anthropology when arguing that user-generated (amateur) new media are integral to contemporary media-personae's global, ongoing struggle to simultaneously secure for their digital identities an ephemeral risk-free media and a ubiquitous, permanent archival and distribution network. Moreover, by aiming to identify why amateur media has an intrinsic primary historical merit per se, the authors have relied on historical perspectives when comparing modes of production, distribution and reception of different amateur media technologies. Finally, the discussion about local, regional and national histories archived and perpetuated across amateur media networks is supplemented with an overview of current online trends in private memory and history making. In light of this, it is hoped that *Amateur Media and Participatory Cultures* offers a reliable theoretical and historical review of the global amateur media literacy alongside possible new research methodologies that could challenge and redefine current theories of media and visual studies, social anthropology and digital culture.

Notes

1 The scene was filmed in the UK (prices are in pounds sterling) and, as indicated by gogogadgetmarijuana in his Tweet thread, it was Anthony Moll@AnthonyMoll18 who allegedly made the original upload on Twitter. Available at https://twitter.com/amenbreakfast/status/998049864981319680 [25 May 2018].

2 See, for instance, Claire Wardle, Sam Dubberley and Pete Brown's research project *Amateur Footage: A Global Study of User-Generated Content in TV and Online-News Output* (2014); Mona Baker and Bolette B. Blaagaard (eds), *Citizen Media and Public Spaces* (Routledge 2016); or Luis Pérez-González, Bolette Blaagaard and Mona Baker (eds), and the Routledge *Critical Perspectives on Citizen Media* series (available at http://citizenmediaseries.org/about-the-series [20 June 2018]).

3 See for more on the heuristic potential of re-enactment in this media archaeology experiment 'Staging the Amateur Dispositif', conducted as a performance at the International Orphan Film Symposium 2014 in: Andreas Fickers, 2018. 'How to Grasp

Historical Media Dispositifs in Practice', in Susan Aasman, Andreas Fickers and Jo Wachelder (eds), *Materializing Memories. Dispositifs, Generations, Amateurs*. New York: Bloomsbury, 85–99. More details about this performance can be found at the blog *Home Movies Project*, available at https://homemoviesproject.wordpress.com/report-staging-the-amateur-dispositif/. An edited video version of the performance, produced by Tim van der Heijden, is available at: vimeo.com/95314562.

Selected bibliography

Aasman, Susan. 2004. *Ritueel van Huiselijk Geluk: Een Cultuurhistorische Verkenning van de Familiefilm* [Ritual of Domestic Happiness: A Cultural History of the Home Movie]. Amsterdam: Het Spinhuis.

Aasman, Susan, Andreas Fickers and Jo Wachelder (eds). 2018. *Materializing Memories: Dispositifs, Generations, Amateurs*. New York: Bloomsbury.

Assmann, Aleida. 2008. 'The Canon and the Archive', *Cultural Memory Studies: An International and Interdisciplinary Handbook*, ed. Astrid Erll and Ansgar Nünning. Berlin/New York: De Gruyter, 97–109.

Andén-Papadopoulos, Kari. 2014. 'Citizen Camera-Witnessing: Embodied Political Dissent in the Age of "Mediated Mass Self-Communication"', *New Media & Society*, vol. 16, no. 5, 753–769. First published online 31 May 2013.

Aronson, Elliot. 2012. *The Social Animal*. New York: Worth Publishers.

Baym, Nancy. 2010. *Personal Connections in the Digital Age*. Cambridge: Polity Press.

Chun, Wendy. 2016. *Updating to Remain the Same: Habitual New Media*. Cambridge, MA: MIT Press.

Couldry, Nick. 2012. *Media, Society, World, Social Theory and Digital Media Practice*. Cambridge: Polity Press.

Doane, Mary Ann. 2002. *The Emergence of Cinematic Time: Modernity, Contingency, the Archive*. Harvard: Harvard University Press.

Elsaesser, Thomas. 2004. 'The New Film History as Media Archaeology', *Cinémas*, vol. 14, no. 2–3 (Spring)), 75–117.

Grau, Oliver (ed.). 2011. *Imagery in the 21st Century*. Cambridge, MA: MIT Press.

Hauben, Michael and Ronda Hauben. 1997. *Netizens: On the History and Impact of Usenet and the Internet*. London: Wiley-IEEE Computer Society Press.

Horak, Jan-Christopher. 1998. 'Out of the Attic: Archiving Amateur Film', *Journal of Film Preservation*, vol. 56, no. 6, 50–53.

Hunter, Dan, Ramon Lobato, Megan Richardson and Julian Thomas (eds). 2013. *Amateur Media: Social, Cultural and Legal Perspectives*. London: Routledge.

Jenkins, Henry, Sam Ford, and Joshua Green. 2013. *Spreadable Media: Creating Value and Meaning in a Networked Culture*. New York: New York University Press.

Kember, Sarah and Joanna Zylinska. 2012. *Life after New Media: Mediation as a Vital Process*. Cambridge, MA: MIT Press.

Kmec, Sonia and Vivian Thill (eds). 2012. *Tourists and Nomads: Amateur Images of Migration*. Magsburg: Jonas-Verlag.

Koltay, Tibor. 2011. 'New Media and Literacies: Amateurs vs. Professionals', *First Monday*, vol. 16, no. 1.

Kowitt, Beth. 2016. 'Why Eating at McDonald's Is about to Undergo A Massive Makeover', *Fortune*, 18 November. Available at http://fortune.com/2016/11/18/mcdonalds-kiosks-table-service/ [29 December 2017].

Margolis, Eric M. and Luc Pauwels (eds). 2011. *The SAGE Handbook of Visual Research Methods*. London: Sage.

Motrescu-Mayes, Annamaria. 2017. 'Paradoxical Legacies: Colonial Missionary Films, Corporate Philanthropy in South Asia and the Griersonian Documentary Tradition', in Ian Aitken and Camille Deprez (eds), *Colonial Documentary Film in South and South-East Asia.* Edinburgh: Edinburgh University Press, 128–147.

Motrescu-Mayes, Annamaria and Heather Norris Nicholson. 2018. *British Women Amateur Filmmakers: National Memories and Global Identities.* Edinburgh: Edinburgh University Press.

Norris Nicholson, Heather. 2012. *Amateur Film: Meaning and Practice, c. 1927–77.* Manchester: Manchester University Press.

Novak, Matt. 2018. 'Is This the Perfect Video?', Gizomodo, 21 May. Available at www.gizmodo.co.uk/2018/05/is-this-the-perfect-video [22 May 2018].

Odin, Roger. 2000. 'Productions cinématographiques familiales et limites de la représentation', in Leonardo Quaresima, Alessandra Raengo, Laura Vichi (eds), *I limiti della rappresentazione (The Bounds of Representation: Censorship, the Visible, Modes of Representation in Film)*, Udine: Forum, 127–140.

Odin, Roger. 2014. 'The Home Movie and Space of Communication', in Laura Rascaroli and G. Young with B. Monahan (eds), *Amateur Filmmaking: The Home Movie, the Archive, the Web.* New York: Bloomsbury, 15–26.

Odin, Roger. 2016. 'Cinema in My Pocket', in Giovanna Fossati and A. van den Oever (eds), *Exposing the Film Apparatus: The Film Archive as a Research Laboratory.* Amsterdam: Amsterdam University Press, 45–53. Parikka, Jussi. 2012. *What is Media Archaeology?* Cambridge: Polity Press.

Prelinger, Rick. 2009. 'The Appearance of Archives', in Pelle Snickars and Patrick Vonderau (eds), *The YouTube Reader.* Stockholm: National Library of Sweden, 268–275.

Rascaroli, Laura, Gwenda Young and Barry Monahan (eds). 2014. *Amateur Filmmaking: The Home Movie, the Archive, the Web.* New York: Bloomsbury.

Schneider, Steven and Kirstin Foot. 2004. *The Web as Object of Study.* London: Sage.

Shand, Ryan and Ian Craven (eds). 2013. *Small-Gauge Storytelling: Discovering the Amateur Fiction Film.* Edinburgh: Edinburgh University Press.

Slootweg, Tom. 2018. *Resistance, Disruption and Belonging: Electronic Video as Alternative in Three Amateur Modes.* PhD dissertation, University of Groningen.

Straw, William. 2010. 'The Circulatory Turn', in Barbara Crow, Michael Longford, Kim Sawchuk (eds), *The Wireless Spectrum: The Politics, Practices and Poetics of Mobile Media.* Toronto: University of Toronto Press, 17–28.

Tepperman, Charles. 2015. *Amateur Cinema 1923–1960: The Rise of North American Moviemaking.* Oakland: University of California Press.

Uricchio, William. 2009. 'Moving Beyond the Artifact', in *Digital Material: Tracing New Media in Everyday Life and Technology*, ed. by Marianne van den Boomen. Amsterdam: Amsterdam University Press, 135–147.

Van der Heijden, Tim. 2018. *Hybrid Histories: Technologies of Memory and the Cultural Dynamics of Home Movies, 1895–2005.* PhD dissertation, Maastricht University.

Vohs, Kathleen D. and Roy F. Baumeister (eds). 2012. *Self and Identity, Volume I: Self-Concept and Self-Esteem.* London: Sage.

Zimmermann, P. 1995. *Reel Families: A Social History of Amateur Film.* Bloomington: Indiana University Press.

Zimmermann, P. 2013. 'An Amateurized Media Universe', Review of Amateur Media: Social, Cultural and Legal Perspectives, ed. Dan Hunter, Ramon Lobato, Megan Richardson and Julian Thomas (London: Routledge, 2013), *Jump Cut: A Review of Contemporary Media*, no. 55, Fall 2013.

1

FROM MARGINAL TO MAINSTREAM

A history of amateur media

Understanding today's media culture cannot be fully achieved without taking the massive presence of user-generated content into consideration. In just two decades, amateur media has transformed from modest and mostly private practices into much more prominent and visible features of media culture. Patricia Zimmermann, who once pitied the way home movies were 'denigrated, despised, ridiculed, trivialized, marginalized, cast off and debased' (Zimmermann 1997, 73), recently concluded that we are 'in the midst of what feels like the amateurization of the entire media universe' (Zimmermann 2013). Amateur media content is available on multiple media platforms, as family vlogs, personal webcam videos, eyewitness reports, Snapchats or as video embedded in Tweets. With amateur media being ubiquitous, it is interesting to explore their history, from marginal to mainstream. By surveying the history of amateur media and mapping the relationships between emerging media technologies and changing amateur media practices, this chapter explores the why and how behind people's choices to use specific technologies at particular moments in time, and how economic, political, social and cultural factors influenced these choices.

It was not until the mid-1980s that historians and archivists started to consider home movies seriously as a rich phenomenon with important and distinct characteristics. Fred Camper pleaded for more research on home movies as a category with 'its own varied set of stylistic motifs, even its own aesthetic, moral and cultural implications' (Camper 1986, 9). Since then, the historiography on amateur media has developed into a prolific field focusing on various aspects. Brian Coe (1981) and, two decades later, Alan D. Katelle (2000) and Leo Enticknap (2005) did important work in tracing the technological histories of amateur film. Patricia Zimmermann's (1995) critical history of amateur film discourses was particularly ground-breaking: based on archival research, she demonstrated how ideological, technical and social constraints influenced the way everyday people made use of the amateur film camera and how notions of amateur film evolved throughout the twentieth century. Her book became an important study for much academic work since. In the 2000s Susan Aasman (2004), Alexandra Schneider (2004) and Martina Roepke (2006) focused on the social and cultural history of home movies in the first half of the twentieth century, while James Moran (2002) specifically studied the arrival of home video. There are multiple regional histories, such as Heather Norris Nicholson's (2012) study of amateur film in northern and northwestern England or Karan Sheldon (2017) dealing with New England (US), national histories about Ireland by Gwenda Young (2014) or Luxembourg by Françoise Poos (2016) and colonial histories on amateur film by Nico de Klerk (2008) about the Dutch East Indies, and Annamaria Motrescu-Mayes (2011–17) about British colonial amateur films made across the world. Other scholars focused on particular types of user: organised in cine-clubs, as the work of Ryan Shand (2008), Ian Craven (2009) and Charles Teppermann (2015) shows; on women amateur filmmakers (Motrescu-Mayes and Norris Nicholson 2018) or on travelling filmmakers, by Martin L. Johnson (2018). Additionally, there exist multiple histories that explore the relations between amateur film and historical avant-garde film cultures as in studies by Malte Hagener (2007) and Greg de Cuir (2014).

A more comprehensive, diachronic study of a century of amateur media was the goal of the research project *Changing Platforms of Ritualised Memory Practices: The Cultural Dynamics of Home Movie Making* (2012–2016). This project has systematically investigated the crucial relationship between amateur media technologies and specific user practices from a longue durée perspective.[1] It explored the dynamic between new technologies of production, dissemination and screening, as well as the changing narrative and aesthetic forms, and varying social and cultural uses and interpretations of home movies in different historical contexts. Van der Heijden (2018) showed that an increasing popularisation of amateur filmmaking collided with a process of convergence and multi-mediatisation of home-movie recording. Moreover, he pointed out that there has been a continuous tension between continuity and discontinuity, which accounts for the hybridity inherent in amateur media history as a technology, practice and discourse. However, media technologies are connected to previous ones not only diachronically, but also synchronically. The identity of a medium comes into being only through engagement with and in relationship to other media. This means that intermediality, or the inherent interrelationship between media technologies, is elementary in the contextual understanding of any medium. Slootweg (2018a) demonstrated how the arrival of amateur video in the 1960s and 1970s can be connected to other contemporary media technologies such as television, with which it shares many features such as the viewing context (television set plus VCR) for watching home videos. Furthermore, Slootweg emphasised the importance of relating the emergence of amateur media to a broader historical context. He contextualised and analysed the arrival of video in the 1960s, 1970s and 1980s by delineating three 'separate, coexistent yet, sometimes, slightly overlapping modes of practice and functioning' (Slootweg 2018b, 204): the 'counter mode', represented by social and political activists who embraced video as an oppositional practice, the home mode, driven by a desire to use video as a technology of memory, and the community mode, represented by self-proclaimed serious organised film amateurs. Practitioners within that last mode perceived the arrival of video as a disruptive force as it endangered longstanding creative and artistic traditions.

These insights in general suggest that it is increasingly challenging to write a media history that does justice to the complex dynamics of changing technologies and emerging amateur media practices within diverse social and cultural contexts. Media historians today are opting for a plural approach rather than abiding by Campers' advice to write a single history of home movies as a practice that has distinct characteristics (Aasman 2013). There is no single perspective that can cover all theoretical angles. Based on this assumption, this chapter discusses the various ways in which people appropriated and embedded consumer-recording technologies in their everyday life. Over the course of 100 years, many rich private and public archives representing human life have emerged, produced with ever-changing amateur media technologies, and these archives represent highly conventionalised tales of family life, offering stories that play out repeatedly the same sort of scenarios of happy lives. At the same time, these archives are filled with endless variations of self-conscious experiments, spontaneous unruly attempts that created idiosyncratic aesthetics and alternative narratives. As such, it is an interesting field of study in which amateur media can be seen against the wider background of 'media culture as a highly participatory activity' (Kelnner 1995, 2), whether applied to media historical contexts such as cinema, television or the Internet. For each of these three broader media historical contexts, we will trace how amateur users explored the opportunities for producing, distributing and screening of amateur media content.

I Amateur media in the age of cinema (1900–1950)

The emergence of home cinema in the early age of cinema

There are valid arguments supporting the hypothesis that the history of amateur film has paralleled that of cinema, as they both are part of a series of technological innovations and developments, cultural experiments and economic and entrepreneurial undertakings from the end of the nineteenth century onwards. The early period, which roughly spans three decades, from the 1890s to the 1920s, was a fascinating one as multiple inventors and entrepreneurs experimented with alternative formats and related technologies designed and marketed for domestic use (Zimmermann 1995; Katelle 2000). Many of the early efforts focused on making film technologies cheaper – as film material was expensive – making film safer – as film was usually nitrate based and therefore highly flammable – and making it easier to use – as handling a camera with a crank or feeding a projector was more difficult than taking a still picture. One of Britain's film pioneers, Birt Acres, launched in 1896 the 'Birtac', one of the first known film cameras-cum-projector to suit the early generation of amateur filmmakers. Acres decided to splice the standard professional 35mm film format in half, thereby creating a 17.5mm film gauge format. This simple innovation resulted in a cheaper film format, which made home-movie making, although still expensive, a feasible option among more affluent consumers.

Building on Birt Acres' success, other manufacturers started to experiment as well. One of them was Heinrich Ernemann, a German manufacturer of photographic equipment. In 1903, Ernemann launched his 17.5mm-based *Kino* system, which included both a camera and a projector. This particular system was in use only for a brief period before it disappeared in 1908 when the company stopped the distribution because of strong competition. Martina Roepke, who traced the history of Ernemann's *Heimkino*, described how this format made its way 'into the private homes of high-ranking members of society, including military officers and the royal family' (Roepke 2007, 345). She reconstructed the case of amateur filmmaker and pharmacist Julius Neubronner who, around 1903, compiled a unique collection of amateur films using *Kino* equipment. He would screen his home movies in combination with pre-produced material from the Ernemann catalogue, including subject matters and genres such as animals, streets and cities or historical (Roepke 2007, 347). In his autobiography, Neubronner looked back, giving a rare glimpse of something as ephemeral as a private screening:

> I could see the Kaiser taking a review of the soldiers right before me and whenever I wished too; I could admire myself performing as mime and magician, I could watch my children at all ages, and yes, even today I can watch my dearest little dog, teckel, digging for ice, although he was buried years ago.
>
> *(Cited in Roepke 2007, 350)*[2]

As Roepke rightly observed, early home cinema developed as a mix of public and private material, of purchased theatrical film with amateur films. From the start, amateur film was just as much about entertainment as about self-performance and memory-making (Chapter 5).

Although there are multiple other examples of amateur film collections, Leo Enticknap is right when he concluded that in the early years of the twentieth century 'amateur cinematography was clearly not a hobby for the faint-hearted', since it was too technical an endeavour for many potential users (Enticknap 2005, 66). Before 1923, creating films never became a widespread amateur practice. On the contrary, many of the initial practices related to small-gauge film were about viewing pre-produced theatrical films selected from a film catalogue. Manufacturers such as Pathé and Kodak tried to develop commercially successful projectors such as the Pathé Kok, based on cellulose acetate 28mm film, or the Edison's Home Kinetoscope, on the same type of film, but 22mm wide. These two systems introduced in 1912 used cellulose acetate safety film in order to replace nitrate film, since the latter was considered too great a risk because of its highly flammable nature. Gradually, the idea of the family being able to view rented films at home became a popular social use of middle-class domestic entertainment that represented a kind of 'playback system for cultural content made outside of the home' (Singer 1998; Wasson 2009, 7). In short, the custom of watching films at home preceded the practice of making films at home. A good comparison would be the popularity of the video recorder in the home for watching rented VHS tapes or home-taped television shows in the 1980s and 1990s, which preceded the popular practice of making your own home videos.

The emergence of amateur film culture in the age of cinema

The early 1920s saw a major change in the use of amateur equipment when in both the US and Europe new amateur media systems were introduced: in 1922 Pathé started producing the smallest and cheapest film gauge since then, namely the 9.5mm film format accompanied by a new projector called Pathé Baby. One year later the company launched a 9.5mm camera, also cheap and relatively easy to use. In the meantime, the Eastman Kodak Company introduced a complete Ciné-Kodak system intended for amateur use in June 1923. Film historians tend to interpret these concurrent introductions of 16mm and 9.5mm as an important watershed moment. By 1926, Kodak had already sold 35,000 cameras and 49 million feet (c. 15 million metres) of film footage.[3]

One explanation for its remarkable success would be its simplicity in use, a concept that had proved to be so successful in transforming the act of taking a picture into an everyday practice. Kodak had acquired much expertise on how to market successfully mass-produced consumer media technologies. They reformulated their well-known photography-related slogan: 'You press the button; we do the rest' into 'You turn the crank, we do the rest'.[4] What is especially interesting about Kodak's concept was the fact that the company stimulated consumers to buy the whole package, more or less steering them to become active filmmakers producing content by themselves. Besides the relative simplicity of these new systems, another explanation for the remarkable success was the moderate cost of small-gauge film compared with more expensive (semi-)professional film formats. The initial costs of the first Ciné-Kodak system was at the time $335 US (the equivalent of $5,000 today), which was expensive compared with that of Pathé Baby, which was around $100 ($1,400 in today's prices).[5] According to Ben Singer, this reduction of the cost of making home movies 'emancipated a popular market' (Singer 1998, 48). From the 1920s onwards, the basics of amateur filmmaking were drastically simplified: it only required the amateur filmmaker to buy the film stock, record whatever he or she wanted, send the reel to a film laboratory and wait for the film to be developed and returned (Sarvas and Frohlich 2011). It provided an easy routine for amateur filmmakers interested in documenting their everyday lives and using their film cameras as a technology of memory. The popularity increased after 1932, when Kodak introduced 8mm as a new small-gauge film format, which quickly developed into the next standard, attracting many new users.

However, for those who loved to tinker with the technical possibilities of film, or wanted to explore the aesthetic power of the medium, this new Kodak way of doing things was too simple. These types of amateurs acquainted themselves instead with professional formats as they loved to experiment with less pre-formatted consumer-oriented processes. They greatly appreciated the hands-on aspects of their hobby as an important characteristic of film amateurism just as it had worked for the development of amateur photography. 'Kodaking' in the sense of just pushing the button could threaten that type of amateur skill. Despite some initial hesitance towards these new developments, the opportunities for do-it-yourself filmmaking stimulated a growing sense of film amateurship, and in various place users started to organise themselves in cine-clubs. These clubs functioned as self-teaching communities, which is why Ryan Shand defined this type of practice as the 'community mode', usually holding an ambiguous position between a more public and a more domestic mode (Shand 2008, 52). Self-improvement combined with the ambition of becoming a film artist, but not limited by a kind of Hollywood commercialism, played an important role in the discursive construction of the 'serious' amateur. Also, cine-clubs offered a social environment and a creative space for collaborative production, shared equipment, film competitions, collective screenings, jury reports, which all were instrumental to the construction of 'highly organized artistic regimes' (Shand 2008, 54).

The early history of amateur cine-clubs started in the 1920s, not long after the introduction of 16mm and 9.5mm film. One of the first amateur cine-clubs to be founded in the UK was the Cambridge Kinema Club, founded in 1923 (Heather Norris Nicholson 2012), but quickly they were established almost everywhere across North America and Europe. In the late 1920s and early 1930s, these local cine-clubs organised themselves into national federations. An amateur film movement really took off in 1930s. In a survey carried out for the amateur section of the magazine *American Cinematographer*, it was observed that in Europe, and especially in the UK, almost every town had a cine-club and these clubs regularly held competitions as 'the spice of things', with 'everybody trying to outdo the other'.[6] According to Lance Bird, this growth 'peaked after the war in the late 40's and early '50s; suffered a decline in the late '50s; were rejuvenated by the introduction of Super-8 film in the late '60s, and died with the widespread use of VCRs in the mid '70s' (Bird 1986, 39). Most organised cine-clubs published monthly magazines such as the British *Amateur Cine World* (1934–1967), the American *Movie Maker* (1926–1954) and the Dutch *Het Veerwerk* (1932–1958). Amateur film magazines quickly earned an important role in the life of an amateur: they offered advice, giving tips and tricks, reviewing the newest gadgets or stimulating their readers to use the scissors and cut long stories short.

Early on, these amateur cine-clubs started to organise themselves internationally. An interesting case that accounts for this growing amateur film culture is the Amateur Cinema League (ACL), which started in New York in 1926 as the first international association for non-professional filmmakers. This league would be mainly US based for a considerable time, while the *Union Internationale du Cinéma d'Amateur*, also known as UNICA (World Organisation for Non-Commercial filmmakers), attracted national federations from all over Europe and including countries such as Canada, Japan, Argentina and the USA.[7] The main attraction of the ACL and UNICA was their yearly gathering of amateurs keen to join in the international competitions. These events deeply influenced the amateur filmmaker's understanding of film narrative, aesthetics, genre and topic, thanks to international circulations of prize-winning films. Nevertheless, when looking not only at the numerous cine-club minutes and jury reports, amateur magazines, but also the 'how-to' amateur filmmaking manuals, it becomes clear that it was not always evident what amateur filmmaking exactly entailed. Over the years, fierce debates on aesthetics, the right skills, the appropriate topics and suitable film formats came to characterise the world of the 'serious' amateur.

From a wider media historical perspective, the emergence of amateur film in the interwar years aligns to the emergence of a broader notion of film culture. On a regional, national and international level, competitions, canons and arguments formatted 'cinema as a discursive field', connecting to a wide variety of film cultures such as narrative film, documentary and avant-garde films, while also including amateur filmmaking (Hagener 2007). In some cases where a homegrown film industry was lacking, amateur film made up for that gap and even joined in constituting a national cinema (Horak 1996). The connection to the avant-garde has been especially interesting; in the USA, but also in smaller European countries such as Yugoslavia, Belgium and the Netherlands, independent film societies and amateur cine-clubs worked closely together and in some instances even merged, sharing a network of filmmakers (Horak 1996; Aasman 2004; De Cuir 2014). This situation did not last – from the 1930s onwards, the once closely connected worlds of the avant-garde, the amateur, the documentary and other cultures gradually dispersed (Hagener 2007).

Amateur film as a technology of memory

Although the amateur cine-clubs multiplied quickly, this growth stood in contrast to the large number of everyday users of film. In the United Kingdom around 1935, estimations pointed to 250,000 amateur film camera buyers, whereas only three to four thousand of them became club members (Rieger 2005). In Germany, around the same time, estimations pointed to approximately 16,000 owners of film camera, of whom only 1,000 held a club membership. In amateur magazines, cine-club members would lament, more than once, the lack of overspill of new users into the club. However, not everyone bought a camera out of love of tinkering with new and complex media technologies. Most consumers, rather, appreciated a user-friendly recording technology that allowed them to shoot rather effortlessly and share moving images. It that sense, the average user was less interested in understanding crucial aesthetic or technical features of the medium of film as such. It was enough to understand the ability to make a visual record of their own lives.

The ideal function of the camera as a tool to capture family life in motion was already evident early on, producing 'living pictures' rather than still photographs of the family. The feeling of magic evoked by home movies seems to be a continuous one, or, as one amateur filmmaker wrote in 1921: '[T]he wonderful sensation to see ourselves, our family members as living creatures quite naturally was deeper, more intense than any photograph could ever evoke' (cited in Aasman 2004, 47). Home-movie making became an important (film) genre for those who strived to construct their own history on film. The amateur's camera – whether it was film or photographic – had the right features: it was spontaneous and it was precise, or, as Albert Crane wrote in the photo magazine *Kodakery*: 'You might call Kodak the boss biographer.'[8] As a new recording tool, it gave its owner the chance to materialise on film potentially valuable memories. Although often sold by marketers as a fun-loving activity, once the camera entered the house, home-movie making quickly became more than that: it turned into a duty that transformed a casual Sunday afternoon into an opportunity to add a new film reel to the family archive.

Home-movie making became part of a strong rise of consumer culture, which was gendered as well. For instance, consumption showed a strong differentiation between husband and wife: she decided about the purchase of a sewing machine or a vacuum cleaner, but he decided about the car or the camera. Buying and using a film camera became predominantly a male practice, although occasionally the industry did try to seduce women to become buyers. For example, in 1928 the manufacturer Bell and Howell attempted to make their film cameras more attractive to women by introducing the Filmo 75 B, in a special 'fashionable' leather lining, available for purchase in four different colours. And, indeed, there were women filmmakers, and renewed historical interest in exploring film archives for women filmmakers reveals a strong presence of important collections (Motrescu-Mayes and Norris Nicholson 2018). However, many of the 'how to do it' amateur manuals treated the making of home movies as explicitly a male activity. He was the 'image hunter', shooting his wife and children with his camera. The mother was to step in only if the father was at work when junior made his first steps.

Not only was a gender divide in the field of consumerism and technology a determining factor, but also the history of the family is an important context to be taken into consideration. To be more precise, one cannot separate the history of amateur film from the history of the family (Zimmermann 1995; Aasman 2004). Amateur film was part of a set of values related to a prevailing ideology of domesticity that not only defined a dominant position of the nuclear family but also included different gender roles within it – with the wife as a mother and domestic caretaker, and the husband as a father and breadwinner, one who aspired to spend his leisure time with his wife and children in the intimate sphere of the home. The family and home thus became the preferred domain for leisure time, fun and consumption. And domestic hobbies such as home-movie making fitted well into this ideology. Making a home movie stimulated active and collective forms of domesticity that assigned every member of the family a (gender-)specific role. It could even be argued that this specific practice of amateur filmmaking stimulated a new kind of fatherhood: one that made men become more involved with domestic life, a role traditionally associated with motherhood. This ideology of domesticity deeply influenced the narrative of many home movies and how the family came to be represented. For instance, the father is almost never visible in home movies since he is mostly behind the camera, as he is looking at his family. Still, the fact that the film is made by him presupposes his presence, and this is usually acknowledged whenever the subjects (his children/his wife) respond, glance at or speak to him. In this way the father is present through 'giving the appearance of participation' (Sontag 1979, 10).

These representations suggest a world in which the social formation of the family retracted from the world, where public life had no role. Even when events associated with 'big' history occurred, home movies usually did not address these moments in an explicit way. Patricia Holland made very clear the fact that home movies create their own space and so '[w]hen family and politics cross, it is always family which takes priority, as if the politics could be denied' (Holland 1991, 10). At the same time, home-movie makers acted as *chroniclers* of their time, going out with their camera and capturing life on the streets and during events. How exactly such contradictory ambitions play out – making a record of the happy life at home while taking the camera out to eyewitness life outside – can be analysed, for instance, during moments of political crises or a war. One such interesting example would be the Dutch home movie *One day based on many days*, which was made during the Second World War – a period in which families suddenly had to deal with new rules imposed on them by the Nazis who had occupied the Netherlands. Theo Festen (1903–1985), a sales manager and father of five, had recorded moments during a year, after which he compiled the separate moments and edited them in a typical 'day-in-the-life' – from morning until late at night – style. This type of narrative was quite popular among home-movie makers, as it offered the prospective viewer a collection of important moments of family life. The film starts with a brief introduction of Festen's family, after which it follows the events of the typical day-to-day life of a Catholic family in chronological order: family members wake up and get out of bed, the children wash their faces (see Figure 1.1), the oldest boys go to an early-morning mass and then to school; the father leaves the house to go to work, etc. In the evening, the family enjoys their evening meal, after which the children go to bed. After a long and busy day, the house is quiet again. Mother stitches some clothes while Father lights his pipe and reads the evening paper. The last frame shows Festen giving a quick, playfully conspiratorial nod at the camera (see Figure 1.2). Another day in their life had passed.

The film proves that Festen was a fairly skilled amateur filmmaker, although he was not a cine-club member. Most of his home movies represent the usual topics, showing the festive moments of his family life: the birth of his children, their first steps, their first school days, etc. However, one scene in his compilation displays a moment of suspense. To explain this, we need some more historical context. At the time, because of the German occupation, it could be dangerous to film outside the house as there were all kinds of curfew rule and safety regulation about

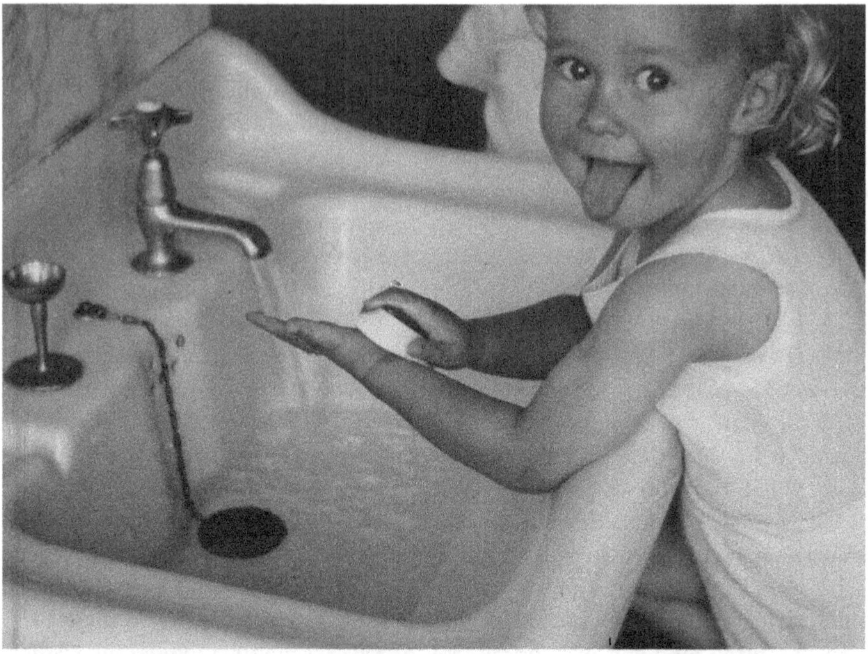

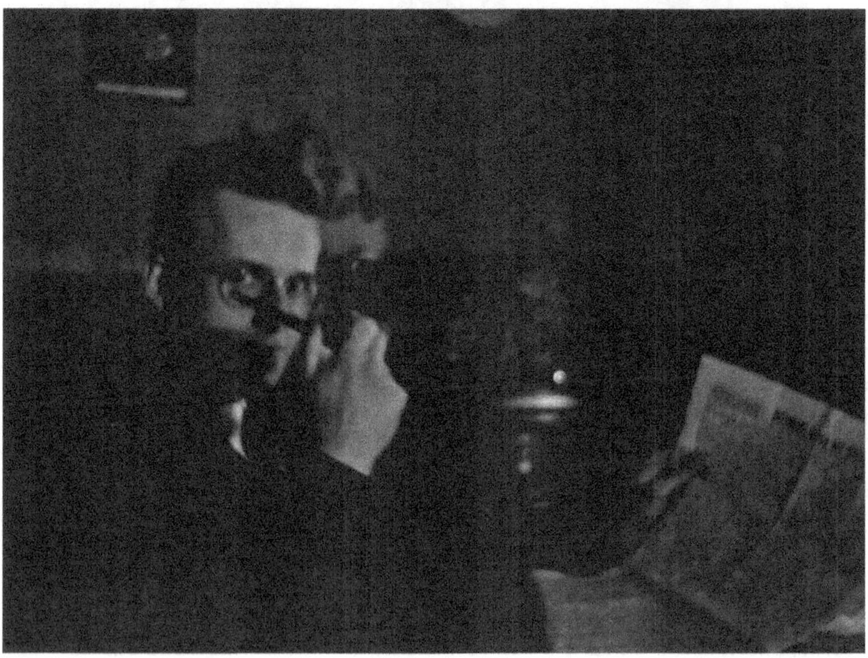

FIGURE 1.1 and **FIGURE 1.2** Stills from *One day based on many days*. 1943. Eye Filmmuseum, Amsterdam.

recording in public areas, especially near military areas. In the home movie, this danger becomes almost tangible when Festen and his wife, cycling through the woods, unexpectedly pass some German soldiers (see Figure 1.3). They quickly turn their bikes around and pick up the camera, which Festen has placed on a fence.

This moment was certainly not planned and it must have been really special for the family to watch these dramatic moments during home screenings. However, what has not been shown in the film is that potential danger was not just outside the house, but it could be at home as well, especially for the father. At that time, he was a reserve officer in the Dutch military and had reason to be afraid of being held as a prisoner of war or being put to work as a forced labourer in Germany. So, when the frequency of German raids rose, the father started staying away during late evenings and nights. The home movie, of course, reveals nothing about his absence during the night. This absence/presence of the filmmaker and his explicit nod at the camera at the end of this movie do point – although very indirectly – towards a crucial meaning of this type of visual document. Home movies are very selective in their representations; they underscore the unity and wholeness of the family, celebrating moments of togetherness.

To understand Festen's compilation, some knowledge of the historical context is important: only then can we start to interpret the experiences created in the movie as well as the functional modality of this type of recording. This goes even further

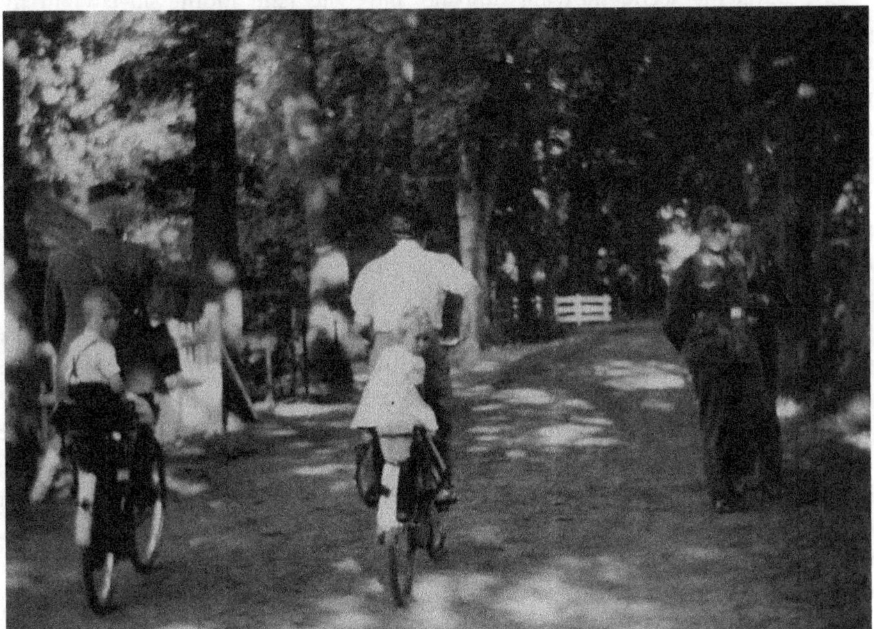

FIGURE 1.3 Still from *One day based on many days*. 1943. Eye Filmmuseum, Amsterdam.

with another example, made around the same time, by a Dutch Jewish filmmaker Max Peereboom (1911–1943). Peereboom was a young man when he started filmmaking in 1932 with his 8mm film camera. For about ten years he recorded his life and that of his parents, his shop in Vlissingen, the Jewish neighbourhood in Amsterdam and from 1937 onwards his life with his wife and their two children. When Nazi Germany occupied the country, Peereboom carried on making home movies. But life outside quickly became more and more restricted for Jews up until the point at which leisure was only possible within the confines of their house. Still, he kept recording his domestic life, close to the end. Somewhere around August or September of 1942, the family was ordered to prepare to leave to the transit camp Westerbork, from where almost every week a train left for the concentration camps in Germany and Poland. It is not entirely clear when the following scene from Peereboom's collection was recorded: it is evening when two women are shown sitting at a table stitching clothes. They are Max's wife and mother-in-law (Figure 1.4). It might be that Peereboom wished to capture the preparations for their journey. He takes his time to carefully register the women's work as he includes some close-ups of their busy hands. Twice Max enters and leaves the frame: the last time he joins the company; he seats himself behind the table while his wife pours him some coffee. He then lights his pipe while picking up the newspaper (Figure 1.5). This is the end of the scene and it was probably the last scene ever recorded by Max Peereboom.

The mundane scene showing husband and wife (and mother-in-law) in the evening recorded by Peereboom resembles the last scene in the Festen home movie, only this time we might wonder why someone would record such a moment, knowing that they have to leave their home and uncertain of what the future holds for them or, indeed, if there would be a future at all. We don't know the answer to these questions. It might be helpful to think of home movies as a practice based on not only the past but also the future. By making home movies, people sent themselves a message in which they state: 'We are doing just fine.' As Annette Kuhn stated: '[T]he promise is of a brighter past in the future, if we only seize the chance today to consume the raw materials of our tomorrow's memories' (Kuhn 1995, 20). As rituals of domestic happiness, home movies can offer a sense of continuity and stability, even if we do not fully understand if it really helps, or, as Barbara Meyerhoff suggested: 'In ritual, doing is believing' (Meyerhoff 1984, 305).

Max Peereboom, his wife and children and most of his family members were sent to Auschwitz. They all died in the gas chambers. Only his brother, Simon Peereboom, survived, and when he returned to the Netherlands after the war had ended, he was able to recover the film collection.[9] Theo Festen went back to work as a sales manager and hardly had time to film his family on average weekdays. From the 1950s onwards, the popularity of making home movies grew exponentially due to social, economic and cultural factors, such as the rise in welfare, suburbanisation and more leisure time, as well as the availability of new consumer technologies that were quickly appropriated by many new enthusiastic users.

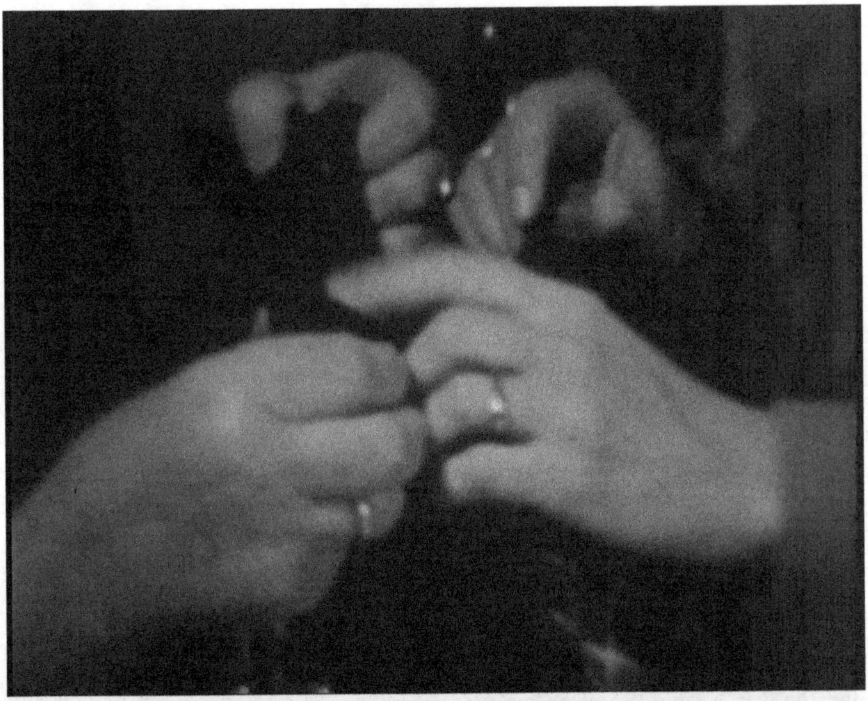

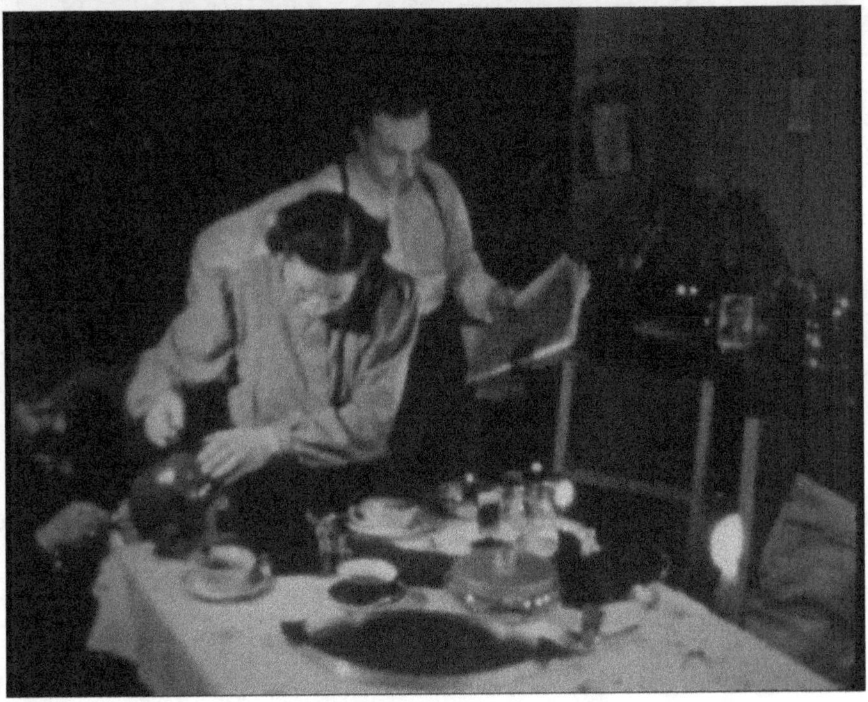

FIGURE 1.4 and **FIGURE 1.5** Stills from Peereboom collection 1942–43. The Netherlands Institute for Sound and Vision.

II Amateur media in the age of television (1950–2000)

During the post-war era, amateur filmmaking practices became part of a changing media culture, in which television gradually emerged as a dominant form of expression alongside cinema. Nevertheless, it took a while before television became the main point of reference in the discourse on amateur media, as it remained closely connected to cinema for many years. Film remained the dominant technology that guided the protocols and routines for the production of images, the types of narrative and the screening context. The introduction of Super-8 film technology in 1965 popularised amateur filmmaking for some decades to come. But gradually television, a popular new mass medium that infiltrated almost every household in two decades, deeply influenced amateur media practices. In particular, the arrival of new media technologies, such as video, made a major impact and became part of divergent, yet interconnected amateur media histories. In particular, the rhetoric of amateur media as a democratic tool able to resist and subvert mass media monopolies became more explicit. Another interesting extension of the home-movie tradition was the transformation from a predominant domestic mode to a more personal approach towards filmmaking.

From domestic to personal

After the war, a rapid rise of welfare and an increase in leisure time, combined with the prevailing domestic ideology, eased the way for a growing popularity of do-it-yourself pastimes. Whether it was about redecorating one's kitchen or making home movies, the domestic sphere became the prime area of leisure and fun such that the post-war 'cultural discourse idealised the home and the nuclear family as more creative labour sites' (Zimmermann 1995, 117). Families more than ever became the target for consumption of commodities and entertainment. The hitherto modest popularity of amateur filmmaking grew significantly. In the USA, Zimmermann traced the rapidly increasing sales of major film manufacturers, such as Bell and Howell, and Kodak. The already growing market for amateur media technologies moved to another level in 1965 when Kodak introduced the Super-8 film system, whereas, at the same time, the Japanese manufacturer Fuji launched Single-8. Both companies innovated the recording technology by replacing open-film reels with cartridges that made loading a camera much easier. This transition was essential to the development and success of the amateur film practice as it combined the advantages of automatisation and miniaturisation with a serious reduction in the cost: this 'cheap and easy to use' rhetoric became strategic in the marketing of Super-8 film technologies, attracting a new generation of first-time users (Van der Heijden 2018).

In addition, the introduction of colour film stock persuaded many new users. Colour film had been an option for amateurs before – e.g. Kodacolor and earlier versions of Kodachrome had been used since the late 1920s – but with the arrival of Kodachrome II and Super-8 affordable colour film became available to a larger group of consumers. Gradually amateur filmmakers embraced Kodachrome and consequently its features shaped generations of collective mediated memories. The rich saturation and clarity of the colours became the recognisable cultural form of the amateur aesthetic of everyday life during the late 1960s and early 1970s. When Kodak, after many decades, ended its production of Super-8 colour reversal film and closed its last Kodachrome lab in January 2011, the response was overwhelmingly that of nostalgia. This decline of Kodachrome in combination with the overall disappearance of Super-8 film stimulated a renewed interest in analogue small-gauge film formats at the end of the 1990s and the early 2000s, mostly by young people who never had first-hand experience of analogue technologies. Van der Heijden (2018) describes this 'analogue response' or 'nostalgic turn' as a counter-reaction to various technological, social and cultural changes, although it ultimately inspired Kodak to re-introduce Super-8 colour in early 2018.

Back in the 1960s and 1970s when Single and Super-8 film became the standard home-movie formats, they did not, however, significantly change the *screen practice* of the home movie. Nor did it fundamentally influence the narrative structures of the home movie. Moreover, home-movie making remained a silent medium for another decade. Since the 1920s, individual amateurs who dared to experiment with available sound technologies had to explore a range of different technologies, including things like pre-striped film, post-striped film or additional devices or projectors that could handle the different sound systems. The option to convert to sound film for home-movie makers became more obvious with the arrival of Ektasound in 1973. With this new format that allowed recorded synchronous sound on a magnetic strip at the edge of the film, Kodak hoped to convince families to work with a camera and film format and a projector that automatically recorded and projected sound pictures. Ektasound did not last long as around 1979 Kodak ended production when video emerged as the new consumer technology for synchronous sound.

It is useful to consider home-movie making in the post-war era in relation to television as the new prime medium. The proliferations of television sets in households showed a yearly exponential growth of sales. In the USA, for instance, the number of sales was by far the largest in the world and the number grew from a modest 9 per cent in 1950 to almost 100 per cent by the end of the 1960s. UNESCO estimated that around 1960 there were about 100 million television sets in the world and around that time North America had 60 per cent and Europe (including USSR) 31 per cent (UNESCO 1963). During this period, television became an important domestic medium integrating in the daily rhythm of life – whether it was broadcasting news, sports, talk shows, sitcoms or drama series. Even more interesting, close resemblances between sitcoms' domestic settings and narrative patterns and the home-movie practice show shared cultural codes (Moran 2002). According to Moran, each genre inspired the other, borrowing and appropriating conventions of representation and patterns of interpersonal communication. Just like home movies, television programmes sought to portray 'families in everyday settings, sentimentalized child rearing, celebrated rites of passage, and advocated togetherness' (Moran 2002, 105). Moran's hypothesis helps take a broader media historical perspective on the intermedial relations between amateur media and television.

With television as the dominant medium of communication, there emerged a growing interest in representing family life, highlighting the everyday in a wide variety of non-fiction television formats. As television became the prime witness of social-historical reality (Ellis 2012), recording and broadcasting everyday life became an important foundation especially in the post-war documentary film tradition. But in the late 1960s and early 1970s the more social engaged, fact-loving genre developed into other directions as well, namely a more autobiographical and personal approach (Lane 2002). Especially in the United States, there was a small but influential group of avant-garde filmmakers experimenting with amateur media technology as a tool for bridging the gap between life and art. In *Window water baby moving* (1959), Stan Brakhage recorded the pregnancy of his wife and the birth of his child with his 16mm camera, whereas Jonas Mekas created his famous diaries *Walden* (1969) also on 16mm film. These films became part of an autobiographical turn in documentary filmmaking, taking the genre of home movie as their source of inspiration. According to Jim Lane, this change towards subjectivity and personal experience was part of a more general societal desire for self-realisation in the late 1960s and early 1970s. This aligns also with a particular mode of radical political discourse in these decades, in which it was believed that social change could only be reached through a process of personal change (Lane 2002).

New amateur media technologies, such as Super-8 film and video, were expected to be the right tools to explore such personal change (Aasman 2014). Throughout the 1970s young artists explored the Super-8, especially since synchronous sound became an option. Almost simultaneously with the introduction of Kodak's Ektasound, documentary filmmaker Richard Leacock, one of the pioneers of 'Direct Cinema', developed, with a grant from the American Massachusetts Institute of Technology (MIT), Super-8 film synchronous sound equipment by modifying available mass-produced amateur media technology. It meant a breakthrough in the development of cheap sync-sound Super-8 systems (at the time, under $800). The highly portable Super-8 system was seen as a medium that offered better affordances for a personal and intimate reflection on life (Chittick 1980). At MIT, in special film courses, and elsewhere through magazines and journals, young aspirational filmmakers learned to appreciate amateur media technology as a tool for personal expression. Several filmmakers, such as Ed Pincus in the USA, Ed van der Elsken in the Netherlands and Joseph Morder in France, explored intimate and autobiographical approaches by using sync-sound Super-8 systems.

Such performances of intimacy, so closely related to home-movie making, extended to video as well. Early on in its development, video was believed to be an excellent opportunity to engage in self-reflection. In particular, the arrival of the Sony's Portapak system, a portable video camera and recorder, at the end of 1960s, attracted new kinds of media makers – initially, avant-garde artists who experimented with its new features. The affordability of synchronous sound recording and the instant feedback loop with a nearby television screen gave its users the opportunity to talk to the camera, having an uninterrupted monologue in which they could share their thoughts and ideas. It enabled and stimulated new genres such as video diaries. The possibility of an instant feedback loop was particularly interesting because video no longer required a development stage in a lab, which not only eliminated the delay in watching the footage, as was the case with film; but also eliminated the possibility of unwanted views of your content. This instant possibility for viewing without any intermediaries stimulated a much more intimate and confessional attitude for documentary filmmakers as well as amateur filmmakers.

It was the 1980s before video really became popular with amateur filmmakers. Early video systems had been heavy and cumbersome, as they required a heavy tube-based camera and a separate video recording machine. The first portable video recording systems (usually called Portapaks to emphasise the portability) that were available from 1965 onwards were still expensive, certainly when compared with Super-8 film. Another setback was the long struggle for the standardisation of consumer video formats (tapes, recorders and cameras), also known as the 'format wars'. During this struggle in the late 1970s and early 1980s, several mutually incompatible video systems competed with each other: Betamax (Sony), Video2000 (Philips) and VHS (JVC). Eventually, the Video Home System (VHS) became the standard for consumers. It was not until the mid-1980s, with the arrival of the camcorder (a camera with an integrated recorder), that video became the preferred device for making family recordings. Estimations show that in just a few years only one in 30 American families owned a video camera, but this figure rose dramatically in the early 1990s to one in six (Buckingham et al. 2007).

A big advantage of video was that a tape – compared with film – was a much cheaper format thanks to the length of the tape: this made the necessity of strict selection criteria of what to record both economically and materially less urgent. Families could tape for hours and these technical and economic changes deeply influenced the traditional practice of home-movie making. Therefore, the textual dimension evolved from fragmentary short stereotypical highlights into long takes, which opened up the potential to provide a 'narratively rich mediation of everyday activities and events' (Slootweg 2018a, 214; Moran 2002). Moreover, due to the length of the videotape and the availability of synchronous sound, the recording of audible emotions became much more a part of the final videotext. Now, alongside smiles and performed-for-the-camera happy family moments, tears or screams of anger entered the videotape (Moran 2002). Even when people did not want to be in the video and tried to keep out of the range of the camera, the microphone would still pick up signals. As such, home video became the – potentially much more – multi-layered successor of the home movie.

From the mid-1980s onwards, new users started exploring this new media technology, one of them being the Petroskey family. This case tells the story of a collection of more than 600 videos produced by Paul Petroskey, who started making his own videos in 1984, as a 14-year-old when his father bought a RCA colour video camera. Two years earlier, the Petroskey family from Pittsburgh got their first video recorder, a Panasonic PV1217. Young Paul immediately bought himself a VHS tape for $12 and started taping television programmes. By the time the video camera entered the family, Paul had already built a modest tape collection that contained his favourite commercials, sketches from *Saturday Night Live*, local television footage (including the weather forecast) and music videos.[10]

The arrival of the home video system represents a shift in generational use of amateur media – it shows the young teenager rather than the father having almost full control of the camera. During their first night, with the new device barely unboxed and with the room filled with giggling children watching themselves on the television screen, while the father starts recording the very first seconds with the new camera, Paul demands to be both the director and the protagonist at the same time (Weird Paul, *First night with the video camera* (1984)). With the camera still recording, Paul shouts at his father who is panning the living room with his newly acquired camera: 'Dad, Dad, don't move that camera, Dad.' With these words, Paul demonstrates his eagerness to be in the view of the camera lens. 'Don't you just love this,' Paul says to the camera. It is also the beginning of a generational struggle regarding who is in control. For instance, halfway during this first video, when Paul keeps standing in front of the camera, blocking the view of the others, his father gets angry and starts screaming, 'Get away from it', to which Paul responds, 'Look at me, look at me, I am a TV star' (Figure 1.6) The videotape eventually ends with Paul standing close to the camera, reciting quite solemnly: 'On this day. It will be remembered. That we got a camera.'

From then on, and not always with the approval of his father, Paul started using the camera himself. It was another year before the family bought a tripod, but during that period Paul would convince his mother or one of his sisters to hold the camera whenever he wanted to be on screen, show his birthday gifts, do music video imitations or just be funny. It is interesting to analyse his many camera appearances: his total confidence in front of the camera indicates how children of his generation have grown up in a television culture characterised by people sharing thoughts, ideas and creative moments in a public domain. His videos also show a complete lack of the traditional, more restricted form of documenting that had become one of the characteristics of the average home movie. Also the more mundane moments of his ordinary life were documented with a youthful swagger wrapped in a loose and almost experimental use of the camera. This meant that the camera was on when his father became angry and shouted at him; when his mother got irritated and screamed at him, and it was on in the bathroom when Paul explored the inside of the toilet. The last scene is only known because Weird Paul recollected his early video-making memories in his YouTube version of this old VHS tape. But at the time of the recording his father had erased these specific images as being inappropriate. Over the years, Paul built a unique video archive, as

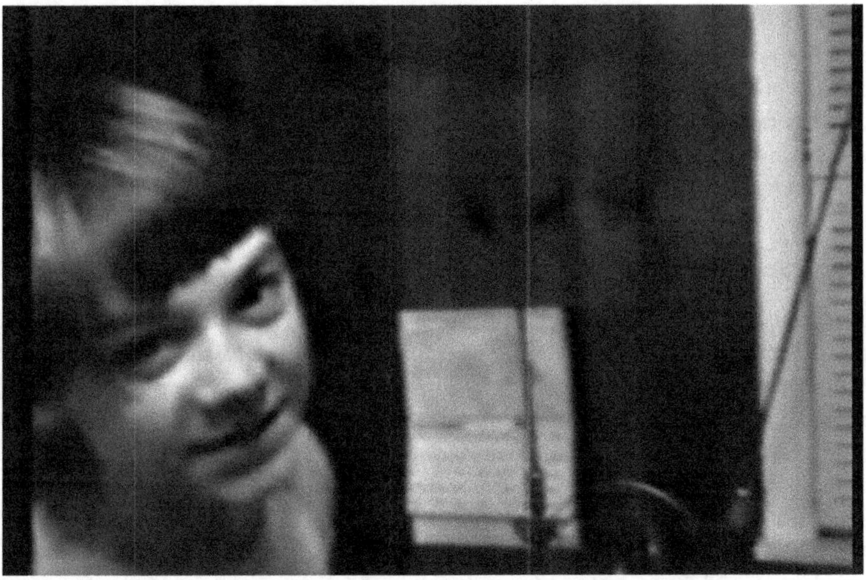

FIGURE 1.6 *First night with the video camera.* 1984. Screengrab via YouTube.

visible evidence of a transformational period in which amateur media making was no longer the prerogative of the parents.

The availability of integrated synchronous sound added an extra and very interesting layer to this work as well. For instance, sound changed the one-dimensional home movie into a multi-layered document, stimulating new themes and directions. When Paul talked to the camera, he created a certain level of intimacy, which is now quite conventional but, compared with the long silent era of amateur film, was still rather new then. Spoken words gave him the option to control the narrative, adding through his voice his strain of thoughts to the video. But the ability of synchronous sound also set new challenges, as the camera would catch every sound, including sounds that were not intended to be captured on tape. For instance, in one video Paul had his family participate to help him re-enact a videoclip by the popular hard rock band Twisted Sister (*We're not gonna take it. Fan Video 1985 Twisted Sister music video*). His father played a character, his brother and sister did their part, but his little baby brother just cried throughout most of the recording. It is exactly this inherent probability of recording unwanted sounds, voices or noises that gave the home mode a greater sense of polyvocal representation (Slootweg 2018a).

In the new era of television, amateur film and video cultures, documentary filmmaking and television mainstream genres all shared these 'patterns of increasing subjectivity' (Winston 2015, 200). As Moran noted: '[P]ersonal lives and public media texts have become almost indistinguishable for a TV generation accustomed to being in front of both a video screen and a lens' (Moran 2002, 147). With the arrival of video, we can indeed trace a transformation of the amateur media practice from a domestic to a more complex multi-layered one. Home videos no longer put the family first. Instead, a much more personal perspective had emerged, which means that the person behind the camera can just as easily point his camera at his family as he can turn the camera 180 degrees to be himself in front of the camera.

Amateur video as an alternative medium

The arrival of video fuelled long-lived ideals about amateur media as an alternative media space for production and dissemination for political and social activists. Moreover, it inspired communities of lo-fi artists who appreciated amateur video technologies as the perfect means that suited their do-it-yourself ethics. The promise of a single media system that was portable and mobile, had synchronous sound and was easy to distribute and screen on television fed emancipatory discourses of democratisation and participation, and these have been present from the 1920s and 1930s onwards. Already in the early history of amateur media oppositional practices had existed, when substandard film gauges such as 16mm film were embraced by political activists: for instance, the Belgium Association of Socialist Amateur Film-Makers (Arbeiders Film Collectief). Many of these groups used amateur film cameras, in the full belief that eyewitness reports could make a difference (Winston 2015). Super-8 film became the next solution. As we have already seen, Leacock and Pincus developed a sync-sound Super-8 film system in order to start a 'deprofessionalisation of filmmaking' (Pincus 1972, 30). In 1975, UNESCO published a report called *Super 8: The Modest Medium*, which predicted an 8mm revolution. This prediction was based on the idea that giving ordinary people access to an audio-visual medium could help them participate in the public sphere. Although this UNESCO report emphasised the opportunities in Third World countries, it promoted the more general idea that Super-8 film could become a counter-technology, insomuch that people could use it as a communication tool to portray a variety of problems (Gunther 1976). However, the opportunities for widespread dissemination remained somewhat limited and almost never reached beyond the marginal communities that produced these images.

With video already on the horizon, its arrival in the mid-1960s was weighed not only for its potential of user agency in terms of production, but also in terms of the potential for dissemination. At this point, there were several options for how amateur video came to be positioned as an alternative medium, which basically came down to focusing on participation *in* or participation *through* media (Bailey et al. 2007; Slootweg and Aasman 2015). The first approach refers to a media infrastructure that enables non-professionals to communicate *within* institutionalised media, such as radio or television. The second approach relates to the means with which self-representation can be achieved *outside* of the realm of institutionalised media. From the onset of its emergence in the consumer market, artists and activists embraced video technology and rapidly attributed itith significance with regard to its political and radical artistic potential, against and outside media. Video was thus seen as a 'specific cluster of technologies [that] was endowed with specific symbolic meanings and affordances by which everyone was believed to appropriate them to radically resist to mass media by mediating everyday life' (Slootweg 2018a, 78). This was particularly the case for American video activists in the 1970s, who were convinced that video offered possibilities to challenge the dominance of powerful media institutions such as television (Boyle 1992). Video activists welcomed portable video as a counter-technology, praising its potential to decentralise the mainstream mass media monopolies and give the ordinary user some level of individual agency (Slootweg 2018a). An interesting example of how idealistic video activists tried to bring video to the people and experimented with democratic video culture is the American video collective Videofreex. From 1972 to 1977, this so-called grassroots organisation ran in its community in New York 'the world's smallest television station'. Using a local channel and a low-power transmitter, the group experimented with alternative models – such as a media bus – for the collaborative production and distribution of television programming, challenging standard claims of professionalism. Meanwhile, in Europe, video activists attempted through similar projects to establish some form of 'Folk TV' (Burch 1997) – for instance, the Dutch video collective Meatball toured the streets with a van, which held a television set and a video recorder in the back (Slootweg 2018a). Video gave a strong impetus to concrete experiments of politically inspired 'do-it-yourself TV', acknowledging a participatory role for the amateur.

Another example of participatory video making, giving the amateur an opportunity to share his or her videos with a wider audience, comes from the BBC in the UK. Jo Henderson (2009) reconstructed the history of access programming at the BBC going back as early as the late 1960s. This policy for more community-oriented programming eventually led to the highly regarded *Video Diaries* series in 1990 in which ordinary people could share their first-person accounts on BBC2. Later, this series was followed by *Video Nation*, again based on a format that allowed amateur self-portraits to be broadcasted on national TV. Overall, however, idiosyncratic aesthetic experiments or private images of the home did not receive public broadcasting unless it was in compilation programmes, such as *America's Funniest Home Movies* (ABC, 1990–present).

However, in some special cases, the amateur video footage was spectacular enough to enter the arena of professional news broadcasting and received wider public exposure, as for instance the *Rodney King Video Tape* (1991), which became one of the most famous examples of a home video. This early example of what later came to be called 'citizen journalism' (Rosen 2008) demonstrated the possibilities of affordable media technologies in producing eyewitness reports. The amateur video was made by George Holliday who stood on his balcony in Los Angeles with his newly acquired camcorder on the evening of 3 March 1991 when five police officers had heavily beaten up an African-American man, who was later identified as Rodney King. Holliday recorded the event and then shared his images with the local news station KTLA. After this first broadcast, the amateur video footage quickly gained nationwide coverage. The public was shocked by the police brutality and, in the weeks and months that followed, a huge debate on racism within the Los Angeles Police Department (LAPD) raged, while most TV stations repeated broadcasts of the footage of King over and over.

The *Rodney King Video Tape* was not the first amateur footage to receive such coverage; three decades earlier, in 1963, amateur filmmaker Abraham Zapruder took his 8mm Bell & Howell camera with him to record the arrival of President Kennedy in Dallas, Texas. By accident, he taped the assassination of the president. His film reel turned out to be the only recording of the actual shooting. Since then, the 'amateurish', unedited and shaky footage has become an iconic example of how eyewitness reports were perceived as authentic and true (Chanan 2000). This was also the case with the *Rodney King Video Tape*. The shaky, grainy, black-and-white handheld camerawork on the videotape was perceived as amateur and thus as authentic, truthful evidence. Video technologies, such as the camcorder, seemed to be able to become an ideal political weapon. However, the tape also came to represent the vulnerability of amateur media as evidence – in court, the videotape was not considered strong enough to be counted as evidence against the police, because, as the prosecutor stated, it only showed a part of the action and not the whole story (Figure 1.7).[11] Based on this evaluation, the jury acquitted the officers but afterwards major riots broke out in Los Angeles, because that part of the audience had interpreted the images in a different way.

However, the idea of amateur media being able to raise awareness and the idea of amateur media makers as citizen journalists or media activists who were able to

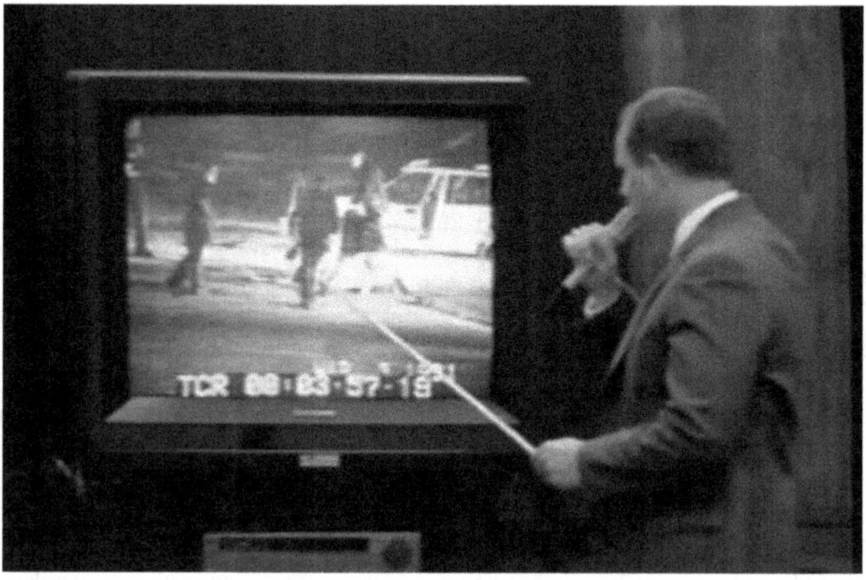

FIGURE 1.7 Still showing the *Rodney King Video Tape* used in court, *Court TV News: California v. Powell, et al.* 1992. Screengrab via YouTube.

produce eyewitness reports on evil being done inspired musician and activist Peter Gabriel to start the human rights organisation WITNESS (1991). According to this organisation, video evidence makes it 'hard for the perpetrators of those abuses to deny and bury what had happened'. The Rodney King incident made it very clear that ordinary people could use video 'to witness abuse and use it to campaign for justice and change' (Gabriel 2014).[12] Despite the rhetoric and the widespread dissemination of this controversial tape that really impacted a broad audience, Laurie Ouellette (1995) heavily downgraded the potential of amateur video at the time – according to her analysis, amateur video failed and certainly was unable to live up to its radical potential. Overall, amateurs were only good enough for broadcasting bloopers or they were dependent on severe selection by professional television programme makers. Zimmermann (1995) concluded in similar vein when she noticed that amateur footage was only valued when there was a lack of professional material.

III From marginal to mainstream: amateur media in the age of Internet

> Imagine a place where other cultures … are available to all; a place where almost anyone … can produce verbal and visual images, where individual or groups can edit, arrange, and rearrange the visualization of their outer and inner worlds, and, a place where these movies, TVs. … can be instantaneously available to anyone who chooses to look. … Imagine this place, for it is where we are at now.
>
> *(Worth 1968)*

In her book on print cultures, Lisa Gitelman posed the question whether amateurs of one era are the same as amateurs of another. To become aware of both the continuities and discontinuities, we should look at how amateurs' 'doings and do-abilities are situated within the broader cultural economy' (Gitelman 2014, 145). One of the continuities that can be observed is the current rise of amateur culture, which recalls the productive and creative energies of early 1930s amateur cinematography. Moreover, the everyday production of domestic images has been a powerful and continuous drive for building family archives. However, the discontinuities are there as well. Amateur media culture has changed dramatically with the emergence of the Internet as an important tool that not just provides the affordances of media distribution but also, and more importantly, marks a social space that makes the amateur visible in a way that they were never before (Seijdel 2010). In the current context of 'doings and do-abilities' that Gitelman mentioned, the amateur has become 'emancipated', meaning that the traditional boundaries and hierarchies between professional and amateur, public and private and commercial and non-commercial have become redefined (Gitelman 2014, 19).

This transformation happened very quickly. Since it became easier to produce amateur images with small digital camcorders (since 1995) or with mobile (cell) phones (since 2000), image production has expanded. In addition, since the Internet entered the Web 2.0 stage in the early 2000s, the circulation of these home produced images has exploded likewise. 'Every time a new consumer joins this media landscape, a new producer joins as well because the same equipment – phones, computers – lets you consume and produce', Clay Shirky stated in 2012.[13] The many innovations in social media tools and Internet have, according to Shirky (2008), removed older obstacles to public expression, and thus changed the way mass media work, resulting in a 'mass amateurization' of the media landscape. The Internet facilitated the transformation from mass consumption to mass cultural production (Manovich 2009), as it broke down the barriers to make room for 'pro-ams' or 'prosumers', each of these new terms trying to characterise a fundamental shift in what used to be professional and amateur. The terminology at the time indicated intense optimism built on a longstanding tradition of relating technological innovation to a democratic potential of access to the means of media. Even more intriguing, it did somehow reflect the words of the anthropologist and filmmaker Sol Worth in 1968, some four decades before YouTube started, when he predicted a media space where mass access would be possible. What is interesting about Sol Worth's quote is that he was referring not only to means of production but, more importantly, to the means of distribution.

In addition, social media, providing for multiple applications that further encouraged all kinds of communication and production as the dominant cultural form, made the Internet the place for disseminating do-it-yourself material. The major difference with previous innovations in amateur media is the ability to now share audio-visual content to a potential wide audience without much effort. Whether it is Facebook, Instagram, Google Video (ended 2009), Vine (ended 2017), Vimeo, Daily Motion, Twitter or YouTube, or any other free video-sharing platform, the Internet has transformed amateur media practices fundamentally in both a public and a global medium culture, making it capable of competing with professional media in its potential for worldwide dissemination. Amateur media has finally integrated into mainstream mass media, demonstrating a 'rapid circulation across a range of social networks' (Jenkins et al. 2013, 39). Indeed, there is a shift from distribution to circulation that can be analysed as a movement towards a more participatory model of culture. In this model, users shape, share and remix media content in a way that was previously unthinkable and also impossible (Jenkins et al. 2013). Seen from a historical perspective, that would mean something like: amateurs moved beyond the home or the club as a social space and joined a global media space, beyond any immediate geographic or social proximity.

Roland Barthes once defined the amateur in terms of absence of audience. He stated: 'The amateur is not necessarily defined by a lesser knowledge, an imperfect technique … but rather by this: he is the one who does not exhibit, the one who does not make himself heard' (Barthes 1991, 230). Today's media culture is bound to invalidate his claim because the new, cultural dimensions of the amateur in the age of the Internet is a place where everyone and the everyday can be heard and thus get signification, acquiring symbolic value. Amateur media production nowadays implies simultaneous dissemination owing to easy sharing of streaming video on large online media platforms. What was previously considered marginal has now entered a completely reconfigured media landscape where amateur and professional converge in a shared media culture that is always *on* and refreshed 24/7, day by day. Amateur media have become a key asset of popular culture, but whether this is the ultimate outcome of a long-lived dream or a nightmare depends on one's view.

Notes

1 The Netherlands Institute for Scientific Research (NWO) supported this research project during the period 2012–2016. It entailed a collaboration between Maastricht University and the University of Groningen and produced two PhD dissertations by Tim Van der Heijden (2018) and Tom Slootweg (2018) and an edited volume by Susan Aasman, Andreas Fickers and Joseph Wachelder (eds), *Materializing Memories: Dispositifs, Generations, Amateurs*. New York: Bloomsbury, 2018.

2 The original German version of this autobiography of Julius Neubrunner, *55 Jahre Liebhaberfotograf von Dr. Julius Neubrunner (1852–1932)*, was partly reprinted in Michael Kuball (ed.) 1980. *Familiekino: Geschichte des Amateurfilms in Deutschland, 1900–1930*. Hamburg/Reinbek: Rowohlt.

3 These numbers were mentioned in a Dutch magazine for amateur photographers: J.C. Mol, 'Filmknipsel', *Lux. Geïllustreerd Tijdschrift voor Fotografie*, 1927, no. 38, 32.

4 'Ciné Kodak for motion pictures', *Kodakery: A Magazine for Amateur Photographers*, 1923, no. 8, 9–11.

5 The prices of these devices differed from country to country and according to year. The advertisements indicating prices in French francs, British pounds or American dollars do not always compare.

6 Arthur Campbell, 'Survey of Foreign Cinephotography', *Amateur Cinematography*, September 1934, 226–233, 226.

7 Officially, a permanent commission with the title UNICA started in 1937 when national amateur film leagues from all over the world came together in Paris. This official start was a follow-up of yearly meetings and film competitions that had been taking place since 1931, when the first gathering of (five) European countries was held in Brussels.

8 Albert Crane Wallace, 'The Year Story', *Kodakery. A Magazine for Amateur Photographers*, 1923, no. 5, 308.

9 The Hungarian Filmmaker Peter Forgács made a gripping documentary of the original footage: *The Maelstroom. A Family Chronicle*, 1997, video 60 min.

10 After 2010 Weird Paul (Paul later named himself Weird Paul when he produced his first record as a lo-fi musician in 1987) digitised his analogue tapes, re-edited them, adding comments, and uploaded them on his YouTube channels. Weird Paul has several channels on YouTube, the main one for this chapter being 'ORIGINAL VLOGGER 80S' WEIRD PAUL' [online]. Available at www.youtube.com/user/weirdpaulp.

11 See Court TV News. 'California v. Powell, et al.', 29 April 1992.

12 Peter Gabriel, 'Tech can make video evidence a cornerstone of justice', *Wired*, 30 December 2014 [online]. Available at www.wired.com/2014/12/peter-gabriel-witness-on-videoevidence. See for more on WITNESS: https://witness.org/.

13 See the transcript of a radio interview TED Radio Hour, 'How can social media make history?', 6 May 2012 [online]. Available at www.npr.org/templates/transcript/transcript.php?storyId=152868437.

Selected bibliography

Aasman, Susan. 2004. *Ritueel van Huiselijk Geluk. Een Cultuurhistorische Verkenning van de Familiefilm* [Ritual of Domestic Happiness. A Cultural History of the Home Movie]. Amsterdam: Het Spinhuis.

Aasman, Susan. 2009. 'Home Movies: A New Technology, a New Duty, a New Cultural Practice', in Sonja Kmec and Viviane Thill (eds), *Private Eyes and the Public Gaze: The Manipulation and Valorization of Amateur Images*. Trier: University of Trier, 45–51.

Aasman, Susan. 2013. 'Impossible Family Portraits: Users, New Media Technologies and the Writing of Amateur Media History', *New Cinemas: Journal of Contemporary Film*, vol. 11, nos 2–3, 111–125.

Aasman, Susan. 2014. 'New Media Technologies and the Desire to Broadcast Yourself, in Marcel Broersma and C. Peterson (eds), *Retelling Journalism. Conveying Stories in a Digital Age*, Leuven:Peeters, 47–65.

Aasman, Susan. 2016. 'The Introduction of Ciné-Kodak: "The Long Awaited Answer"', in Annie van den Oever and Giovanna Fossati (eds), *Exposing the Film Apparatus: The Film Archive as a Research Laboratory*. Amsterdam: Amsterdam University Press, 119–131.

Bailey, Olga, Bart Cammaerts and Nico Carpentier. 2007. *Understanding Alternative Media*. Maidenhead: Open University Press.

Barthes, Roland. 1991. *'Réquichot and His Body', Responsibility of Form. Critical Essays on Music, Art and Representation* (translated Richard Howard), (original 1973). Berkeley: University of California Press.

Bird, Lance. 1986. 'A Letter to the Editor: Cinema Clubs and the World of Tomorrow', *Journal of Film and Video*, vol. 38, nos 3–4, 39.

Boyle, Deirdre. 1992. 'From Portapak to Camcorder: A Brief History of Guerrilla Television', *Journal of Film and Video*, vol. 44, nos 1–2, 67–79.

Buckingham, David, Maria Pini and Rebekah Willett. 2007. '"Take Back the Tube!": The Discursive Construction of Amateur Film and Video Making', *Journal of Media Practice*, vol. 8, no. 2, 183–201.

Burch, Elizabeth. 1997. 'Getting Closer to Folk TV Production: Nontraditional Uses of Video in the U.S. and Other Cultures', *Journal of Film and Video*, vol. 49, no. 4, 18–29.

Camper, Fred. 1986. 'Some Notes on the Home Movie', *Journal of Film and Video*, vol. 38, no. 3–4, 9–14.

Chanan, Michael. 2000. 'The Documentary Chronotope', *Jump Cut*, vol. 43, 56–61.

Chittick, John. 1980. *Evolution of a Filmmaker*, MA dissertation: MIT.

Coe, Brian. 1981. *The History of Movie Photography*. Westfield, NJ: Eastview.

Craven, Ian. 2009. 'A Very Fishy Tale: The Curious Case of Amateur Subjectivity', in Ian Craven (ed.), *Movies on Home Ground: Explorations in Amateur Cinema*. Newcastle-upon-Tyne: Cambridge Scholars, 1–33.

Cuir, Greg de Jr. 2014. 'Early Jugoslav Ciné-Amateurism. Cinéphilia and the Institutionalization of Film Culture in the Kingdom of Yugoslavia During the Interwar Period', in Malte Hagener (ed.), *The Emergence of Film Culture*. New York and Oxford: Berghahn, 162–179.

Ellis, John. 2012. *Documentary: Witness and Self-Revelation*. New York: Routledge.

Enticknap, Leo. 2005. *Moving Image Technology: From Zoetrope to Digital*. London: Wallflower Press.

Gitelman, Lisa. 2014. *Paper Knowledge: Toward a Media History of Documents*. Durham, NC and London: Duke University Press.

Gunther, Jonathan. 1976. *Super 8: The Modest Medium*. Lausanne: UNESCO.

Hagener, Malte. 2007. *Moving Forward, Looking Back. The European Avant-garde and the Invention of Film Culture, 1919–1939*. Amsterdam: Amsterdam University Press.

Henderson, Jo. 2009. 'Handing Over Control? Access, "Ordinary People" and Video Nation', in David Buckingham and Rebekah Willet (eds), *Video Cultures, Media Technology and Everyday Creativity*. London: Palgrave Macmillan, 152–172.

Hill, Chris (ed.). 1996. *Rewind: Video Art and Alternative Media in the United States, 1968–1980*. New York: Video Data Bank.

Holland, Patricia. 1991. 'History, Memory and the Family Album', in Patricia Holland and Jo Spence (eds), *Family Snaps: The Meanings of Domestic Photography*. London: Virago, 1–14.

Horak, Jan-Christopher (ed.). 1996. *Lovers of Cinema: The First American Film Avant-Garde 1919–1945*. Madison, WI: University of Wisconsin Press.

Jenkins, Henry. 2006. 'Confronting the Challenges of Participatory Culture: Media Education for the 21st Century (Part One)', Blog Confessions of an ACA-Fan, 19 October. Available at http://henryjenkins.org/blog/2006/10/confronting_the_challenges_of.html.

Jenkins, Henry, Sam Ford and Joshua Green. 2013. *Spreadable Media: Creating Value and Meaning in a Networked Culture*. New York: New York University Press.

Johnson, Martin L. 2018. *Main Street Movies: The History of Local Film in the United States*. Bloomington: Indiana University Press.

Katelle, Alan. 2000. *Home Movies: A History of the American Industry, 1897–1979*. Nashua, NH: Transition Publishing.

Kelnner, Douglas. 1995. *Media Culture*. London: Routledge.

De Klerk, Nico. 2008. 'Home Away from Home: Private Films from the Dutch East Indies, in Karen L. Ishizuka and P. Zimmermann (eds), *Mining the Home Movies: Excavations in Histories and Memories*. Berkeley and Los Angeles: University of California Press, 148–162.

Kuhn, Annette. 1995. *Family Secrets: Acts of Memory and Imagination*. London: Verso.

Lane, Jim. 2002. *The Autobiographical Documentary in America*. Madison, WI and London: University of Wisconsin Press.

Luckett, Moya. 1995. '"Filming the Family": Home Movie Systems and the Domestication of Spectatorship', *The Velvet Light Trap*, vol. 36 (Fall), 21–32.

Manovich, Lev. 2009. 'The Practice of Everyday (Media) Life: From Mass Consumption to Mass Cultural Production?', *Critical Inquiry*, vol. 35, nol. 2, 319–331.

Matthews, Glenn E. and Raife. G. Tarkington. 1967. 'Early History of Amateur Motion-Picture Film', in Raymond Fielding (ed.), *ATechnological History of Motion Pictures and Television*. Berkeley, Los Angeles and London: University of California Press, 130–131.

Meyerhoff, Barbara. 1984. 'Rites and Signs of Ripening: The Intertwining of Ritual, Time and Growing Older', in David Kertzer and Jennie Keith (eds), *Age and Anthropological Theory*. New York: Cornell University Press, 305–328.

Moran, James. 2002. *There's No Place like Home Video*. Minneapolis, MN: University of Minnesota Press.

Motrescu-Mayes, Annamaria. 2011. 'Imperial Narratives Displaced by Subaltern Indian Identities in Early Amateur Films', *Journal of Early Popular Visual Culture*, vol. 9, no. 2,107–121.

Motrescu-Mayes, Annamaria. 2014. 'Imperial Imagination and Colonial Cities in Inter-War Amateur Films', in A. Choné, A. Granchamp-Florentino and F. Repussard (eds), *(In)visibles cités coloniales. Stratégies de domination et de résistance de la fin du XIXe siècle à nos jours*. Paris: Orizons, 103–114.

Motrescu-Mayes, Annamaria. 2014. 'Uncensored Imperial Politics in British Home Movies from 1920s-1950s', in Laura Rascaroli, G. Young, with B. Monahan (eds), *Amateur Filmmaking: The Home Movie, the Archive, the Web*. New York: Bloomsbury Academic, 95–107.

Motrescu-Mayes, Annamaria. 2015. 'Britische Frauen mit imperialer Mission und ihre Amateurfilme", in S. Mattl, C. Lesky, V. Ohner and I. Rechner (eds), *Abenteuer Alltag: Zur Archäologie des Amateurfilms*. Synema: Österreichisches Filmmuseum, 172–182.

Motrescu-Mayes, Annamaria. 2016. 'Ethnographies of Trauma and Migrant Emotions: South Asian Visual Narratives of War and Displacement', *Pakistan Journal of Historical Studies*, vol. 1, no. 1, 1–17.

Motrescu-Mayes, Annamaria. 2017. 'Paradoxical Legacies: Colonial Missionary Films, Corporate Philanthropy in South Asia and the Griersonian Documentary Tradition', in Ian

Aitken and Camille Deprez (eds), *Colonial Documentary Film in South and South-East Asia*, Edinburgh: Edinburgh University Press, 128–147.

Motrescu-Mayes, Annamaria and Norris Nicholson, Heather. 2018. *British Women Amateur Filmmakers: National Memories and Global Identities*. Edinburgh: Edinburgh University Press.

Norris Nicholson, Heather. 2012. *Amateur Film. Meaning and Practice, 1927–1977*. Manchester: Manchester University Press.

Ouellette, Laurie. 1995. 'Camcorder Do's and Don'ts: Popular Discourses on Amateur Video and Participatory Television', *The Velvet Light Trap*, vol. 36 (Fall), 33–44.

Pincus, Ed. 1972. 'One Person Synch Sound. A New Approach to Cinema Verité', *Film-makers Newsletter*, vol. 6, no. 2, 24–30.

Poos, Françoise. 2016. *The Making of a National Audio-Visual Archive: The CNA and the Hidden Images Exhibition*. PhD dissertation, DeMontfort University, Leicester.

Rieger, Bernard. 2005. *Technology and the Culture of Modernity in Britain and Germany, 1890–1945*. Cambridge: Cambridge University Press.

Roepke, Martina. 2006. *Privat-Vorstellung.Heimkino in Deutschland vor 1945*. Hildesheim: Georg Olms Verlag.

Roepke, Martina. 2007, 'Tracing 17.5mm Practices in Germany (1902–1908)', *Film History: An International Journal*, vol. 19, no. 4, 344–352.

Rosen, Jay. 2008, 'A Most Useful Definition of Citizen Journalism', PressThink, 14 July. Available at http://archive.pressthink.org/2008/07/14/a_most_useful_d.html.

Ruoff, Jeffrey. 2002. *An American Family: A Televised Life*. Minneapolis, MN: University of Minnesota Press.

Sarvas, Risto and D. Frohlich. 2011. *From Snapshots to Social Media: The Changing Picture of Domestic Photography*. London: Springer.

Schneider, Alexandra. 2004. *Die Stars sind wir: Heimkino als filmische Praxis*. Marburg: Schüren.

Seijdel, Jorinde. 2010. *De Waarde van de Amateur* [The Value of the Amateur]. Amsterdam: Fonds voor Beeldende Kunsten, Vormgeving en Bouwkunst.

Shand, Ryan. 2008. 'Theorizing Amateur Cinema: Limitations and Possibilities', *The Moving Image*, vol. 8, no. 2, 36–60.

Sheldon, Karan. 2017. 'A Place for Moving Images: Thirty Years of Northeast Historic Film', in Martha J. McNamara and Karan Sheldon (eds), *Amateur Movie Making: Aesthetics of the Everyday in New England Film, 1915–1960*. Bloomington: Indiana University Press, 17–39.

Shirky, Clay. 2008. *Here Comes Everybody: The Power of Organizing Without Organizations*. New York: Penguin.

Singer, Ben. 1998. 'Early Home Cinema and the Edison Home Projecting Kinetoscope', *Film History*, vol. 2, no. 1, 37–69.

Slootweg, Tom. 2018a. *Resistance, Disruption and Belonging: Electronic Video as Alternative in Three Amateur Modes*. PhD dissertation, University of Groningen.

Slootweg, Tom. 2018b. 'Home Mode, Community Mode, Counter Mode: Three Functional Modalities for Coming to Terms with Amateur Media Practices, in Susan Aasman, Andreas Fickers and Jo Wachelder (eds), *Materializing Memories: Dispositifs, Generations, Amateurs*. New York: Bloomsbury, 203–216.

Slootweg, Tom and Susan Aasman. 2015. 'Democratic Television in the Netherlands', *VIEW, Journal of European Television History and Culture*, vol. 4, no. 7, 21–37.

Sontag, Susan. 1979. *On Photography*. London: Penguin.

Tepperman, Charles. 2015. *Amateur Cinema 1923–1960: The Rise of North American Movie-making*. Oakland, CA: University of California Press.

UNESCO. 1963. *Statistics on Radio and Television, 1950–1960*. Paris: UNESCO.

Van der Heijden, Tim. 2018. *Hybrid Histories. Histories. Technologies of Memory and the Cultural Dynamics of Home Movies, 1895–2005.* PhD dissertation, Maastricht University.

Wasson, Haidee. 2009. 'Electric Homes! Automatic Movies! Efficient Entertainment!: 16mm and Cinéma's Domination in the 1920s', *Cinéma journal*, vol. 48, no. 4, 1–21.

Winston, Brian. 2015. *The Documentary Film Book.* London: BFI.

Worth, Sol. 1981. 'Toward An Anthropological Politics of Symbolic Form', in Larry Gross (ed.), *Studying Visual Communication.* Philadelphia: University of Pennsylvania Press, 85–86.

Young, Gwenda. 2014. 'Glimpses of a Hidden History: Exploring Irish Amateur Collections, 1930–1970', in Laura Rascaroli, Gwenda Young and Barry Monahan (eds), *Amateur Filmmaking: The Home Movie, the Archive, the Web.* New York and London: Bloomsbury, 81–95.

Zimmermann, Patricia. 1995. *Reel Families: A Social History of Amateur Film.* Bloomington: Indiana University Press.

Zimmermann, Patricia. 1997. 'Democracy and Cinema: A History of Amateur Film', in Nancy Kapstein (ed.), *Rencontres autour des inédits/Essays on Amateur Film.* Charleroi: Association Europeenne Inédits, 73–81.

Zimmermann, Patricia. 2013. 'An Amateurized Media Universe', *Review of Amateur Media: Social, Cultural and Legal Perspectives*, ed. Dan Hunter, Ramon Lobato, Megan Richardson and Julian Thomas (London: Routledge, 2012), *Jump Cut: A Review of Contemporary Media*, vol. 55, Fall 2013.

2

EVERYDAY COMPLEXITIES AND CONTRADICTIONS IN CONTEMPORARY AMATEUR MEDIA

In April 2017, DaddyOFive, a popular YouTube channel hosted by Christopher Martin and his family in Maryland, USA, became embroiled in a global controversy when other YouTubers accused the parents of being both physically and verbally abusive to their five children and of exploiting them for advertising revenues.[1] Until then, the couple had been successfully vlogging regularly about their daily life. They were particularly popular for the pranks they pulled on their kids. By 2017, they secured more than 700,000 subscribers, which made them successful enough to rely on vlogging as their main source of income. However, the upload of *Invisible Ink Prank! (Epic Freakout)* (DaddyOFive, 18 April 2017), showing one of the youngest children as the target of his parents' yelling and screaming, received instant severe criticism.[2] The backlash forced the parents to deny the accusations and explain their methods of both parenting and vlogging. Soon afterwards, they removed the video and posted instead an apology on YouTube.[3] A few days later, they renewed their apology in an interview with *Good Morning America* (28 April 2017).[4] Eventually, the parents decided to remove all their videos from their YouTube channel.

This is one of the many examples of how families nowadays use YouTube as a public platform to share their daily activities through self-made videos. Family vloggers like the Martins rely on their own lives as the main, unlimited source of narrative and key subjects. This change from home mode playfulness and amateur video making to semi-professional media production is taking place quite rapidly, making such families of vloggers swap a past-time group activity for a regular daily task. Their hobby soon becomes work. Christopher Martin (the father in DaddyOFive) put it best: 'It started out as family fun, but then it was just about making a video and then making the next video more crazier' (Luscombe 2017). The burden of becoming and remaining a star on YouTube and the fun of doing family stuff somehow clashed along the way. As the father observed in his explanation video: 'I am still new to this.'[5]

Vlogging was certainly not a new phenomenon in 2017. Ever since the Internet originated, users have explored new opportunities of distributing homemade audio-visual content, and so foregrounded the practice of amateur media in this participatory environment. Among the very early examples of vlogging is American student Jennifer Ringley's famous attempts in 1996 to life-cast her everyday life while a student at Dickinson College in Carlisle, Pennsylvania, US. She installed a webcam in her dorm and started broadcasting pictures of herself on 'JenniCam'; her website became an instant success, attracting up to 4 million paying viewers a day. As a guest on CBS's *David Letterman Show*, Ringley reflected on exposing her life and sharing it with millions of strangers looking at her. Letterman argued that her act seemed to be the perfect idea for the Internet, since people want to see life taking place somewhere else. Echoing Letterman's opinion, Ringley added: 'On *Wild America* you can watch lions and antelopes eating and sleeping and doing what they do. But, for some reason, wanting to see people doing the same thing is considered sick and perverse.' Scholars researching everyday use of the webcam argued that the success of JenniCam went beyond being just a curiosity; it predicted the expansive use of webcams soon to be used by millions of amateurs around the world (Andrejevic 2004). Ringley's success confirmed the validity of an alternative media model, one in which amateur media makers' 'uncut, uncensored and unedited reality' could reach global audiences and not just their families and friends (Andrejevic 2004, 193). Therefore, the webcam in combination with the Internet became integral parts of a crucial social and technological transformation, which made private spaces such as a student's dorm or a family's kitchen 'stages' for new media productions and contexts for a wider public distribution.

Nevertheless, video blogging and the online sharing of other types of self-made moving images remained for a while relatively limited, owing to major technical constraints related to different types of video players that were incompatible or to difficulties with uploading and downloading large media files. It was only with the launch of YouTube in 2005 that online users finally had access to simplified and reliable protocols for video uploading. This was a turning point in an already strong emerging online participatory culture, securing an even greater increase of highly active media content creators. The impressive rise of active content creators inspired *Time* magazine to choose 'You' – Yes, you' as the person of the year 2006, thereby acknowledging the cultural promise of user-generated content (Grossman 2006). Statistics for YouTube show that the number of uploads by users has been growing at a staggering rate. By 2018, the number of uploads reached around 50 million, with an average of 30 million visitors per day and 3.25 billion hours of video watched each month.[6] In this context, some key research questions become imperative such as: How should we assess the millions of amateurs creating content on such a impressive scale and such a rapid rate? How can we understand the impact of YouTube and other video websites as platforms that provide infrastructures for mediating our daily life and monetising daily life for global audiences? How do we understand amateur media in the age of YouTube culture?

By the end of the twentieth century, amateurs' use of media technologies expanded quickly in terms of production, distribution and reception. Basically, media are everywhere as we are witnessing 'the mediation of everything', including social institutions such as the family (Livingstone 2009, 54). Indeed, more than ever, the family has become a mediated community as well as an enacted space, wherein every moment, whether it is the mundane or the unique, is a potential resource to be recorded and shared. Some scholars suggested that we are not so much living *with* media as *in* media: 'Who you are, what you do, and what all of this means to you does not exist outside of media. Media are to us as water is to fish' (Deuze 2012, x). This 'media everywhere universe' can be described as an 'increasingly seamless and altogether ambient lived experience of multiple media as we navigate everyday life' (Deuze 2016, 328). In order to understand this 'mediatized world', a term that Andreas Hepp and Friedrich Krotz (2014) use to point to 'the everyday concretization of media cultures and media societies', we need to focus on people's media use in very specific contexts and with very specific intentions (Hepp and Krotz 2014, 14).

This chapter aims to understand this mediatisation in relation to some particular forms of amateur media use. Specifically, it sets out to explore the ongoing transformation of formerly fixed home movies or home videos (i.e. filmmaking or videotaping at those special ritualised moments) into a ubiquitous practice deeply embedded in our daily life. By looking at some concrete examples, it is possible to get a grasp on the highly individual and, at the same time, very complicated social arrangements we are part of, and in which the availability of media technologies and platforms play a constructive role. The focus is on one particular mediatised world: the home. According to Andreas Fickers, and many other media scholars discussing domestication of media technology, 'the home is the privileged locus for the appropriation and use of communication and media technologies', such as webcams, smartphones, and video-sharing websites (Fickers 2018, 91; Silverstone and Hirsch 1992). Moreover, the chapter addresses the issues of what happens once the home mode leaves the living room and joins public platforms.

First, it is essential to have a clearer definition of our object of study as current amateur media technologies and practices are more fluid and flexible than ever before. These more recent developments can be discussed in terms of 'media ensemble' (Morley 2000) or 'polymedia' (Madianou and Miller 2013), while a historical reflection about amateur media also points towards processes of 'hybridity' (Van der Heijden, 2018) and of 'intermediality' (Müller 2010; Slootweg, 2018). Each of these terms suggests specific approaches to understanding the proliferation, transformation and processes of convergence of media technologies. While hybridity emphasises the process whereby media technologies, user practices and discourses not only succeed each other in time, but also increasingly interrelate, interact or even transform each other; intermediality foregrounds the embeddedness of media technologies in a larger network or cluster of related media technologies in a given time. Overall, these approaches share an awareness of how these technologies are embedded in and shaped by manifold contexts – historical, social, cultural, technological, political and economic.

The multiplicity of technologies and their overlaps have not only become manifold in form and use but also full of interpretative complexities and contradictions, which make these media practices ever more fascinating as they represent a wide variety of new social and cultural practices (Uricchio 2009). New media technologies tend to disrupt traditional ways of communication as they prompt contradictive uses, thereby transgressing previous genre-related protocols. With online home videos, for instance, the filmmaker communicates with an intended audience such as his or her family, while at the same time the video is also available to an unknown public. In this respect, a strict sense of what is private and what is public becomes blurred (Baym 2010). As such, these complexities and contradictions have become part of everyday life as 'people incorporate digital media into their routine practices of relating' (Baym 2010, 5). This particular development is certainly not new. James Moran addressed this issue when he explored the functional modalities of analogue amateur video practices in terms of 'sets of intentions' (Moran 2002, 69–70). Moran explained that most of the time these intentions can be clarifying as well as confusing as they are not stable but fluid and dynamic.

Several analytical perspectives should be considered when studying the constellations of contemporary amateur media practices. For one, this chapter analyses communicative interactions as long as they are inscriptive media practices – meaning they are material and semiotic, stable and savable – because only then do they begin to act as representations (Gitelman 2006). As Lisa Gitelman has noted, mediated interactions start circulating while acquiring both material and semiotic meaning:

> Media are socially realised structures of communication, where structures include both technological forms and their associated protocols, and where communication is a cultural practice, a ritualised collocation of different people on the same mental map, sharing or engaged with popular ontologies of representation.
>
> *(Gitelman 2006, 7)*

In order to understand the variety of social, economic, cultural and material relationships that are underlying these protocols, the concept of *dispositif* can help to explore these intimately connected dimensions (Kessler 2007; Fickers 2014; Albéra and Tortajada 2015). The concept of *dispositif* provides an analytical perspective that allows us to understand complex interrelations between the different aspects of home-movie and video making; it addresses the material dimensions of the technologies that make the production and sharing of images possible, the textual dimension that includes specific aesthetics or specific genres, with the perceptual dimensions of users viewing and responding to the text within certain socio-technical screening contexts (Aasman et al. 2018). The challenge is to be able to explore amateur media practices in specific communicative spaces that are constantly changing, as they have become more fluid, networked and ubiquitous than ever. According to Roger Odin, the many new devices available, combined with also new family constellations has led to an 'upsurge of dispositifs' (Odin 2018, 29). Or, as Henry Jenkins once remarked: 'Our lives, relationships, fantasies, desires also flow across media channels. Being a lover or a mommy or a teacher occurs on multiple platforms' (Jenkins 2006, 17).

This perspective makes it possible to explore the new spatial and temporal dimensions of social family gatherings in current digital home video practices. The chapter discusses this process by exploring how people appropriated non-traditional camera devices such as webcams, computer applications (video-calling technologies) and smartphones, and how this changes not only our concept of connectivity but also challenges our deep archival desire to record and store those brief moments of connection. It traces what happens when users turn to non-traditional ways of sharing and screening home videos, by making use of online video platforms, thereby entering a communication space that is no longer private. How does this changing *dispositif* influence the specific modes of address and the expectations of its meaning-making potential for viewers, subjects and the video makers? Finally, the broader issue of the political economy of amateurs joining this new public and highly commercialised space has to be addressed, even if that means that we have to rethink whether 'amateur media' is still the most relevant term or category.

The domestic as a virtual media space

Video-calling services such as Skype, Facetime and WhatsApp are crucial technologies, as they have become part of a broad ensemble of everyday communication and media technologies. Although these popular tools were never invented as recording technologies – they were originally designed as communication devices offering free and easy access to video conversations – users gradually started to appropriate this new set of affordances as a technology of memory (Aasman, 2012, 2013). By recording, editing and narrating live conversations, users transform live video events in traditional home video-like documents. However, when analysing such new media practices, it becomes clear how current communication technologies redefine the material, textual and perceptual dimensions of what was formerly known as a home-movie *dispositif*. We shall focus on an interesting selection of home videos that represent everyday yet complex constellations in traditional *topoi* (birthday parties), new communication technologies (Skype, Facetime), multiple recording devices (webcam plus video camera), distribution channels (YouTube) and changed screening settings (pc/laptop/smartphone).

Take for instance *Nana's Birthday Surprise* (dir. 7ac2dc3, 2012), which shows a birthday party organised through a Skype setup, recorded via multiple cameras (webcam plus video camera) and uploaded on YouTube. In this case, a grandmother visits the house of her son and grandchildren to celebrate her 60th birthday. Before she arrives, the owner activates a video camera positioned high on a tripod so as to get a good overview of the room. The children are encouraged to make funny faces into the camera (Figure 2.1). One of them approaches the lens so closely that the only thing visible is an eye. This scene shows that a camera, even in

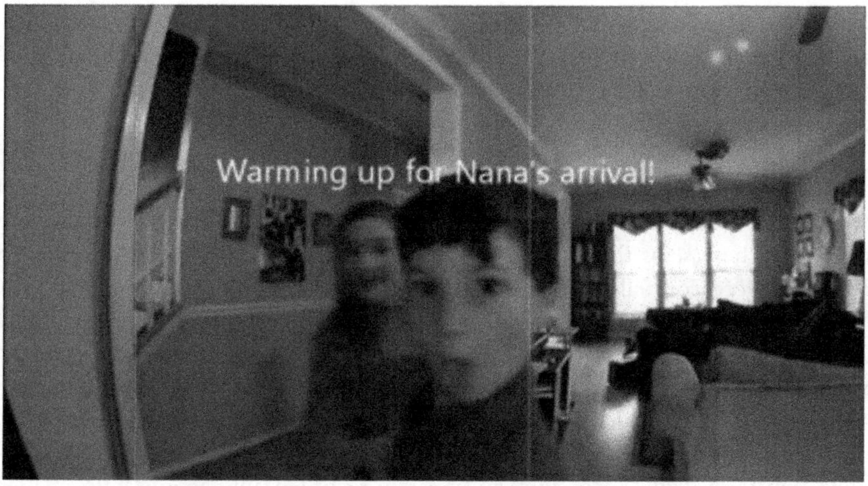

FIGURE 2.1 *Nana's Birthday Surprise*. 2012. Screengrab via YouTube.

the twentieth century, still seems to have a magic appeal and has, therefore, not yet completely disappeared as an invisible tool in everyday life. When the doorbell rings, the family lines up and starts singing 'Happy Birthday'. After just a few lines, even more family members join in. As it turns out, to the grandmother's great surprise, the new joiners are singing via Skype on a laptop. Now, the family and the grandmother are standing together in front of the laptop while all are cheering and singing. Nana blows the candle on her cake and starts unpacking the gifts. Afterwards, the filmmaker edited the recorded Skype material, adding music and titles, to create a sense of narration to the scene.

In film history, the camera has always been a main instrument in recording special moments of family life. Events such as birthday parties represent the traditional *topoi* of home-movie history, as this is typically an occasion to mark a memorable moment in which the family comes together. As discussed in Chapter 1, bringing out the camera at such moments became a 'ritual of domestic happiness', entailing a promise to become a future memory. This particular quality of the camera ensured that home-movie making could become a special and dear practice, a duty even, as was the case with domestic photography. They functioned on the level of what Pierre Bourdieu (1965) once termed 'les grand moments de la famille' celebrating special moments rather than the mundane or the ordinary. Therefore, Richard Chalfen (1987) categorised this practice as a form of home mode communication. As this example shows, the convergence of media and communication technologies did not fundamentally change the selection of *topoi* but rather reinforced the importance of the event, by setting up complicated media ensembles to bring the family together in one mediated space.

There are many other examples that show the way this new video routine is enacted – for instance, the video *Let's Party on Skype! Ben in Australia* (dir. Rural Cork 2015). In this video the main event is situated in Cork (Ireland) while the son – who is celebrating his birthday – is in Australia. As the house is filled with people partying, the absent son appears on Skype via a laptop in order to 'join' the cheerful crowd. Then they show the son his birthday cake. There is a paradox noticeable in this particular moment, where, on the one hand, the casual relationship with technology is evident, while, on the other hand, the tool evokes a magical moment by being able to bring the son 'home'. 'Is this the first Skype party ever?' the filmmaker wondered in his video description. This was surely not the case as there are various examples that reveal likewise or even far more advanced constellations. Mark Deuze (2012) suggested that many everyday media users become creative in one way or another without necessarily realising it, preparing, recording, editing and eventually uploading the media content. Some users exploit the Skype technologies even further, by taking the affordances of the Skype *dispositif* to create a shared space in which there is no longer a preferred place wherein the other is the guest. Other examples show how long-distance relations transform live video conversations in recorded interactions after which these precious moments are created into a home video. Through the combined acts of video calling and recording, users create audio-visual albums of specific moments of interaction that would have otherwise existed only in a virtual media space.

What these technologies offer to their users is the ability to create a sense of connectedness. As such, they can be considered to be 'technologies of the hearth', functioning as 'imperfect instruments, by which people try to maintain and also save something of the security of cultural location' (Tomlinson 2001, 17). It shows that the meaning is in the production of a symbolic space of the home and family in a globalised world. At the same time, this type of mediated connectedness is not a new phenomenon within the home-movie tradition; early in the twentieth century, amateur media became a prime instrument used in bringing the family together. Time and again new media technologies were tried and tested to uphold family life that was not specifically localised in a particular place. Whether it was small-gauge film in the 1930s, accommodating travellers and immigrants to produce a 'home away from home' (De Klerk 2008), or electronic video in the 1980s supporting expatriates going abroad (Slootweg 2018) or US soldiers going to Iraq in the 2000s using their cell phones to make videos to stay in touch (see Chapter 5), amateur media technologies played an important role as a recording and communication device. However, compared with earlier home-movie and video practices, the protocols needed for enabling video calling, and its storage, reflect the changing social and cultural contexts of today's globalised world. These recorded moments of tele-presence not only transformed the domestic in a mediated virtual space but also allowed for these mediated but live interactions to be kept safe. The traditional cultural format of the home movie was thus redefined as the new *dispositif* of home video production, which, through a diverse set of tools, recreated traditional topics in innovative ways and enabled new types of family portrait of birthdays and other special moments in family life. In other words, being a social practice as well as a mode of representation, these moments transformed new types of experiences of virtual co-presence as 'part of the fabric of everyday experience' (Harrison 2009, 3).

Bringing the family online

Each of the home videos discussed so far in this chapter was uploaded on YouTube in order to be shared. By that particular act, users brought their families online, and thereby changed the practice of the home video on multiple levels. Once a video is posted on an open, online video platform like YouTube, the 'space of communication' (Odin 2014) is by default very different from the traditional home mode. It needs to be analysed how the particular use of technology interacts with the textual and perceptual dimensions while acknowledging that there may be contradictory implications, once the home video is deprived of its familiar screening context. According to Roger Odin, 'the modalities of textual construction change in relation to context' (Odin 2008, 255), or, in other words, the context of the communication space matters. This perspective emphasises not only that textual meaning is important, but also that 'the affect and the interactions during production and reception must be analysed' (ibid.).

In the case of online videos, and because of this online context, we need to understand how (new) affective relationships with the spectator are shaped. For instance, this perceptual dimension of online home videos includes the possibility of having to deal with 'viewers' who are not members of the family, or even necessarily known to the family, and whose numbers might exceed any expectation. Even with 'just' a few hundred views, an online video has a potentially radically different scale of distribution compared with the time when the living room was the main space for screening. A crowd of 100 people can transform a small social circle of family and friends into something that can be categorised as 'an audience'. These people might not necessarily be related to the family as they have clicked on the video randomly. By the same token, some of those viewers who are watching the clip online might indeed be related. However, since they are watching the video online, they do not necessarily physically share a space with the family members who are on screen. Either way, compared with the traditional home-movie viewing (screen *dispositif*) – which enables people to collectively be seated in front of the moving images – the new setup/ensemble accepts viewings of people being disparate in space and time. A side effect is also noticeable. As live commenting in a face-to-face situation is now less likely to happen, sharing thoughts and memories is done through adding written comments online, which makes these moments of interaction less ephemeral, as they become fixed and textual. An example of this can be found in a response to the *Let's Party on Skype! Ben in Australia* video posted on YouTube: 'Well done Tony! Had a great time. First time ever at a party when the birthday boy was at the other side of the world. Thank God for Skype.'

As stated, private home videos uploaded on YouTube might reach a large number of viewers, even though the uploader might not always be aware of this.

An early example is the famous home video *Charlie bit my finger – again*, which was uploaded by Howard Davies-Carr in 2007. This 56-second clip recorded in the UK shows a funny little scene of two young boys. It unexpectedly went viral, eventually reaching an audience of billions.[7] The father later explained that he had meant to send the clip by email to the children's grandfather. However, the video file was too large so he uploaded it on YouTube. He soon realised how naïve he was about using YouTube for not thinking that viewers outside his own small circle of family and friends could also watch the video. Once the clip went viral, as Davies-Carr explained: 'There was nothing I could do.'[8] *Charlie bit my finger – again* became one of the most viewed amateur videos and gained an iconic reputation of what simple unedited homemade or user-generated content could achieve. Along the way, as Davies-Carr gradually found out, uploading a home video was not some isolated individual act, but rather happened within a larger network of users (Jenkins et al. 2013).

The video not only received thousands of likes and comments but was shared numerous times and featured in a wave of remixes produced by young and old alike, re-enacting the dialogue, or mashing up the scene through thousands and thousands of Lego animation parodies. Although the original video was uploaded in 2007, after which millions of remixes saw the light of day, new additions are still being made and uploaded to this day. Together, these videos make up a still ongoing networked document, drawing attention to YouTube as a platform were new highly networked cultural forms emerged. As with many other early famous YouTube videos, *Charlie bit my finger – again* marked a shift that indicates the potential of content circulation on YouTube.[9] Moreover, this example shows how entirely new patterns of social interaction have emerged. According to Jenkins (2013), the affordances of YouTube reconceptualised the social logic of this cultural practice of home videos with regard to cultural and political participation (users joining in by re-enacting or remixing) and economic expectations (ultimately, the Davies-Carr family was able to monetise on the clip). This development redefined ideas of social relations as something that could entail virtual connections between people who might never have met each other before. In the case of *Charlie bit my finger*, the affection felt by viewers was quite strong and overwhelming. Shortly after the upload, and given the immense success, the father felt compelled to create new videos about his children because so many viewers, curious about how the boys were doing, requested more material. Davies-Carr eventually created a YouTube channel where subscribers to the channel and others could be regularly updated by new footage of the children growing up.[10]

Serialised families

As was shown, Howard Davies-Carr accidentally, or at least not on purpose, developed a relationship with his viewers by recording and then sharing more and more home videos of his family on YouTube. Both aspects, connecting with unknown viewers and regularly uploading a series of videos, became essential characteristics of a new amateur genre: the family vlog. Vlogging has become the emblematic form of YouTube participation (Burgess and Green 2009) although it bears traces of other cultural forms, from before YouTube, such as video journals and webcam diaries. As such, the genre is also closely related to personal blogging and, more generally, is embedded in – as we have seen in the first chapter – a broader confessional media culture. The family vlog represents a cultural format, which can be described as the result of 'situated creativity' (Burgess and Green 2009). It is a type of creativity that is set in a specific social context, which involves a social process that reflects the observations Roepke (see Chapter 1) made for the early twentieth-century home movies. She described the process of home-movie making as a social practice that engages all the members of the family and not just the one behind the camera.

The vlog's popularity is due to the low threshold that YouTube offers. The simplicity of circulating homemade audio-visual material clearly stimulated millions of amateurs to join in making online family videos. When searching for the term 'family vlog', YouTube generates more than 20 million results. Some of these vlogs succeed in developing into long-term commitments; other vlogs do not last longer than one or two updates. Family vlogs in particular come in all kinds of languages, types of families; different socio-economic classes, races, religion, genders, family structures, etc. Active participants can be young, even one-year-olds, or they can be old, sometimes even 80+ years old. The very popular family YouTube channel *The Shaytards*, which ran from 2008 until mid-2017, and then restarted in 2018, is a poignant example of a vlog that made a long-term commitment to a large audience.[11] Over the years, the family produced more than 2,000 vlogs. This American family, consisting of father Shay Carl Butler, his wife Colette Butler and their five children, was, for a while, the most popular YouTube family; their vlog inspired many others to do the same. As the opening video explained to new viewers: the vlog, on a daily basis, will take them on a real-life journey to almost everywhere. With this level of commitment, the Butlers were able to build an audience of almost 5 million subscribers and billions of viewers following their everyday life while cooking, cleaning, going out, partying or welcoming yet another child to the family.

One of the episodes, titled *The kids are vlogging* (2015) features a rather non-eventful day in the life of this family. Contrary to the title, the father is in charge in this vlog, although he allows the oldest children to take the camera and participate in the process of filmmaking for some minutes. Most of the time, however, Shay Carl moves around the house with his camera mounted on a selfie-stick. On one level, the video is in line with the procedures of a regular home video, coming from a longstanding tradition of recording everyday life. Conversely, however, the vlog is a much more multi-layered text, in which the role of audio and the relationship between the filmmaker(s) and the subject(s) are less one-sided. The mode of address in the video, for example, alternates between a first-person documentary mode, the observational mode and the home mode. As Odin (2008) explained, a documentary works at a different level to a home movie, wherein the former tries to communicate to an audience, while the latter invites family members to remember and participate in performing the family. Vlogs do both: they seek to establish a relationship with the visitors of the channel while, simultaneously, they engage in the home mode by addressing and performing the family.

This particular dynamic occurs on multiple occasions in *The kids are vlogging*. No matter who is behind the camera, there is always some interaction with the other members of the family in front of the lens. The children are constantly aware of being recorded on camera, acknowledging its presence by looking and talking to it, and thereby also becoming secondary narrators. This was also common practice in previous forms of home video making. However, this vlog differs from home video making, for instance, in the manner in which the father is talking to and with the camera. On numerous occasions, Shay Carl swings the camera back and forth on a 180-degrees axis, alternating between filming himself in a selfie style, at arm's length, and a first-person perspective (Figure 2.2). Moreover, as the father talks, he can shift the mode of address in just one sentence to either his kids or to his YouTube viewers. The vlog is thus at once observational and highly performative in the sense that everyone involved in the filmmaking process, but also those who are watching, is constantly aware of, and takes part in, the making of the vlog.

The Shaytards were able to build a close relationship with their numerous viewers who not only watched the family but also wrote comments explaining how much they loved the family or went to 'meet and greet' sessions with the whole family present. To their subscribers, the Butlers felt like family. Of course, these types of relationship were shaped earlier as well through soap operas, sitcoms and reality TV shows, thanks to the serial character – through weekly appearances on TV – of fictional families that could evoke feelings that mixed fandom with a sense of being member of the family. However, vlogging holds the promise that it

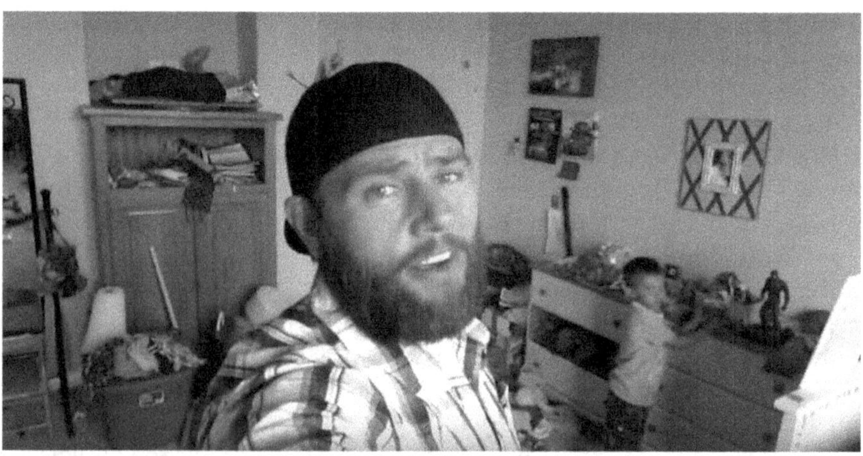

FIGURE 2.2 *The kids are vlogging*. 2015. Screengrab via YouTube.

shares real people living real lives. The idea of being authentic and true to life, however, came under pressure in 2017 for the Butlers. After Shay Carl confessed to cheating on his wife, as well as having an alcohol problem, he became the subject of a scandal. The family decided to stop vlogging for a year. The temporary disappearance of the family disturbed the many devoted viewers who publicly regretted no longer being unable to follow the whereabouts of the family.

These new types of viewing practices raise the question of whether we can label the family vlog as a particular subgenre of what used to be a home movie. Are vlogs comparable to home movies, even though the dissemination of these images is scaled up beyond the traditional domestic boundaries? Shay Carl, having a moment of self-reflection in one of his posts, emphasised that his daily recordings are basically about 'freezing these moments' (*#WhyIVlog*, 2016). This statement shows a dual set of intentions of the filmmaker at work. The intentions shift between constructing a family archive and developing a commercially viable channel that accommodates two different spaces of communication. It reveals the hybridity of the genre nowadays, full of contradictions and expanding the rules of what Richard Chalfen (1987) once defined as home mode communication. Chalfen explained how the home mode favours very restrictive, highly conventionalised moments. His characterisation seems to contradict the content of vlogs. The latter includes recordings of a wide range of moments from everyday life even as they are somewhat uneventful, such as doing the dishes, cooking a meal or cleaning the house. On the other hand, there is definitely a selective strategy at work. Not everything is recorded, not everything is kept in the final edit. In case of the Shaytards, the use of the camera was restricted to a maximum of 30–45 minutes a day, after which the editing further reduces those 45 minutes to 15–20 minutes vlog (screen) time. So, one could argue that the overall narrative of the channel is still that of the traditional audio-visual family album, representing the happy family starting as a couple, having kids, getting rich and finally moving to a big house.

In March 2018, after one year of absence, *The Shaytards* returned to YouTube. In one of his first uploads, Shay Carl explained that he wanted to try something he had never done before: uploading the vlog without editing and relying less on a high production value. It is not clear whether the upload of this more 'amateurish' non-polished *i did not edit this vlog* (2018) had to make up for the previous lack of honesty, restoring some sense of authenticity and re-establishing the relationship with his subscribers. His fans were happy with the reappearance of the family and the new style; as one of the subscribers approvingly wrote: 'Honestly minimally edited vlogs are more genuine.'

Monetising the home mode

So far, we have discussed YouTube as a more or less neutral space, providing affordances for easy and free video content sharing, something that is perfectly suitable for amateurs who love the opportunity to distribute self-made videos beyond the confines of a closed circle of family and friends. However, once a home video is uploaded on YouTube, it enters the public domain while simultaneously becoming part of a specific infrastructure that is highly commercialised. Jenkins et al. suggested that the web enabled the emergence of a much more 'hybrid model of circulation, where a mix of top-down and bottom-up forces determine how material is shared across and among cultures in for more participatory (and messier) ways' (Jenkins et al. 2013, 1). Media content produced in a context of social exchanges (e.g. family events), but now circulated on a platform like YouTube, become part of a process of market exchange. This hybrid status of digital content, moving between different kinds of transaction, is a constant negotiation of different systems of evaluation (Lessig 2008; Jenkins et al. 2013). Especially since Google bought YouTube in 2007 and introduced the partnership programme, the media platform enabled and stimulated the practice of monetising 'user-generated' content. To understand this monetisation as an integral part of the YouTube *dispositif*, an analysis of the affordances of this particular platform is necessary. In other words, we should account for the protocols and routines that are in place when people start distributing content.

Initially, YouTube had a strong base in a peer community-driven platform that believed in a true democratic opportunity for even and fair distribution of user-generated content. But as José Van Dijck (2013) suggested, YouTube developed into a platform with a far more complex interwovenness of not just what users do or hope or what technologies enable, but also the particular business models and specific rules of governance that underpin this whole system (cf. Van Dijck et al. 2018) According to Van Dijck et al., YouTube is a perfect example of a website that deploys automated technologies and business models to organise data streams as part of measuring economic interactions, while providing social exchanges between users of the Internet. The main mechanisms that determine the operation of these platforms are datafication, commodification and selection, which means that every activity, transaction or piece of information is commodified because of its transformation into data. Once these social and cultural activities become data, algorithms filter these, producing automated selection, e.g. personalisation, rankings, reputation (Van Dijck et al. 2018). Users who are uploading videos on YouTube are not only sharing creative content, but also generate data with potential economic value if they are able to attract enough (and preferably returning) viewers. Once the user is able to get into the algorithm that selects and ranks the uploaded video, it will automatically be selected again and again. And the algorithm will earn both the uploader and YouTube money from advertisements. This model worked out well for the Shaytards who became millionaires thanks to their daily recordings of their everyday life. This family quickly learned the benefits of the right YouTube production values by attracting many viewers who expect regular new content while the 'content provider' expects their viewers to subscribe and like the new uploads.[12]

This form of 'self-commodification' (Van Dijck 2013, 46) implies a strategy towards the self as a prerequisite for acquiring social or professional capital, and as such it became the business model for many trained amateurs who learned to see themselves and their mediated lives as products with economic value. This need for self-promotion has become so central that it has transformed the recordings of everyday life into *content* and the amateur into a *content creator*, which is furthermore enabled through the commercial infrastructure that intermediates between the user/producer and his or her public. Given these characteristics, being an amateur or content creator has become hard work. Living your life and raising your children while recording it, has become the main source of income and in that business model YouTube functions as the first window of opportunity in 'small media' industries, connecting to other social media platforms such as Instagram, Twitter and Facebook, carefully constructing ordinary YouTubers to develop into 'microcelebrities' (Senft 2008, 2013). With this term, Theresa Senft addressed the fact that everyday users now experiment with online performances using webcams, making vlogs or Facebook posts, in order to build an audience. In addition, Alice Marwick explored the techniques of self-presentation and pointed out that these 'microcelebrities' often 'view themselves as a public persona to be consumed by others, use strategic intimacy to appeal to followers, and regard their audience as fans' (Marwick 2015, 333). For all the performativity that has been inherent in the home mode from its very beginning, this new way of addressing an audience, rather than a circle of friends or family, is a fundamental move away from earlier domestic *dipositifs*.

Beyond the home mode – beyond the amateur

How fundamental is the change in amateur media practices and discourses? Are today's 'content creators', 'users' or vloggers yesterday's amateurs?[13] How to evaluate amateurism in the age of YouTube? According to Burgess and Green, there is a 'murkiness between professional and amateur' (Burgess and Green 2009, 103), which they situate as a co-existing or co-evolving culture of market and non-market culture. Especially in its early stage, YouTube 'thrived on enthusiasm of users as they ran and operated their new virtual spaces, which were often regarded as experiments in online citizenship and a reinvention of the rules for democratic governance' (Burgess and Green 2009, 15). Scholars like Benkler (2006) believed a networked public sphere, characterised by a non-market peer production, was possible. The early days of the web saw a level of enthusiasm for the promise of a so-called 'pro-am' revolution, which is famously summarised by the concept of 'participatory culture' by Henry Jenkins (2006). However, this ideal of participation and democratic communities was questioned by many users after Google acquired YouTube in 2006. Although Google had originally promised to keep the community-based identity of the platform intact, the gradual introduction of regulations (e.g. the partnership programme in 2008) that enabled some form of monetisation ultimately changed the character of YouTube (Van Dijck 2013; Aasman 2018). Burgess and Green indicated how the different roles of being a social network, a media archive or a commercial platform caused 'discomfort and uncertainty with the meaning and uses of YouTube' (Burgess and Green 2009, 5).

As a result, ever since YouTube started, a discursive struggle has ensued as to what makes YouTube a place for amateurs.

The case of Casey Neistat, a popular YouTuber who has been vlogging for several years, demonstrates the discursive struggle of what it means to be an amateur in the age of YouTube. Neistat took to the platform in October 2017 to make a passionate plea to YouTube to reconsider its policy measures with regard to their new rules of advertisement. As a response to a withdrawal from advertisers, YouTube applied a new algorithm demonetising videos based on certain characteristics of inappropriate content (violence, sexual behaviour, etc.) that did not meet advertiser-friendly guidelines. However, the machine-learning process was struggling to be precise and as a result a wide array of diverse types of video content was flagged. Using caps lock to emphasise his message *DEMONITIZED DEMONITIZED DEMONITIZED* (2017), Neistat complained how the new YouTube rules had a devastating effect on the income of most of the 'content creators'. According to Neistat, he and his fellow YouTubers were unable to make a living and this might endanger 'the community'. As Neistat reminded his millions of viewers: 'I genuinely don't feel YouTube does enough to care of and look after their community.' He warned YouTube to be alert to its disruptive actions, because 'community is the one thing that none of its competitors has been able to copy'. To illustrate what he meant, Neistat filmed himself wearing a suit of self-made armour with the words 'YouTube community' attached to it, symbolising YouTubers' position as the defence to keep the soul of YouTube alive (see Figure 2.3).

What is interesting about this vlog is how the terminology 'content creators', '(de)monetisation' and 'community' applied by Neistat resonated with his millions of subscribers.[14] Many of his followers applauded him for speaking up against YouTube, and thus Google. They expressed how thankful they were that this 'elite' content creator stood up and spoke for them – the 'small creators' or 'small YouTubers' (the rhetoric used here has an interesting connotation to small film, a

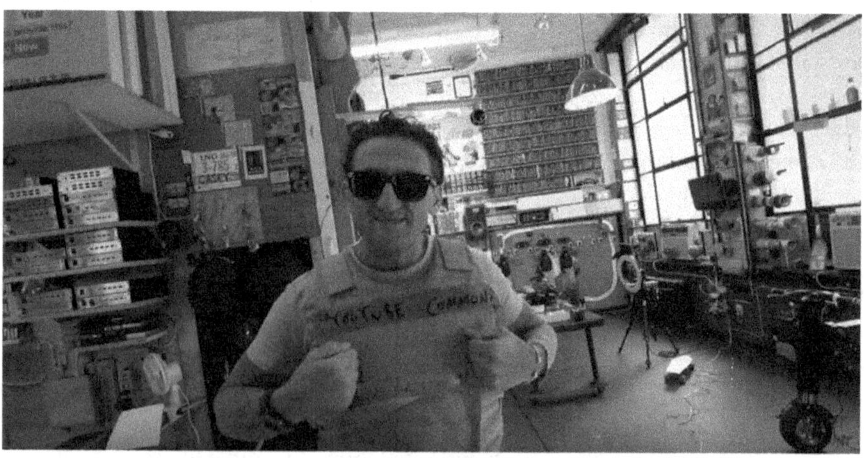

FIGURE 2.3 *DEMONITIZED DEMONITIZED DEMONITIZED*. 2017. Screengrab via YouTube.

historical term indicating amateurs on sub-standard film format such as 8mm) – as they described themselves. However, not all commentators agreed with Neistat's analysis and predominantly disliked the emphasis on monetisation. Indeed, they considered the act of monetising to go against the old YouTube ideal, or in the words of one of Neistat's critics of the vlog post:

> Completely wrong, YouTube back in the day … was thriving with all the creators doing it for free and the love of creativity. Once they started offering money that was the beginning of the end of YouTube. I hope YouTube crashes and we see a redemption of the old days.

And another critic added: 'YouTube died when it stopped being a hobby and started becoming about the money.' So, when Neistat complained against YouTube's policy of *demonitisation*, he spoke for the happy few, the small group of successful YouTubers, and not the dedicated amateur users who resisted *monetisation*. To them, demonetisation would be a blessing, if that meant the return of the *old* YouTube: the once active community of alternative, unruly users generating their own cultural form, with 'its informal way of addressing the audience and its haphazard editing' (Van Dijck 2013, 119). This discussion was repeated in many other conversations elsewhere on YouTube, and it shows the passionate, often quite divergent, positions of users about the identity of the 'real' YouTuber. Also, it was not the first time that YouTube was declared dead as a lively community of passionate users. The history of YouTube shows that there were several waves of change, each stage showing distrust and discontent towards YouTube and Google, or, as Van Dijck described it: 'YouTube's users were anything but complacent dudes' (Van Dijck 2013, 111). For instance, in 2012, several videos claimed that 'YouTube amateur hour is over', referring to the once popular American TV show for amateurs.[15]

Did amateurship turn out to be about making money and, therefore, are amateurs the new professionals? According to Jean Burgess (2014), this is indeed the case. She signalled how YouTube gradually became the site where a process of 'professionalisation and formalisation of amateur media production' has taken place (Burgess 2014, 54). But the degree of this formality is not so straightforward. In their introduction to the role of user-generated content in formal and informal media economies, Hunter et al. (2014) explored how, both in past and in today's media culture, the amateur can be both part of informal, as in outside the official consolidated and regulated media industries, and part of, or at least share various attributes of, formal economies. But once home videos shift from a private space to a more public terrain, for instance by entering YouTube, partaking in this highly commercialised media space does have consequences, even for those who just use the platform to distribute home videos easily to family and friends. For instance, one implication is that amateur users can become subject to formal legal governances as a result of YouTube's end-users agreement (Hunter et al. 2014). Families have to make sure that the images meet the requirements of YouTube's guidelines, avoiding the use of strong language, graphic violence or even copyright infringement. In a worst-case scenario, everyday activities, such as singing 'Happy Birthday' during a birthday party, could become – once uploaded on YouTube – 'a new site of tension [that] appears at the edge of the formalised economy' (Hunter et al. 2014, 13) Until 2016 the entertainment company Warner Brothers held the copyrights to the song 'Happy Birthday' and every time the song was used in a movie without the company's consent, it was a potential copyright infringement. Vlogs or home videos like *Nana's Birthday Surprise*, in which the family sing this song, potentially ran the risk of being deleted by YouTube. All of a sudden, the private space could become a dangerous zone related to problems connected to more formal and commercialised media spaces.

The amateur moment

In her study about YouTube, José Van Dijck (2013) noted that the idea that YouTube is a platform for amateurs should be demystified: amateurs as active producers contributed just a fraction of the total content. She indicated a significant shift from active user agency to passive consumer behaviour as a result of 'its interface features and underlying algorithms – increasingly gravitated toward viewer-based principles and away from community-oriented social networking' (Van Dijck 2013, 117). However, despite the fact that YouTube does indeed stimulate and instigate new hierarchies between producers and users, which led to a decreasing percentage of user-generated content, the platform still holds billions of amateur-produced uploads. Even if everyday users only produce a tiny fraction of the total amount of content, the absolute numbers of videos will still be overwhelming. If we look, for instance, at the number of users who upload baby's first steps, this entails a staggering 22,700,000 uploads (for the English version). While some of these videos will only attract one viewer and others 1 million, the fact remains that YouTube is the preferred platform for distribution. Not all users try to earn money or want to become a celebrity.

These aspects of present-day media culture indicate that we are in the midst of what William Uricchio (2015) characterised as 'moments of innovation' that, thanks to the new set of technologies and changed cultural appreciation of the amateur, inspire intriguing experiments and stimulate new forms of producing content. Many of the homemade videos we explored in this chapter can be considered part of this experiment: people constructing their online stories about their lives, expanding to new forms of connectedness, creating virtual domestic and commercial spaces, crossing the boundaries of what once was a home movie.

Notes

1 DaddyOFive was a YouTube channel and online alias of Michael Christopher 'Mike' Martin. The channel was active from 2015 until 2017. In 2018, Martin started a new family channel, named 'FamilyOFive', this time without the participation of his

youngest two children. See: www.officialfamilyofive.com [31 May 2018]. Not long after the restart, YouTube decided to terminate this channel for violating YouTube's Terms of Service (18 July 2018). For an overview of the controversial videos, responses on YouTube and the apologies, see the online blogpost: Don Caldwell, 'DaddyOFive Prank Controversy', *Know your meme* (2017). Available at http://knowyourmeme.com/memes/events/daddyofive-prank-controversy [17 December 2017].

2 The original video is removed, but some of the original content is still visible in other vlogs addressing the video, such as Phillip de Franco's *Wow. We need to talk about this*, 17 April 2017.

3 DaddyOFive, *DaddyOFive Founders Issue Public Apology*, 28 June 2017, www.youtube.com/watch?v=yeraLEdNOBA&t=7s [17 December 2017].

4 The deleted explanation video was re-uploaded by other YouTubers. See Polly Anner, *DaddyOFive explanation deleted video* (22 April 2017), www.youtube.com/watch?v=pwcorpHu8WQ. The interview on *Good Morning America* can be found at: www.youtube.com/watch?v=t2hDM_I25mE.

5 See the *DaddyOfive explanation deleted video*, re-uploaded 22 April 2017. Available at www.youtube.com/watch?v=pwcorpHu8WQ.

6 www.blogkens.com/blog/youtube-video-statistics-infographic.

7 HDCYT Channel, 856,393,882 views on 12 December 2017.

8 Maurice Chittenden, 'Harry and Charlie Davies-Carr: Web gets taste for biting baby', in *The Times*, 1 November 2009.

9 There are many websites that list the most viewed or the most influential YouTube videos. If it comes to the most viewed, music videos are on every top list. *Charlie bit my finger – again* is one of the most viewed non-music videos in 2007. See https://en.wikipedia.org/wiki/List_of_most-viewed_YouTube_videos. When YouTube celebrated five years, *Charlie* was selected as one of the best 50 YouTube clips: http://content.time.com/time/specials/packages/completelist/0,29569,1974961,00.html.

10 HDCYT. Available at www.youtube.com/user/HDCYT [Accessed 12 December 2017].

11 The Shaytards Channel: www.youtube.com/channel/UCJZ7f6NQzGKZnFXzFW9y9UQ.

12 Socialblade.com (2017) [online]. Available at https://socialblade.com/youtube/user/shaytards/similarrank [15 December 2017].

13 YouTube speaks consequently of content creators since it installed the Creators Academy in 2018.

14 Since 2017, the debate about 'demonitisation' and 'adpocalypse' has been widespread among the many 'content providers' of YouTube. For an overview of YouTube's changing policies in making the platform more 'ad-friendly', see Julia Alexander, 'The Yellow $: a comprehensive history of demonetization and YouTube's war with creators', *Polygon*, 10 May 2018, www.polygon.com/2018/5/10/17268102/youtube-demonetization-pewdiepie-logan-paul-casey-neistat-philip-defranco.

15 See, for instance, unclenats, *Is YouTube Amateur Hour Over?*, uploaded on 5 October 2012. Available at https://www.youtube.com/watch?v=d4C9146WKCg.

Selected bibliography

Aasman, Susan. 2012. 'Smile, Wave or Blow a Kiss. Home Movies and Tele-Technologies from the Hearth', in SonjaKmec and VivianeThill (eds), *Tourists and Nomads: Amateur Images of Migration*. Marburg: Jonas Verlag, 161–169.

Aasman, Susan. 2013. 'Impossible Family Portraits: Users, New Media Technologies and the Writing of Amateur Media History', *New Cinemas: Journal of Contemporary Film*, vol. 11, no. 2 & 3, 111–125.

Aasman, Susan. 2018. 'Becoming YouTube's Grandad: Media, Age, and Generation in a Virtual Community', in Susan Aasman, Andreas Fickers and Joseph Wachelder (eds), *Materializing Memories: Dispositifs, Generations, Amateurs*. New York: Bloomsbury, 151–169.

Aasman, Susan, Andreas Fickers and Joseph Wachelder (eds). 2018. *Materializing Memories: Dispositifs, Generations, Amateurs*. New York: Bloomsbury.

Albéra, François and Maria Tortajada. 2015. *Cine-Dispositives: Essays in Epistemology across Media*. Amsterdam: Amsterdam University Press.

Andrejevic, Mark. 2004. 'The Webcam Subculture and the Digital Closure', in Nick Couldry and Anna McCarthy (eds), *Media Space: Place, Scale and Culture in a Media Age*. London: Routledge, 193–209.

Baym, Nancy. 2010. *Personal Connections in the Digital Age*. Cambridge: Polity Press.

Benkler, Yochai. 2006. *The Wealth of Networks: How Social Production Transforms Markets and Freedom*. New Haven andLondon: Yale University Press.

Bourdieu, Pierre (ed.). 1965. *Un art moyen: Essai sur les usages sociaux de la photographie*. Paris: Les Éditions de Minuit.

Buckingham, David, M. Pini and Rebekkah Willet. 2009. '"Take Back the Tube!": The Discursive Construction of Amateur Film- and Video-Making', in David Buckingham and Rebekah Willett (eds), *Video Cultures: Media Technology and Everyday Creativity*. New York: Palgrave Macmillan, 51–71.

Burgess, Jean. 2014. 'YouTube and the Formalisation of Amateur Media', in R. Lobato, J. Thomas and Dan Hunter (eds), *Amateur Media: Social, Cultural and Legal Perspectives*. London: Routledge, 53–59.

Burgess, Jean and Joshua Green. 2009. 'The Entrepreneurial Vlogger: Participatory Culture beyond the Professional–Amateur Divide', in Pelle Snickars and Patrick Vanderau (eds), *The YouTube Reader*. Stockholm: National Library of Sweden, 89–108.

Burgess, Jean and Joshua Green. 2013. *YouTube: Online Video and Participatory Culture*. Cambridge: Polity Press.

Chalfen, Richard. 1987. *Snapshot Versions of Life*. Bowling Green, OH: Bowling Green State University Press.

Deuze, Mark. 2012. *Media Life*, Cambridge: Polity Press.

Deuze, Mark. 2016. 'Living in Media and the Future of Advertising', *Journal of Advertising*, vol. 45, no. 3, 326–333.

Fickers, Andreas. 2014. '"Neither Good, nor Bad, nor Neutral": The Historical Dispositif of Communication Technologies', in Martin Schreiber and C. Zimmermann (eds), *Journalism and Technological Change: Historical Perspectives, Contemporary Trends*. Frankfurt am Main and New York: Campus, 30–52.

Fickers, Andreas. 2018. 'How to Grasp Historical Media Dispositifs in Practice', in Susan Aasman, Andreas Fickers and Joseph Wachelder (eds), *Materializing Memories: Dispositifs, Generations, Amateurs*. New York: Bloomsbury, 85–99.

Gitelman, Lisa. 2006. *Always Already New: Media, History and the Data of Culture*. Cambridge, MA: MIT Press.

Grossman, Lev. 2006. 'Yes – Yes, You – Are TIME's Person of the Year', *TIME*, 25 December 2006. Available at http://content.time.com/time/magazine/article/0,9171,1570810,00.html [10 March 2018].

Harrison, Steve. 2009. *Media Space: 20+ Years of Mediated Life*. London: Springer.

Hepp, Andreas and F. Krotz (eds). 2014. *Mediatized Worlds: Culture and Society in a Media Age*. Basingstoke: Palgrave MacMillan.

Hunter, Dan, R. Lobato, M. Richardson and J. Thomas (eds). 2014. *Amateur Media: Social, Cultural and Legal Perspectives*. London: Routledge.

Jenkins, Henry. 2006. *Convergence Culture: Where Old and New Media Collide*. New York: New York University Press.

Jenkins, Henry, S. Ford and J. Green. 2013. *Spreadable Media: Creating Value and Meaning in a Networked Culture*. New York: New York University Press.

Kessler, Frank. 2007. 'Notes on Dispositif'. Published online. Available at www.frankkessler.nl/wp-content/uploads/2010/05/Dispositif-Notes.pdf.

De Klerk, Nico. 2008. 'Home Away from Home: Private Films from the Dutch East Indies', in Karen L. Ishizuka and P. Zimmermann (eds), *Mining the Home Movies: Excavations in Histories and Memories*. Berkeley and Los Angeles: University of California Press, 148–162.

Lessig, Lawrence. 2008. *Remix: Making Art and Commerce Thrive in the Hybrid Economy*. New York: Penguin Press.

Livingstone, Sonia. 2009. 'On the Mediation of Everything: ICA Presidential Address 2008', *Journal of Communication*, vol. 59, no. 1, 1–18.

Luscombe. Belinda. 2017. 'The YouTube Parents Who are Turning Family Moments into Big Bucks', *Time*, 18 May 2017. Available at http://time.com/4783215/growing-up-in-public/?xid=time_socialflow_facebook.

Madianou, Mirca and Daniel Miller. 2013. 'Polymedia: Towards a New Theory of Digital Media in Interpersonal Communication', *International Journal of Cultural Studies*, vol. 16, no. 2, 169–187.

Marwick, Alice. 2015. 'You May Know Me From YouTube: (Micro)-Celebrity in Social Media', in P. David Marshall and S. Redmond (eds), *A Companion to Celebrity*. Hoboken, NJ: John Wiley & Sons, 333–350.

Moran, James. 2002. *There's No Place Like Home Video*. Minneapolis, MN: University of Minnesota Press.

Morley, David. 2000. *Home Territories: Media, Mobility and Identity*. London: Routledge.

Müller, Jürgen E. 2010. 'Intermediality Revisited: Some Reflections about Basic Principles of this Axe de Pertinence', in Lars Elleström (ed.), *Media Borders, Multimodality and Intermediality*. Houndsmills and New York: Palgrave Macmillan, 237–252.

Odin, Roger. 2008. 'Reflections on the Family Home Movie as Document: A Semio-Pragmatic Approach', in Karen L. Ishizuka and Patricia R. Zimmermann (eds), *Mining the Home Movie: Excavations in Histories and Memories*. Berkeley, Los Angeles and London: University of California Press, 255–271.

Odin, Roger. 2014. 'The Home Movie and Space of Communication', in Laura Rascaroli and G. Young with B. Monahan (eds), *Amateur Filmmaking: The Home Movie, the Archive, the Web*. New York: Bloomsbury, 15–26.

Odin, Roger. 2016. 'Cinema in My Pocket', in Giovanna Fossati and A. van den Oever (eds), *Exposing the Film Apparatus: The Film Archive as a Research Laboratory*. Amsterdam: Amsterdam University Press, 45–53.

Odin, Roger. 2018. 'Amateur Technologies of Memory, Dispositifs and Communication Spaces', in Susan Aasman, Andreas Fickers and Joseph Wachelder (eds), *Materializing Memories: Dispositifs, Generations, Amateurs*. New York: Bloomsbury, 19–35.

Senft, Theresa. 2008. *Camgirls: Celebrity and Community in the Age of Social Networks*. New York: Peter Lang.

Senft, Theresa. 2013. 'Microcelebrity and the Branded Self,' in John Hartley, Jean Burgess, and Axel Bruns (eds), *A Companion to New Media Dynamics*. London: Blackwell, 346–354.

Silverstone, Roger and Eric Hirsch (eds). 1992. *Consuming Technologies, Media and Information in Domestic Spaces*. London and New York: Routledge.

Slootweg, Tom. 2018. *Resistance, Disruption and Belonging: Electronic Video as Alternative in Three Amateur Modes*. PhD dissertation, University of Groningen.

Tomlinson, John. 2001. 'Some Cultural Implications of "Global" Technologies', *Global Media Cultures Working Papers*, number 13.

Uricchio, William. 2009. 'Moving Beyond the Artifact', in Marianne van den Boomen (ed.), *Digital Material: Tracing New Media in Everyday Life and Technology*Amsterdam: Amsterdam University Press, 135–147.

Uricchio, William, 2015. *Mapping the Intersection of Two Cultures: Interactive Documentary and Digital Journalism*, MIT Open Documentary Lab. Available at http://opendoclab.mit.edu/interactivejournalism/Mapping_the_Intersection_of_Two_Cultures_Interactive_Documentary_and_Digital_Journalism.pdf.

Van Dijck, José. 2013. *The Culture of Connectivity: A Critical History of Social Media*. Oxford and New York: Oxford University Press.

Van Dijck, José, T. Poell and M. de Waal. 2018. *The Platform Society: Public Values in a Connective World*. Oxford and New York: Oxford University Press.

Van der Heijden, T. 2018. *Hybrid Histories: Technologies of Memory and the Cultural Dynamics of Home Movies, 1895–2005*. PhD dissertation, Maastricht University.

Zimmermann, Patricia. 2017. 'Toward a Theory of Participatory New Media Documentary', in *Afterimage: The Journal of Media Arts and Cultural Criticism*. Available at http://vsw.org/afterimage/2017/06/19/dossier-toward-a-theory-of-participatory-new-media-documentary.

3

THE NON-EPHEMERAL AMATEUR MEDIA AND CONSTRUCTIONS OF SELF

In January 2015, and then in February 2016, two women's stories funnelled news streams, polarised audience(s) and muddled media theorists' perspectives on what proved to be, unquestionably, non-ephemeral media. Both women were highly active netizens, 18- and 22-years-old respectively, living in the United States, and both possessed a zealous command of their self-made media *persona* through mobile phone films and live-streaming. By April 2016, the younger of the women was sentenced to nine months in prison for 'kidnapping, rape, sexual battery and pandering sexual matter involving a minor' (McPhate 2016), while the other secured over 12 million viewers and global fame on YouTube by repeating *ad nauseam* a direct-to-camera statement – 'I am Poppy'.[1] Marina Lonina, a Muscovite teenager barely adjusted to her new home (Ohio) and its social networks, but fluent in her use of the Periscope app – a Twitter-owned live-streaming service (Roettgers 2016)[2] – filmed and broadcasted a 10-minute long video showing her friend being raped by a man whom they met only a few hours before the attack. She later confessed that what she filmed 'wasn't anything out of the ordinary' and that, at the time of the attack, she 'was on Periscope, hanging out with people online'. Moreover, she argued that although she appears in front of the camera several times as if taking a selfie *with* the rape scene in the background, she was in a 'completely different realit[y]' to that of the attacker and her friend.[3] The other newsworthy woman, Moriah Perriera, became the YouTuber called Poppy by deftly recycling Mars Argo's (Brittany Alexandria Sheets's stage name) claim – 'my life is incredibly boring and I need to broadcast that to the world' – and her partnership with musician and video director Titanic Sinclair (Corey Michael Mixter's stage name). Seen by some as a 'parody commentary of what pop stars today go through',[4] Poppy quickly acquired a *vox dei* viewpoint with *Everybody wants to be Poppy* (Figure 3.1),[5] and by ordering her online viewers to *Delete your Facebook* – another of her Dada-style, hypnotically repetitive YouTube clips.[6]

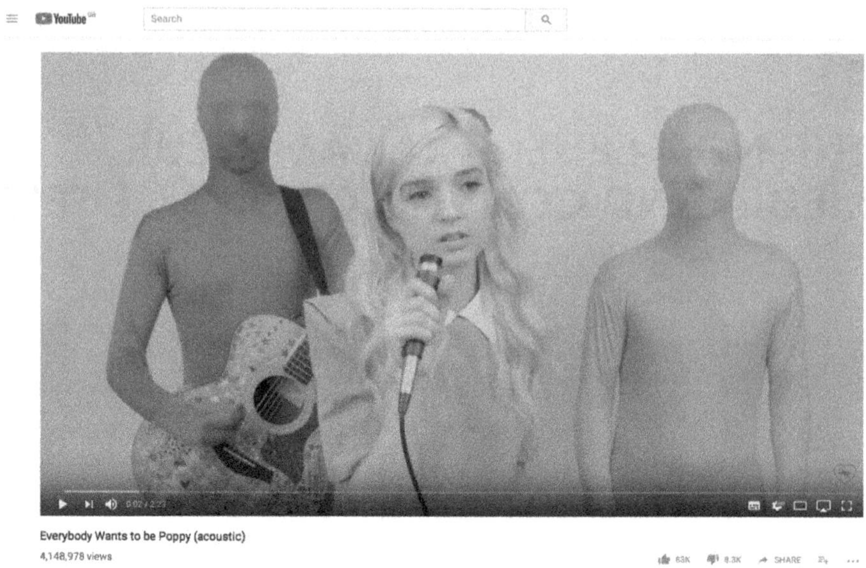

FIGURE 3.1 *Everybody wants to be Poppy*, 2015. Screengrab via YouTube.

These examples of young women manipulating or misusing new media technologies – from making surreal word/music YouTube videos to live-streaming their daily routines and traumas – raise key questions about the ephemerality of online identity,[7] fame and disgrace, collective memory and shifting legal frameworks. Such theoretical perspectives often overwrite enquiries into technological developments and their *shelf life* in terms of archival capability and new media users' interest. Importantly, their stories are not gender, race, citizenship or age related, but find common ground in two behavioural strands. First, the freedom to have an online persona, sometimes with the benefits as well as risks of a blended (real vs. online) identity – 'you can create a [web]page and be a completely different person from who you are in your real life'.[8] Second, the right to use or challenge the alleged ephemerality (read, temporary, briefly streamed/broadcast and quickly erased or forgotten) of certain examples of social and new media.[9]

This chapter focuses on one of the core themes explored in the book, that of theoretical approaches that position ephemeral (new and amateur) media as both a functional social tool and a deceptive theoretical and technological construct. Issues of amateur new media makers opting for anonymity and the ephemerality, or time-restricted modes of distribution, of their records indicate a choice for a renewable, non-punishable freedom of expression. This production-distribution framework often mediates, for instance, examples of political, sexual or racial abuse and hate speech, to name just a few strands, that can reach high levels of (involuntary) online archivability.[10] This is due to either active legal frameworks or to pervasive cultural and visual priming processes that preserve the original media records – from selfies translating impudence and narcissism, to scenes documenting acts of terrorism or domestic crime. The authors of this volume are less concerned with a review of media-recording developments that, at some point, have unavoidably reclassified 'new media' technology as obsolete and impractical, and its feasibility as just another ephemeral recording mode.[11] Instead, they explore how several pervasive cognitive and cultural frameworks allow the current amateur new media (*periscoping*) behaviour – one in which media makers use the shelter of their online *persona*, whether through in-character performance, media channel-specific digital avatars, or ad-hoc and in-situ journalism to self-(obsess)observe, mirror trope identities and meteoric cultural trends, and to identify and expose crucial social and political appeals.

While considering visual literacy's role in preserving means of expression that overwrite, by default, new representational features offered by the latest recording technologies, several examples are discussed throughout the chapter – ranging from selfies to allegedly ephemeral media recordings and orphan media (a different type of media ephemerality) – with the aim to propose a research framework that could be of interest to future media scholars.

For instance, a seemingly benign Periscope video can raise issues of ethics, cognitive psychology and media distribution and consumption. While Marina Lonina live-streamed on Periscope the rape of her friend for a predominantly male audience, she was simultaneously receiving live requests such as 'Don't stop filming!' and 'Film it! Film it' – a peer pressure difficult to ignore and, importantly, one which she later admitted made her 'feel significant'. This online self-significance is a common ground for YouTubers such as Poppy, granted 201,000 likes for *I am Poppy* three years after the original upload, or for Germán Garmendia whose more than 33 million subscribers to one of his channels – HolaSoyGerman – continue to secure his place among the top four YouTube celebrities.[12] This media context, experienced *live* and kept 'alive' through new viewings, shapes the personality of amateur media makers through a continuous online performance of their techno-selves, whether sheltered by the alleged anonymity of a username or under the mask of their digital identity (Luppicini 2012). The online avatars of vloggers, YouTubers or Facebook users, to name just a few social media personae, are defined by a reversible act of voyeurism: they are simultaneously their own subject <u>and</u> the object of their digital scopophillic pleasure owing to an almost undeviating act of self-creation and self-observation. Theirs is a demiurgic perspective from within a self-made identity, and also one resulting from peer pressure and cultural priming since most of their digital identity is a response to what their audience demands or expects to see. The narrative tensions found in Marina's or Moriah's live-streamed images or Moriah's edited videos combine routine elements of the social performance of the self in specific contexts (Goffman 1956), the need to produce a visual 'mortuary mask' (Bazin 1960), and the simultaneous appeal of the (alleged) non-archivability features offered by new media technologies such as Sobrr – the 'anti-Facebook app' (Gross 2014) – Instagram stories – which led to Finstagram vs. Rinstagram contrasting online user identities – and Snapchat.[13] Of note is the rapid development of #Finstagram or Finstas ('fake', read secondary, pseudo-anonymous and closed-network Instagram accounts) due to their short availability (images disappear 24 hours after upload), its self-media purging feature ('prevents the detritus of [our] digital life from becoming overwhelming'; Hern 2017), and the option to post images that are not required to meet the ever-growing aesthetic standard of Instagram.[14] This guaranteed ephemerality and 'sense of urgency', as well as the opportunity to share daily moments of less-performed self-representation – often Finstas are used to post unflattering and 'crying-selfies' (Diamond 2017) – have made Instagram stories 'one of the last refuges of the authentic online self' (Carman 2018). These 'shelters' allow young online users 'to feel it's helping [them] create a healthy balance in their social-media lives' (Hubby 2017). Justifiably, in less than a year after the launch of the app, there was a traffic of 200 million daily users (Wolfson 2017) (Figure 3.2).[15] Representative of the core users and audience of Finstagrams, one high-school blogger declared as early as 2015: 'It is not just normal to have a Finsta, it is expected' (Eric 2015). A few months later, another teenager, and Instagram 'star' with more than 800,000 followers, renamed her Instagram account as 'Social Media Is Not Real Life' (Bromwich 2015), and then closed it a few days later due to peer pressure for performing-the-self on Instagram: 'I made myself into a machine that gave others what they wanted from me, never knowing or valuing my true self' (Safronova 2015).

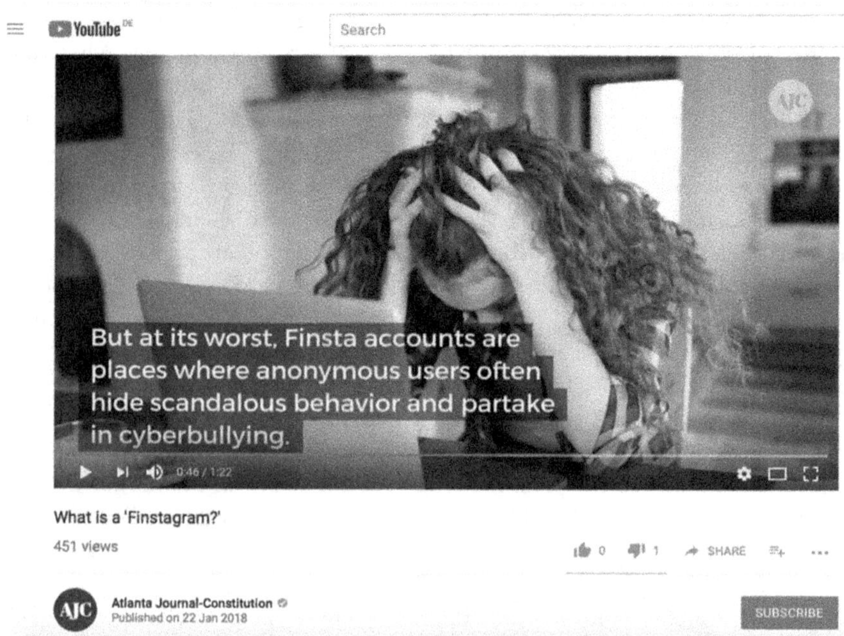

FIGURE 3.2 *What is a 'Finstagram'?* YouTube tutorial, 22 January 2018. Screengrab via YouTube.

From this perspective, most amateur new media distributed across social media networks could be defined as an attempt to secure recognition by means of primed or ingenious performance of anonymity, away from public judgement and safe in the knowledge that most self-representations are ephemeral (Suler 2004; Konnikova 2013). Just before serving her sentence, when asked whether there is a moral to her story, Marina admitted: 'I should have said No.' However, in the broader context of user-generated media studies, and of the applicable, albeit too volatile, legal framework, it is unclear when and to whom she should have said 'No'. To the media appeal of creating a Periscope account? To her male online viewers on Periscope demanding *live* detailed images of the rape scene? To her friend, before this one started flirting with a man they had just met, or to the aggressor during the rape scene? She filmed in-the-moment and explicitly for a mostly unknown, wide audience with whom she shared a 'Periscope reality'. Marina's mobile phone footage was therefore meant to be an ephemeral recording of a scene similar to other sexually themed, and bordering abuse and cruelty content available on Periscope.

Paradoxically, the driving force in her narrative was similar to Moriah's production and promotion of her digital avatar, Poppy. They both addressed and responded to a particular global audience, each defined by the network of a specific media channel, while using or challenging the implicit ephemerality of their digital identities. While Marina pursued a niche, short-lived albeit resounding online fame – the equivalent of 'likes' on Periscope are floating hearts, which were rapidly multiplying during her live-streaming of the sexual attack – Moriah continues to fight the precarious digital fame within YouTube's content surplus by performing her netizen avatar in a flawless exercise of media priming. Nonetheless, neither of them faces oblivion. This is not because of their using Periscope or YouTube, a digital space wherein their identities are the sum of awarded 'hearts' or 'likes'.[16] Nor is this because of their exercise in selfies panopticism – a digital, online identity construction somewhat similar to 24-hour activity trackers such as Fitbit or Garmin except that, instead of having the Self defined by cheering, punitive or competitive statistics showing numbers of steps taken or (un)burnt calories, this framework uses new media self-surveillance protocols documenting one's visual and behavioural memes (Rayner 2012).[17] It is, in fact, the Internet's media ecology and technological affordability that makes 24-hour live-broadcast, instant visual messages and self-destructing recordings – currently features common to apps like Snapchat, Sobrr, Wickr, Mirage, Dust, Confide, or Facebook Messenger – permanent legal liabilities. Sam Shamansky, Marina Lonina's lawyer, after having secured her eligibility for expungement of her criminal charges, admitted that, in the new global media networks, such legal frameworks are superfluous since 'what is never erased is the media attention. You Google [her] name [and] all this crap is gonna appear *forever*' (emphasis added to reflect the change in his voice pitch).[18] This type of ongoing, unmanageable digital notoriety trades traditional protocols for self-surveillance – i.e. 'the attention one pays to one's behaviour when facing the actuality of virtuality of an immediate or mediated observation by others' (Vaz and Bruno 2003) – for the new media-driven self-voyeurism when the subject of visual, online surveillance is the amateur media maker (Mayer-Schönberger 2011). It also revokes the marketing and technological claims made by apps such as Sobrr or Snapchat, for guaranteed ephemerality of new media records. Netizens interested in joining social networking apps that promise a perpetually renewed *carpe diem* digital world by making all their records, such as 'photos, messages, and, even, friendships' expire in 24 hours,[19] are caught in a Sisyphus-like identity formation mode where issues of visibility impact on the individual's right and sense of privacy and self (Niewiadomski and Anderson 2017).

In the context of this iconographic circularity of means of production and reception, can a visual record (all media) still be categorised as an ephemeral image? There are several perspectives from which to draw a list of definitions of ephemeral media, especially in relation to their ever-shifting meaning 'within cycles of time and circuits of value'. For instance, Paul Grainge defines the ephemeral in media as it is in life itself: transient, brief, short-lived (Grainge 2011). A good example is found in Snapchat's transitory twenty-first-century image-making process. At the same time, some media archaeologists and media archivists have recently specialised in collecting, broadcasting and reworking 'orphan films',[20] the type of anonymous media records that, due to their intrinsic no-copyrighted, non-attributed status, are bound to attain the status of 'ephemeral media' as a visual 'meaning' – rather than a process that is constantly located in between media categories. Moreover, in the theoretical framework established by film theorists of the last century such as André Bazin – see, for instance, his chapter on 'The Ontology of Photographic Image' (1960) – photographic practice and filmmaking are also evaluated as light-moulded mortuary masks – *embalming* the living into images.[21] So, irrespective of whether the discussion centres on a 20,000-year-old iron-oxide-sprayed image of human hands or a vlog posted on YouTube just a few minutes ago, it is imperative to assess the human survival skills involved, processed and expressed in the respective image-making process. In this context, it might be possible to argue that the ephemeral in its visual form is the very expression of its own denial, as in the need to capture, preserve and hopefully disseminate in perpetuity the transient immediacy of a specific present tense, as well as elements of its historical and cultural significance. The original meaning of the visual record is then lost across various interpretive modes – all related to the culturally specific visual literacies of subsequent audiences.

Moreover, technologies of ephemeral media need to be evaluated within frameworks addressing innovations and modes of redistribution across private, public and academic disciplines as, for example, when amateur films transitioned from being *just* ephemeral (private) media first into the core, primary research sources for commercial media productions, and second into 'visual manuscripts' used by historians and social anthropologists. This brings into discussion the need for a new hierarchy of visual ephemerality, one established by assessing the 'transient value' – media preservation stability – of various forms of media such as media 'in stone' (iron-oxide pigment, indeterminable or at least 90,000 years), media on celluloid (around 100 years), media on magnetic tape (up to 30 years), media as data storage (the data storage 'time warranty' is yet to be confirmed).[22] In her detailed discussion of early newsreels – *actualités* – Mary Ann Doane (2002) pays an indirect tribute to André Bazin when she argues that media making is, after all, an intrinsic system of documentation able to harness the transience of life. Doane comments on the intuitive need shared by producers and users of early (as well new) media to identify, repeat and thus archive what seems irrefutably lost at the very moment of its expression (projection) – the ephemeral thus demands archiving protocols. Consequently, the identification and re-presentation of fleeting moments that appear or prove to have historical merit function within a polarised network of social and historical relations. For instance, the ongoing open-source Ephemeral Films Project aims at archiving as well as streaming online numerous amateur, instructional, educational and industrial films documenting to various extent the spread of National Socialism in Austria in the twentieth century. The project's aim is to demonstrate that such ephemeral films had a 'limited purpose – not meant to endure – and [so …] have received little scholarly attention or systematic preservation'; nevertheless, 'they contain valuable cultural and historical information'.[23] To some extent, this could be an example of paradoxical research practice. As discussed, if the recording device doesn't limit or deny access to particular images by becoming technically obsolete, it is often the case that the 'media detritus' consisting of non-commercial, hobbyist or industry-specific media productions is identified *ab initio* – i.e. at the level of the intent to produce it – as ephemeral. And yet it is precisely this marginal locality of intent and distribution that confers historical merit to the 'ephemeral' media. Moreover, this is not because such films have not been researched before – a framework that poses the risk of applying pre-established interpretative canons, and ones which are usually borrowed from the critical apparatus applicable to mainstream productions. Instead, it is the representation of social interactions, whether private or communitarian, found in such films that had, by default, to rely on specific visual literacies, which emulated popular narratives while simultaneously establishing coherent documentary prerogatives. The implied ephemerality of such media productions is a superfluous theoretical exercise since they share with commercial, mainstream films the same drive for fixing and re-presenting the instantaneity of life.

At the opposite pole of interpreting accidental or planned recordings of social interactions is the controversial use of body cameras, portable surveillance devices and data- and information-sharing and retrieval technologies such as police dash cams, BodyWorn, SceneDoc, Vievu or Spartan GoPro and Go!Cam, to name just a few. While designed to ensure accurate records of ephemeral albeit potentially crucial information, from hunting and exploration to criminal offences, such recording protocols often create a boomerang effect of media exposure by transforming the media maker into a by-product *of* the recording. For instance, American policemen claimed recently that they feel 'besieged by videos of arrests and other procedures proliferating on YouTube, … [and that they] get taunted by youths holding up their iPhones'[24] – a new disciplinary and punitive context in which, indeed, the use of mobile phone films and their live-streaming on Facebook often reveals agonising examples of transgression and abuse of power. For instance, Diamond Reynolds' phone video showing her partner, Philando Castile, being shot dead by a policeman at a traffic stop in Falcon Heights, Minnesota, in July 2016, instantly took by storm not only Facebook but on global news networks too. If accepting the hypothesis that the World Wide Web is 'a unique mixture of the ephemeral and permanent'

(Schneider and Foot 2004), then this should be the ideal place to archive social *presence* as the lived-*in*, online expression of life – whether documenting horrific miscarriages of justice or acts of blatant bravados (Figure 3.3).

Considered from a wide-angle theoretical perspective, it appears that, most often, it is a matter of access (i.e. technology, distribution, in-situ discovery) and of perception that determines the ephemerality, common interpretative ground, and the subsequent historic merit of images, be they the amateur video showing several members of the LAPD beating Rodney King, an African-American taxi driver, in March 1991 (see Chapter 1), Taliban drone footage of suicide bombings released online (Stanekzai 2016), or prehistoric cave paintings. Indeed, access to communication and new media dialogue is crucial and identity-defining, whether personal, regional or global. For instance, major circulation publications, such as *The Economist*, bank nowadays on implicit visual synecdoche about ubiquitous technological and cultural frameworks found in otherwise mundane images – a case in point is the illustration selected for the article 'Technology in Africa, The Pioneering Continent' (2015, 45): it shows a young Massai man holding a mobile phone high above his head and looking at it as if to take a selfie or to check the network 'bars'. In this context of permanently re-mediatised narratives, it becomes thus possible to argue that, were contemporary recording technologies to stop being available, the visual priming inherited across various societies, and the culturally primed (all) media constructions of self and collective memories, will nevertheless still succeed in preserving and promoting collective narratives. This prompts the question whether it is feasible to categorise an image – all genres and all means of production – as ephemeral media since they would usually *survive*, in one form or another, even when deprived of their initial

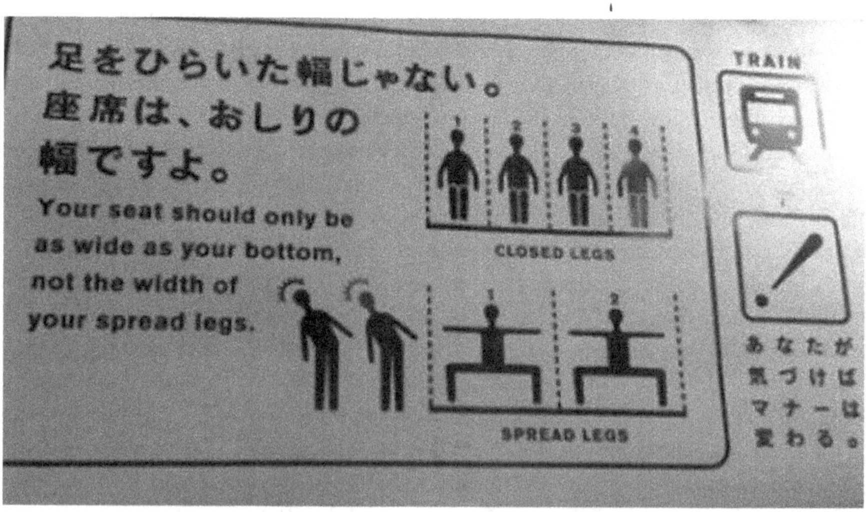

FIGURE 3.3 Tokyo subway commuter etiquette poster. Tokyo subway: rules on seating (Credit: monika.monika). Screengrab via Flickr.com.

technological and cultural means of production and reception. For instance, is it possible to define stone-age rock paintings of hands, animals and hunting techniques found in, for instance, the Chauvet cave (France), Cueva de las Manos (Argentina), Cuciulat cave (Romania), Altamira cave (Spain) and Bradshaw rock paintings (Australia), as examples of *accidental* ephemeral media because they have been hidden from view for several millennia, and hence visually 'extinct' until their rediscovery by the modern world? If yes, then a similar historical validation of non-ephemerality is equally applicable to what today is considered old media – i.e. nitrate film, 9.5mm amateur film stock or analogue recording video cassette – since the visual narratives found across such productions have withstood technological redundancies and remained, in nuanced and updated versions, fixtures of enduring popular visual cultures.

Most non-mainstream, occasional and limited-distribution media productions – from home movies to TV ads and web dramas – that have been recently classified as ephemeral media or 'moving image detritus' do indeed operate within cycles of time and circuits of value' (Grainge 2011, 2–3). These are media form(at)s that circulate *between, beyond* and *below* what screen studies usually prioritise as core research sources, such as long-established film and TV genres. In order to experiment with theories of ephemeral or new media, it helps to remember that such concepts are crucially dependent on regimes of knowledge defined by perception studies and theories of cognitive psychology. The ephemeral, as an intellectual, emotional and cultural construct, is always experienced across specific registers of identity, from the personal self to the political self, from regional and national communal identities to global hierarchies of knowledge. As such, preliminary insights into theories and justifications of human behaviour, emotion and thinking can be structured around a few key perspectives on, for instance, survival instinct in humans, visual priming and visual literacy. For example, borrowing from recent research in pathopsychology regarding visual agnosia, it could be argued that an individual's or a group's visual literacy is equally dependent on the ability to interpret images within or tangential to their culturally specific context. The clinical inability to interpret images adequately (visual agnosia) operates at two levels: the apperceptive level which involves an impaired object (subject) recognition, and the associative level which involves an impaired object (subject) identification (Ferreira et al. 1998; Heilman 2002; Biran and Coslett 2003; Delvenne et al, 2004; Wolfe et al. 2014). This classification model is also useful in determining media literacy across social networks (on- or offline) and groups of people experiencing apperceptive cultural agnosia for various reasons. Primarily, their visual literacy only allows a segmented, incomplete recognition of narrative frameworks and hierarchies of meaning, with some groups experiencing associative cultural agnosia when, in spite of recognising elements of a given iconography, they fail to create a coherent or meaningful narrative. Why would such terms borrowed from pathopsychology be important to discussing technologies, theories and distribution of new media? First, because it is alleged that visual recognition takes precedence among the factors affecting an observer's attitude towards a speaker (Mehrabian 1972). Second, because new media (including their 'ephemeral' expressions) are usually deliberately produced these days for a global audience, their meaning and protocols for memory-building would, in principle, need to be free of impaired recognition. This then leads to the next level of interpreting how people are being taught, at all levels of social interaction, to read images; of understanding, for instance, how they become visually literate in any given context, whether geographically or socially confined – i.e. isolated indigenous people in the Amazonian rainforest, refugees and internally displaced people, or disabled individuals – or globally media-associated communities such as Facebook, VK (VKontakte), Instagram or Twitter communities.

Therefore, in what ways can this theoretical framework help us explore instances of ephemeral media? For instance, new media theoreticians are questioning whether, in the alleged 'absence of hierarchy' of the World Wide Web, social media technologies and networks are either or a 'message and a medium' (Manovich 2015). Moreover, open-ended questions about the ways in which media tools such as Instagram are 'a window into a different reality or only its own reality' (ibid.),[25] raise questions about authorship and medium-specific content. In turn, cognitive psychologists, and scholars working with cognitive theories of perception, have highlighted that the process of visual literacy is a two-part route and that it relates to well-defined visual priming processes (Bar and Biederman 1998).[26] It involves the heuristic processing – occurs whenever an individual relies on shortcut decision-making ruling to construct an attitude within a given context – and the cognitive systematic processing, which involves a contemplative, analytic and responsive attitude within a given context (Kroll and Schepeler 1985; Dillard and Peck 2000). Importantly, visual idioms are like any other language: they update, change, die and recycle other iconographies. Consequently, 'accents' in visual literacy are interpretative cultural grafts that adapt, enrich or limit the original visual narrative.

It is from this perspective that this cross-theoretical exercise in defining common modes of production, distribution and reception, whether discussing prehistoric cave art or vlogs, allows for a credible and reliable critical efficacy. First, understanding how most people become visually literate helps to identify patterns of interpretation and meaning, especially since most visual narratives rely on a set of inherited cultural assumptions. Second, being aware of how the process of visual priming functions at both individual and collective levels can help identify and, importantly, manipulate specific visual literacies such as when producing restorative narratives of collective memories or antagonistic public campaigns. Third, the core visual literacy that most people share transcends other forms of communication – i.e. the ubiquitous use of emoticons across most online and digital social networks. Finally, the core functionality of global visual literacy is anchored in five constant features: it has the highest incidence of universal meaning (emoji, human facial expression), it is usually free (street signs, advertisement billboards, etc.), it is mobile (whether within a geographically defined community or online), it is self-empowering (amateur media productions for analogue or online distribution) and has a high rate of educational applicability. For example, the poster for Tokyo subway commuter seating protocol and the recommended 'zero angle' formed by one's knees when seated (Figure 3.3). Or, the 2015 Russian Interior Ministry official guidelines for taking safer selfies – a governmental intervention prompted by an increase in the number of people killed or hurt while taking mobile phone self-portraits. Other public warnings issued by international officials aiming to secure safer selfie-taking etiquettes prohibit taking a selfie while pointing a gun to your head, this being a cause of injury or death on a par with those caused by individuals taking selfies at the edge of train or subway platforms.[27] Monitoring and prescribing social interactions and cultural representations is employing primarily tropes of globally accessible visual literacy, which, in turn, determines people's visual constructions of their world, whether explicitly archivable or meant for a limited and temporary distribution.

Borrowing from Paul Grainge's conceptual registers that help with critical analyses of ephemeral media, it is possible to explore additional perspectives on, for instance, amateur media self-ethnographies such as vlogging, domestic videos of parental misconduct, or accidental mobile phone films that have become persuasive political *agents*.[28] Grainge proposes two regimes within which to group several conceptual registers: '*regimes of time* (duration, shortness, speed) and *regimes of transmission* (circulation, storage, value)' (Grainge 2011, 9) (emphasis in original). By elaborating on these conceptual regimes, it could be argued that new and amateur media are equally defined by and define their respective narratorial and iconographic genres in as much as any other visual production practice. However, it seems that the point of departure could be found in regimes of authorial intent which classify the accidental/unintentional/allegedly ephemeral media recording against the planned/directed/commercially distributed media production. The latter being a deceptive binary of media records defining either localised historical and archival marginalisation or global networks of reception and archival protocols respectively. In the case of contemporary new media production, distribution and reception networks – as in early twenty-first-century recording technologies, and in contrast with what has been hailed as new media in the early 1900s or late 1980s – these finely delineated regimes of time, transmission and authorial intent fuse into one – the regime of online recycled identities. Furthermore, these identities present consolidated protocols of technological and narrative modes that reconfigure key issues of, for example, chronology – accidental recordings of the mundane vs. continuous streaming of social protests; the relationship between the recording equipment and the human body – from heavy, tripod-fixed film cameras to GoPro cameras or Google Glass; the relevance of developments in recording technologies to visual anthropology studies, and how they shaped understandings of recording practices and their historical validation in relation to ongoing risks of analysis and misdistribution (i.e. lack of cultural sensitivities). Ultimately, the regime of online recycled identities introduces media scholars to the uncharted territory of evolving new visual literacies.

Whether recorded on 35mm film or by using, for instance, the Slorr app, visual records of people *embalm* by default their identities, whether at an intimately secluded level or within narratives of collective historic timeframes. They also reveal across different interpretative contexts (social or temporal) the shifts in authorial agency and informative trajectory. For example, ethnographic films made in the early and mid-twentieth century were seen as timely and highly revelatory visual documents that used the observers' demiurgic-like perspective to detail various registers of otherness, whether within a nation's social fabric or across imperial and early post-colonial cultures. The concept of 'tribal' identity, common to twentieth-century ethnographic observations about what was considered marginal, niche or emerging cultural communities – the us-about-them narrative – has recently shifted from being the subject of observation to becoming the self-observing object as is currently demonstrated by the YouTubers' constructions of identity and by other online behavioural patterns. Examples of early twenty-first-century new global tribal media represented at the power of Selfie are found, for example, in *Tarnation* (dir. Jonathan Caouette, USA, 2003), *Capturing the Friedmans* (dir. Andrew Jarecki, USA, 2003), *The Stories We Tell* (dir. Sarah Polley, CA, 2012), *Meine Keine Familie* (dir. Paul-Julien Robert, AT, 2012), as well as in the self-ethnographies proposed by vloggers such as PewDiePie, the Shaytards, Jenna Marbles or Charles Trippy (Figure 3.4).[29] These narrative patterns present across new and amateur media productions are driven by a self-congratulatory global 'tribal' media, one expressed within the I-about-me-on-behalf-of-us visual tropes.[30]

It is therefore this (allegedly) new visual literacy that reaffirms common understandings of how both old and new recording technologies continue to define identities. Whether considering a cave, oil or watercolour painting, an MRI scan of someone's mental images or a screengrab of a Slorr entry by someone documenting Friday night debauchery, each of these images is in itself a (self-) archival process. Each visual record thus defines and anchors the respective identity, whether on the specific medium or through its reiterations. Consequently, both images and the imbedded identities become non-ephemeral. Nevertheless, their non-ephemeral feature does not exempt them from being subjected to ongoing regimes of critical

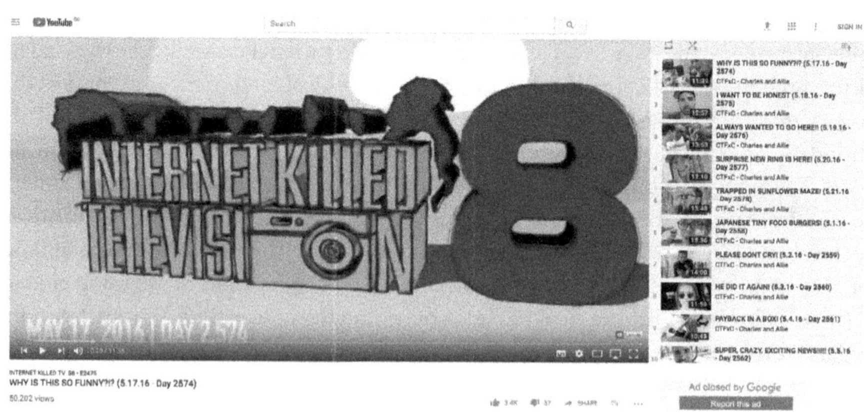

FIGURE 3.4 *Internet Killed TV, S8, E2475, Why is this so funny?!? (5.17.16 – Day 2574),* 17 May 2016. Screengrab via YouTube.

interpretation, often with nuanced or even paradoxical results, since, as visual products, they remain the primary source for visual and cultural (historical) priming processes. A case in point is found, for instance, when comparing popular visual interpretations across imperial and post-colonial cultures which often reveals divergent contemporary perspectives on a shared historical past. In his British studies seminar delivered at the University of Texas at Austin on 24 April 2015, Andrew O'Shaughnessy presented a compelling comparison of the front covers chosen by British and American publishers for his book *The Men Who Lost America* (2013). While featuring different subtitles, both covers relied on details from John Singleton Copley's life-size mural *The Siege of Gibraltar* (1783–1791). The US edition was titled *The Men Who Lost America: British Leadership, the American Revolution, and the Fate of the Empire* and included a close-up excerpt of the British commander George Augustus Eliott's equestrian portrait. In turn, the British publisher opted for *The Men Who Lost America: British Command during the Revolutionary War and the Preservation of the Empire* and a different visual excerpt: the right half of Copley's painting in which most of the British army is depicted as a 'rugby scrum of red coats looking triumphant'. In both cases, while promoting the same historical discourse, the subtitles and the carefully chosen details from Copley's painting resonate with distinctive popular beliefs and national identity ethos: an American celebratory narrative and a British diplomatically revisionist account.[31]

Importantly, old and new media leave cultural traces, as in para-texts, that are highly *recyclable* across socio-geopolitically specific visual priming process and the respective ensuing visual literacies. Part of this process is the constant reclaiming of historical details, a process that often results in recovered visual para-texts, be they the apparent *fake* (possibly kitsch) façade of a repainted Greek temple (Figure 3.5), or the self-referential memory-building exercise perfected by netizens such as Weird Paul (see also Chapter 6),[32] or by YouTubers posting edited compilations under the theme of 'Conversations with old selves' (Figure 3.6).[33]

These examples of recycled personal 'media debris' – i.e. family home movies – document the shift in amateur media practice from being the object of visual enquiry to becoming the self-referential subject of it. The reclusive intimacy of private family viewing of amateur films has gradually been transformed into an extrovert online global exposure of *becoming* the film camera. This is often the case with amateur media made by young netizens, as when children make mobile phone videos of their games (Figure 3.7), use the Periscope application in lieu of a playground partner (Figure 3.8), or when teenagers livestream videos of parental misconduct (Figure 3.9) – an unexpected example of a reversed visual badge of honour, especially when comparing such mobile phone uploads on YouTube with, for instance, 1960s home videos of proud parents filming their children's parties. Confronted with such clashes and shifts in visual literacies and moral ethics, scholars of new and amateur media require innovative methodologies to help them explore uncharted regimes of authorial intent and of specific digital identities that are currently being recycled by global ephemeral cultures.

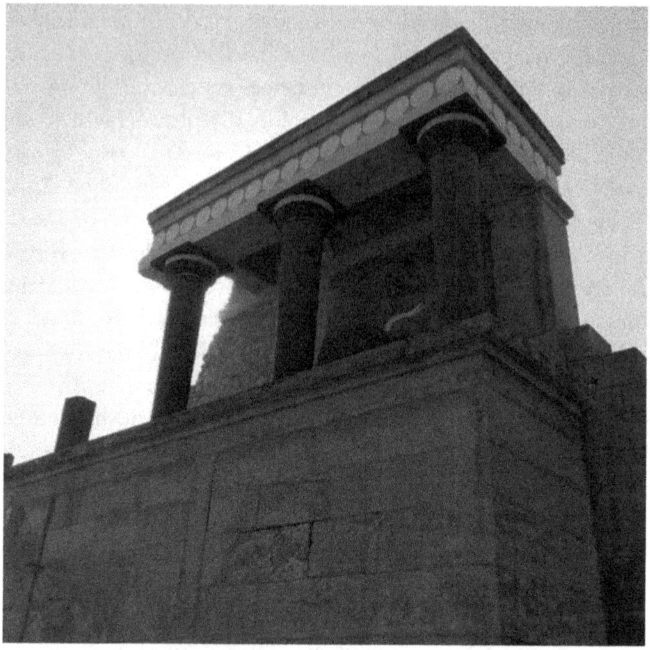

FIGURE 3.5 Knossos temple, Crete, 2016. Courtesy of Eric Mayes.

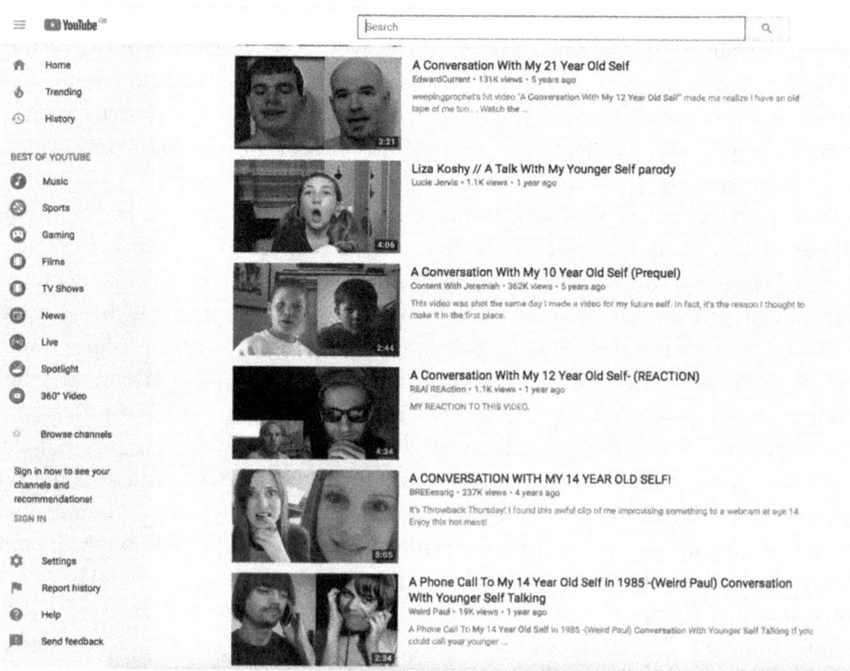

FIGURE 3.6 *Conversations with my … old self*, 2018. Screengrab via YouTube.

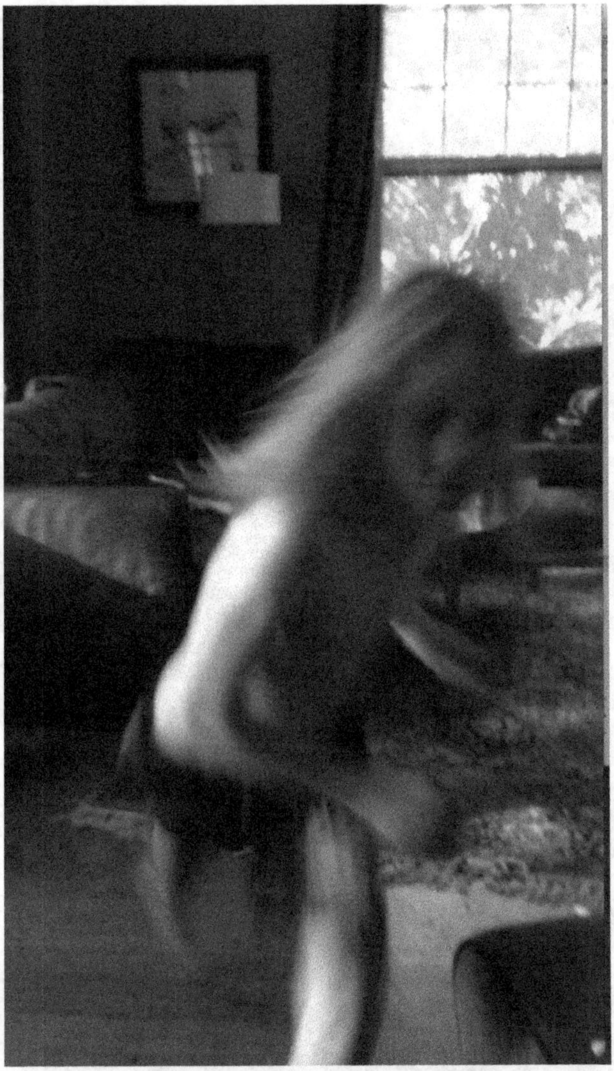

FIGURE 3.7 Mayes boys' mobile phone video. 2016. Courtesy of Wilson Mayes.

Thus, it is then crucial to investigate further whether and to what extent scholars can rely on theories of perception when attempting to define, salvage and anchor the *ephemeral* in (new) media. Will Straw has highlighted in his discussion of media and modes of communications, the imperative obligation to consider the ways in which new media produces (emotional and perception) tensions between stasis and mobility, stability and impermanence, substantial and evanescent, and monumental and momentary (Straw 2010) In addition, there is a status quo of perpetual simultaneity since images are both subsequent and antecedent – a thesis proposed by Martin Shultz (2011). Consequently, it could be argued that new media empower

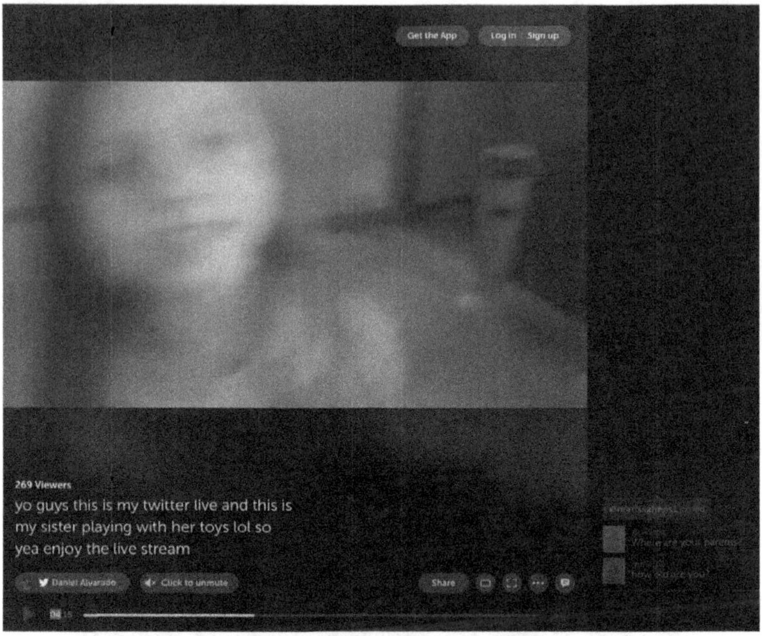

FIGURE 3.8 *yo guys this is my twitter live and this is my sister playing with her toys...*, 2017. Screengrab via Periscope.

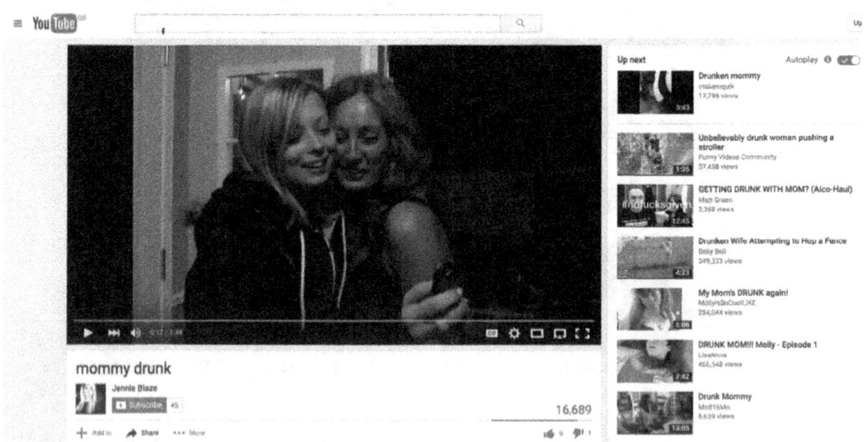

FIGURE 3.9 *mommy drunk*, 13 April 2012. Screengrab via YouTube.

their audiences beyond the ephemeral. For instance, the image of the Massai man holding his mobile phone up high might be read at first as a visual record that in itself prompts an analysis of ephemerality in terms of technology, access to network and possible accidental sharing of data. However, when viewed alongside the caption reading 'self-improvement', the same image anchors the discussion about ephemeral technology and ephemeral media into registers of progress and permanence. A similar interpretative issue can be considered when discussing the ongoing development of the netizens' technologies of memory, all centred on the core function of storyfying *live* their mundane activities and their (often recycled) visually *embalmed* past. By ways of concluding this chapter and announcing further analyses on this theme, both in this volume and elsewhere, it is perhaps pertinent to enquire if, as a visual representational mode, and irrespective whether produced by means of obsolete, traditional or new recording devices, new media empower their makers and users beyond the limits of contextualised meanings (Straw et al. 2011).

Notes

1 Available at www.youtube.com/watch?v=fpCXxqiTjqE [23 June 2017].

2 Periscope users usually stream directly from their phones or GoPro cameras, and the service has recently been extended to selected drones (Graham 2016).

3 Filmed interview with Marina Lonina included in *Don't Stop Filming* (dir. Peter LoGreco, 2017) – the sixth episode of season one *Hot Girls Wanted: Turned On*, a Netflix original series launched in 2017 (–ongoing).

4 See Michael McCrudden's YouTube show *POPPY – Before They Were Famous*, 7 August 2017. Available at www.youtube.com/watch?v=ByALPykLvDU [2 October 2017].

5 Poppy, *Everybody Wants to be Poppy*, 22 September 2015. Available at www.youtube.com/watch?v=qjCSH2e-cOo [5 January 2017].

6 Poppy, *Delete Your Facebook*, 23 January 2017. Available at www.youtube.com/watch?v=k_Jq38JKN3A [5 November 2017]. Some of the comments to this video include 'I feel brainwashed' by Timeya bear; 'delete your web history cuz ur mom is comingg [sic] to check your web history!' by D!scovery; 'It all sounds edited, like poppy didn't say the words together. I think it's because poppy would never really tell us to delete our facebook. She loves the Internet and social media' by kitty kat. These and other comments posted on this webpage offer a valid research source for mapping YouTubers' identity patterns.

7 See also Amalia Ulman's three-part Instagram project *Excellences & Perfections* (2014) with which she challenged social media constructions of identity: 'I felt very uncomfortable with the idea of self-branding, so my anti-capitalist approach to this was to destroy my online persona, to the point of creating this fake truth that I couldn't even fight with. It was all about the power of the image' (Kissick 2014).

8 Filmed interview with Marina Lonina in *Don't Stop Filming* (dir. Peter LoGreco, 2017). More recently, Waitrose, a British supermarket, included in its weekend magazine an editorial cautioning teenagers to 'wait until [being] 13 to use social media' and to '[r]emember – everything you post online is permanent and may come back to bite you!' (Kirkley 2018, 8).

9 Almost a decade ago, William Uricchio presented a detailed analysis of regimes and registers of media ephemerality, and of shifting theoretical perceptions, in his lecture 'The recurrent, recombinatory and the ephemeral: thoughts on a textual system in transition', which he delivered as part of the Ephemeral Media Workshop held at the Institute of Film and Television Studies, University of Nottingham, June–July 2009. Available at www.youtube.com/watch?v=Zmt9HbgPrYY [13 September 2017].

10 This online archivability could be defined both as temporary *and* ongoing online availability since access to data remains dependent on the management and functionality of the archives' servers and websites.

11 A survey of amateur media technologies and modes of reception is discussed in Chapter 1.

12 Available at www.youtube.com/user/HolaSoyGerman [8 May 2018].

13 Social media networks such as Snapchat and Sobrr, which are defined by their seemingly archival brevity, raise questions about unforeseeable risks of compromised online identities and privacy, as well as copycat visual narratives of abuse and trauma. See, for instance, 'Teacher admits sex with students and sending nude photos on Snapchat'. Available at www.independent.co.uk/news/world/americas/teacher-admits-sex-with-students-sending-nude-photos-snapchat-america-ohio-latest-a8050521.html [3 December 2018]; 'Chicago woman is accused of filming friend's rape and posting it to the victim's Snapchat account after the two "argued over a man they met at a party"'. Available at www.dailymail.co.uk/news/article-4844294/Woman-filmed-friend-s-rape-posted-Snapchat.html?cmp.consent=true [8 October 2017]; and 'This App Wants You To Forget Your Friends After You Make Them'. Available at www.businessinsider.com.au/this-app-wants-you-to-forget-your-friends-after-you-make-them-2014-7 [9 March 2017].
14 See *What is a 'Finstagram?'* YouTube tutorial, 22 January 2018. Available at www.youtube.com/watch?v=LkOwCutgsAY [15 May 2018].
15 Recent research has highlighted the 'migration' of teenagers from their Facebook accounts to almost exclusively using Snapchat and Instagram – a possible indication of the shift from Facebook's 'archivability' feature to the more ephemeral, unjudgmental and ad-hoc aesthetics of these limited-archivability and self-cancelling distribution social media (Solon 2018).
16 A topic explored with alarming credibility in *Nosedive* (dir. Joe Wright, 2016), first episode, third series of *Black Mirror*, a science fiction TV anthology (Netflix, 2016–ongoing).
17 There is still scope for scholars to undertake a thorough discussion of how this framework – selfies panopticism – can be applied to new and amateur media, especially from a visual and social anthropological point of view. See, for instance, *Selfiecity* (http://selfiecity.net/#) – a project that studied the selfies culture in Bangkok, Berlin, Moscow, New York and Sao Paolo. One of the project's research findings highlighted that there seems to be a higher number of gender-based than demographic-defined selfies [last accessed 22 April 2018].
18 Sam Shamansky interview in *Don't Stop Filming* (dir. Peter LoGreco, 2017).
19 Sobrr, available at http://blog.sobrr.me/post/90218046282/fabulously-answered-questions [6 June 2017].
20 Of particular relevance are the archival (experimental) documentaries made by Yervant Gianikian and Angela Ricci Lucchi, such as *Images d'Orient – Tourisme Vandale* (2001), *Fragments électriques n. 2, Viêt-Nam* (2002), *Fragments électriques n.7, Afghanistan* (2012) or *Pays Barbare* (2013), as well as works by Péter Forgács such as *The Maelstrom: A Family Chronicle* (1997) or *The Danube Exodus* (1998).
21 The use of social media as a means for visually *embalming* one's life while simultaneously having it acknowledged *live* by an alleged global audience can often have fatal consequences, and change the meaning of the ephemeral from archival settings to protocols of civic liability. For instance, on 22 May 2018, a minibus driver livestreamed on Facebook his irresponsible over-speeding on a Hungarian highway and the subsequent car crash that resulted in his own death as well as that of his passengers (nine migrant workers) (White 2018).
22 New media-savvy TV programmes such as *Mr Robot* and *Black Mirror* approached such topics in episodes that soon after their original air date have shifted genres, from science fiction to credible re-enacted documentary; see, for example, 'eps1.3_da3m0ns.mp4' (episode 4, season 1, *Mr Robot*, 15 July 2015), and *The Entire History of You* (episode 3, series 1, *Black Mirror*, 18 December 2011).
23 Excerpt from *Ephemeral Films Project*, Available at http://efilms.ushmm.org/about_the_project [4 January 2016].
24 'Paralysed by YouTube', *The Economist*, 31 October 2015.
25 See, for instance, the research findings proposed by several new media projects such as *The Exceptional and the Everyday* (available at www.the-everyday.net, 9 April 2014), which analysed 'all publicly available Instagram images shared during February 17–22, 2014 in the central part of Kiev' – a total of '13,208 images shared by 6,165 Instagram

users' during the 2014 Ukrainian Revolution. Also relevant is *On Broadway*, a project proposing that '[t]oday, a city "talks" to us in data' and which relied on a research corpus of '660,000 Instagram photos shared along Broadway during six months in 2014, Twitter posts with images, Foursquare check-ins since 2009, Google Street View images, 22 million taxi pickups and drop-offs in 2013, and economic indicators from US Census Bureau (2013)'. Available at www.on-broadway.nyc [9 April 2014].

26 See also Robert Stufflebeam's *The Mind Project* based at Illinois State University. Available at www.mind.ilstu.edu/index.php [13 March 2018].

27 See 'Death Warning Over Railway Track Selfies', Sky News, 26 October 2015. Available at https://news.sky.com/story/death-warning-over-railway-track-selfies-10341807 [15 December 2017]; 'South coast cliff falls spark #BeCliffAware selfie alert', BBC News, 25 May 2018. Available at www.bbc.co.uk/news/uk-england-sussex-44253155 [4 June 2018].

28 See, for instance, *Internet Killed TV* (Charles Trippy). Available at www.youtube.com/channel/UCsbD_e9o9zMdU0aSrxZrlIg [5 January 2018]; 'mommy drunk' (available at https://www.youtube.com/watch?v=uyUsteVTV1g, 13 April 2012 [3 November 2017]), and the shooting of Philando Castile on 6 July 2016, live-streamed on Facebook by Diamond Reynolds – see CNN compilation of the Minnesota police dashcam video and of Reynolds' Facebook Live video. Available at https://edition.cnn.com/videos/us/2017/06/22/philando-castile-facebook-and-dashcam-full-mashup-video-ctn.cnn, 22 June 2017 [27 December 2017]. In recent years, police bodycam footage often makes front page news. See, for instance, the highly controversial footage showing a New Jersey officer assaulting Emily Weinman; it was later revealed, when compared with the mobile phone film made by a by-stander, that several scenes had been edited out from the police bodycam film (Eltagouri et al 2018). See 'Paralysed by YouTube' (2015) for a brief analysis of how US Policemen respond to the use of bodycam while on duty.

29 Available at www.youtube.com/user/PewDiePie, www.youtube.com/channel/UCJZ7f6NQzGKZnFXzFW9y9UQ, www.youtube.com/user/jennamarbles, www.youtube.com/channel/UCsbD_e9o9zMdU0aSrxZrlIg [6 March 2018].

30 Founded in 1969 (and closed in 2017), CompuServe was the first online service provider on the US market, mostly covering chats and messaging. In the 1980s, it ran advertisement headlines that would suitably fit, for instance, Facebook's marketing campaigns, such as 'How people with common interests find an interesting common ground'.

31 Podcast *The Men Who Lost America* (24 April 2015). Available at http://liberalarts.utexas.edu/britishstudies/Lectures/Audio-Recordings.php [7 August 2015]. A detailed discussion of this case study is found in Motrescu-Mayes (2017).

32 See Weird Paul's YouTube channel. Available at www.youtube.com/user/weirdpaulp. [2 January 2016].

33 See, for instance, *A Conversation With My 12 Year Old Self: 20th Anniversary Edition* (available at www.youtube.com/watch?v=XFGAQrEUaeU, 5 July 2012 [10 March 2017] and *A Conversation With My 21 Year Old Self* (available at www.youtube.com/watch?v=AcZ5qmRM-UM, 8 September 2012 [2 March 2017].

Selected bibliography

Bar, Moshe and Irving Biederman. 1998. 'Subliminal Visual Priming', *Psychological Science*, vol. 9, no. 6 (November), 464–469.

Bazin, André. 1960. 'The Ontology of the Photographic Image', *Film Quarterly*, vol. 13, no. 4, 4–9.

Biran, I. and H.B. Coslett. 2003. 'Visual Agnosia. Current Neurology and Neuroscience Reports', *Jump Up*, vol. 3, no. 6, 508–512.

Bromwich, Jonah Engel. 2015. 'Essena O'Neill, Instagram Star, Recaptions Her Life', *New York Times*, 3 November. Available at: www.nytimes.com/2015/11/04/fashion/essena-oneill-instagram-star-recaptions-her-life.html [5 April 2018].

Carman, Ashle. 2018. 'Instagrams Are one of the Last Refuges of the Authentic Online Self', The Verge, 3 April. Available at: www.theverge.com/2018/4/3/17189912/fake-instagram-finsta-account-whyd-you-push-that-button [30 April 2018].

Delvenne, Jean Françoise, Xavier Seron, FrançoiseCoyette and Bruno Rossion. 2004. 'Evidence for Perceptual Deficits in Associative Visual (Prosop)agnosia: A Single-case Study', *Neuropsychologia*, no. 42, 597–612.

Diamond, Amelia. 2017. 'We Asked a Teen About Fake Instagrams and Crying Selfies', Man Repeller, 2 August. Available at: www.manrepeller.com/minor_cogitations/fake-instagram.html [8 January 2018].

Dillard, James Price and Eugenia Peck. 2000. 'Affect and Persuasion Emotional Responses to Public Service Announcements', *Communication Research*, vol. 27, no. 8/1, 461–495.

Doane, Mary Ann. 2002. *The Emergence of Cinematic Time: Modernity, Contingency, the Archive*. Cambridge, MA: Harvard University Press.

Eltagouri, Marwa. 2018. 'She was Suspected of Underage Drinking. Video Shows an Officer Punching Her in the Head', *Washington Post*, 29 May. Available at: www.washingtonpost.com/news/post-nation/wp/2018/05/28/she-was-suspected-of-underage-drinking-video-shows-the-officer-punching-her-in-the-head/?noredirect=on&utm_term=.deff9ae8152a [1 June 2018].

Eric. 2015. 'Finstagram: The Instagram Revolution.' Blog available at: https://medium.com/bits-pixels/finstagram-the-instagram-revolution-737999d40014 [2 March 2018].

Farah, Martha J. 2000. *The Cognitive Neuroscience of Vision*. London: Blackwell Publishers.

Farah, Martha J. and Graham Ratcliff (eds). 1994. *The Neuropsychology of High-level Vision: Collected Tutorial Essays*. London: Psychology Press.

Ferreira, C.T., Mathieu Ceccaldia, Bernard Giusianoa and Michel Ponceta. 1998. 'Separate Visual Pathways for Perception of Actions and Objects: Evidence from a Case of Apperceptive Visual Agnosia', *Journal of Neurology, Neurosurgery, and Psychiatry*, vol. 65, no. 3, 382–385.

Goffman, Erving. 1956. *The Presentation of Self in Everyday Life*. Edinburgh: University of Edinburgh.

Graham, Jefferson. 2016. 'Periscope Adds Live Streaming from Drones', *USA Today*, 9 May.

Grainge, Paul (ed.). 2011. *Ephemeral Media: Transitory Screen Culture from Television to YouTube*. Basingstoke: Palgrave Macmillan.

Grau, Oliver (ed.). 2011. *Imagery in the 21st Century*. Cambridge, MA: MIT Press.

Gross, Doug. 2014. 'Meet Sobrr, the Anti- Facebook app', CNN, 21 August. Available at: https://edition.cnn.com/2014/08/21/tech/mobile/sobrr-app/index.html [7 April 2018].

Heilman, K.M. 2002. *Matter of Mind*. New York: Oxford University Press.

Hern, Alex. 2017. 'Why Instagram Would Rather Posts Disappear than be Deleted by Users', *The Guardian*, 30 May. Available at: www.theguardian.com/technology/2017/may/30/instagram-snapchat-stories-posts-disappear-delete [20 February 2018].

Horton, Alex and Marwa Eltagouri. 2018. 'You're About to Get Dropped!' an Officer Shouted before Punching a Woman's Head at an N.J. Beach', *Washington Post*, 31 May. Available at: www.washingtonpost.com/news/post-nation/wp/2018/05/31/youre-about-to-get-dropped-an-officer-shouted-before-punching-a-womans-head-at-a-n-j-beach/?noredirect=on&utm_term=.fa307ac9760a [1 June 2018].

Hubby, Kristen. 2017. 'Inside Finstagram, the Private World of "Fake" Teen Instagram Accounts', Daily Dot, 7 July. Available at: www.dailydot.com/debug/finstagram-fake-instagram [8 May 2018].

Jenkins, Henry, Sam Ford and Joshua Green (eds). 2013. *Spreadable Media: Creating Value and Meaning in a Networked Culture*. New York: New York University Press.

Kirkley, Paul. 2018. 'Online Dependency Is a 'Form of Addiction', *Waitrose Weekend*, 10 May 2018, 8–9.

Kissick, Dean. 2014. 'From Plastic Surgery to Public Meltdowns, Amalia Ulman Is Turning Instagram into Performance Art', *i-D*, 24 October. Available at: https://i-d.vice.com/en_uk/article/7xvbg9/from-plastic-surgery-to-public-meltdowns-amalia-ulman-is-turning-instagram-into-performance-art [5 November 2017].

Kolb, Bryan. and Ian Q. Whishaw. 2009. *Fundamentals of Human Neuropsychology*, 6th edn. New York: Worth Publishers.

Konnikova, Maria. 2013. 'The Psychology of Online Comments', *New Yorker*, 23 October. Available at: www.newyorker.com/tech/elements/the-psychology-of-online-comments [9 January 2017].

Kroll, N.E. and E.M. Schepeler. 1985. 'Visual Priming Effects as a Measure of Short-Term Visual Memory', *American Journal of Psychology*, vol. 98, no. 3 (Fall), 449–468.

Luppicini, Rocci (ed.). 2012. *Handbook of Research on Technoself: Identity in a Technological Society*. New York: IGI Global.

McPhate, Mike. 2016. 'Teenager Is Accused of Live-Streaming a Friend's Rape on Periscope', *New York Times*, 18 April. Available at: www.nytimes.com/2016/04/19/us/periscope-rape-case-columbus-ohio-video-livestreaming.html [23 May 2016].

Manovich, Lev. 2015. 'Instagram Is a Window into People's Thoughts and Imagination', *STRELKA Mag*, 3 June. Available at: https://beta.strelkamag.com/en/article/interview-lev-manovich [27 December 2017].

Mayer-Schönberger, Viktor. 2011. *Delete: The Virtue of Forgetting in the Digital Age*. Princeton, NJ: Princeton University Press.

Mehrabian, Albert. 1972. *Nonverbal Communication*. Chicago: Aldine-Atherton.

Motrescu-Mayes, Annamaria. 2017. 'Re-Illustrating the History of the British Empire', in William Roger Louis (ed.), *Effervescent Adventures with Britannia: Personalities, Politics and Culture in Britain*. London: I.B. Tauris, 209–219.

Niewiadomski, Robert and Dennis Anderson. 2017. 'The Panopticism of Cyberculture: Could Privacy-Invasive Social Media Stifle Innovation?' *Computers in Entertainment*. Available at: https://cie.acm.org/articles/panopticism-cyberculture-could-privacy-invasive-social-media-stifle-innovation [5 December 2017].

'Paralysed by YouTube'. 2015. *The Economist*, 29 October. Available at: www.economist.com/united-states/2015/10/29/paralysed-by-youtube [15 February 2018].

Rayner, Tim. 2012. 'Foucault and Social Media: Life in a Virtual Panopticon', Philosophy for Change, 21 June. Available at: https://philosophyforchange.wordpress.com/2012/06/21/foucault-and-social-media-life-in-a-virtual-panopticon [3 December 2016].

Roettgers, Janko. 2016. 'Periscope Adds Permanent Archive for Broadcasts, Search and Drone Support', *Variety*, 9 May. Available at: http://variety.com/2016/digital/news/periscope-archive-search-dji-support-1201769007 [7 June 2016].

Safronova, Valeriya. 2015. 'On Fake Instagram, a Chance to Be Real', *New York Times*, 18 November. Available at: www.nytimes.com/2015/11/19/fashion/instagram-finstagram-fake-account.html [5 April 2018].

Schneider, Steven and Kirstin Foot. 2004. *The Web as Object of Study*. London: Sage.

Shultz, Martin. 2011. 'The Unmasking of Images: The Anachronism of TV-Faces', in Oliver Grau (ed.), *Imagery in the 21st Century*. Cambridge, MA: MIT Press, 37–55.

Solon, Olivia. 2018. 'Teens Are Abandoning Facebook in Dramatic Numbers, Study Finds', *The Guardian*, 1 June. Available at: www.theguardian.com/technology/2018/jun/01/facebook-teens-leaving-instagram-snapchat-study-user-numbers [1 June 2018].

Stanekzai, Zainullah. 2016. 'Taliban Release Drone Footage of Suicide Attack', Reuters World News, 22 October. Available at: www.reuters.com/article/us-afghanistan-taliban/taliban-release-drone-footage-of-suicide-attack-idUSKCN12M0LD [22 December 2017].

Straw, William. 2010. 'The Circulatory Turn', in Barbara Crow, Michael Longford and Kim Sawchuk (eds), *The Wireless Spectrum: The Politics, Practices and Poetics of Mobile Media*. Toronto: University of Toronto Press, 17–28.

Straw, William, Sandra Gabriele and Ira Wagma. 2011. *Intersections of Media and Communications: Concepts and Critical Frameworks*. Toronto: Emond Montgomery Publications.

Suler, John. 2004. 'The Online Disinhibition Effect', *CyberPsychology & Behaviour*, vol. 7, no. 3, 321–326.

'Technology in Africa, The Pioneering Continent', *The Economist*, 25 April 2015, 45.

Van Dijck, José. 2013. *The Culture of Connectivity: A Critical History of Social Media*. Oxford: Oxford University Press.

Vaz, Paulo and Fernanda Bruno 2003. 'Types of Self-Surveillance: From Abnormality to Individuals "at Risk"', *Surveillance & Society*, vol. 1, no. 3, 272–291. Available at: www.surveillance-and-society.org [2 March 2017].

White, Debbie. 2018. 'Nine Passengers and Minibus Driver Are Killed in Head-On Crash Livestreamed on Facebook', MailOnline, 24 May. Available at: www.dailymail.co.uk/news/article-5767693/Nine-passengers-minibus-driver-killed-head-crash-livestreamed-Facebook.html [25 May 2018].

Wolfe, Jeremy, Keith Kluender, Dennis Levi, Linda Bartoshuk, Rachel Herz, Roberta Klatzy, Susan Lederman and Daniel Merfeld. 2014. *Sensation & Perception*, 4th edn. Sunderland, MA: Sinauer Associates, Inc.

Wolfson, Sam. 2017. 'Instagram Stories Has Turned Life into a Slideshow of Content', *The Guardian*, 21 November. Available at: www.theguardian.com/commentisfree/2017/nov/21/instagram-stories-life-slideshow-contents-snapchat [5 February 2018].

4

THE POLITICS OF ETHICAL REPRESENTATION IN AMATEUR MEDIA

Political activism comes in different shades of ethical actions, moral commitments and across nuanced visual literacies, especially when the subject of the media gaze is empire, war, unending or accidental trauma and crimes against humanity. In 1969, Harun Farouki ensured that his experimental, essayistic documentary *Inextinguishable Fire* kept the audience (then and now) eyes shocked-open – he used his left forearm as an ashtray for a lit cigarette but only after priming his viewers to fight the instinct to look away. He was criticising the horror and superfluous political meaning of the Vietnam War but, most importantly, he confirmed the standard psychological reaction provoked by images of terror: 'First you'll close your eyes to the pictures. Then you'll close your eyes to the memory. Then you'll close your eyes to the facts. Then you'll close your eyes to the entire context' (Farouki 1969). Farouki's words are as ethically relevant today as they were in the late 1960s, especially when discussing, for instance, imperial and post-colonial ethnographic films, the recent White Helmets' mobile phone footage of the Khan Shaykhun chemical attack on civilians in Syria on 4 April 2017,[1] or first-person video recordings of coups d'état in Eastern Europe in the late 1980s and early 1990s. Looking at trauma and/or being looked at while experiencing trauma are core features of identity-defining visual narratives, a framework particularly relevant in the study of social media – a case in point being Giorgio Lambri's photograph discussed below or Yervant Gianikian and Angela Ricci Lucchi's use of found footage in their archival documentary, *Dal polo all'equatore* (1987): in particular, the scene showing First World War soldiers being shot dead while advancing to capture an enemy post. On such occasions, it is important to explore the moral and perception criteria dependent not on seeing close-up or medium shots of people experiencing pain, fear, anger, but examples of *essentialised* trauma as, for instance, in the scene of the ghostly silhouettes of soldiers crawling or charging towards imminent death. Also, in this film, Gianikian and Ricci Lucchi offer additional research questions on the theme of witnessing and experiencing trauma while viewing images of terror and death in a hypnosis-like state.

People's engagement with a contextualised discourse, be it religious, national or domestic, by means of their personal narratives involves simultaneous acts of reconstruction of a community's master narrative and thus of its respective identity dynamics. Social and media psychologists agree that selfhood is often defined by individuals' ongoing dialogue with their respective in-group stories, a dialogue that helps reproduce or repudiate master narratives (Hammack 2012). Also, technological developments in media production and distribution can at times favour in equal measure both processes as when social media networks allow amateur media makers to either echo or denounce mainstream governmental ideologies and warfare strategies. For instance, in 2016, social and media networks reached new heights of conflicting political engagement and expression during the US presidential elections and UK referendum. Within this type of participatory culture emerge online identities that succeed in defining cultural and political shifts (of opinion and of policies) as well as counter-narratives of ethical protocols. For example, several Instagram postings in 2014 showed Crimean civilians posing with Russian (invading) soldiers (Brady 2014), while two years later a similar observance of media counter-narratives is found in the campaign ran by *Indecline*, an American activist collective, against the then Republican presidential nominee, Donald Trump, by offering passers-by in New York, San Francisco, Los Angeles, Seattle and Cleveland the opportunity to take selfies with a life-size naked statue of him (Holley 2016). As in the case of amateur media production, it is often the case that amateur media consumption, and feedback within common ethical protocols, also highlights or side-tracks particular online master narratives. A case in point is found in the footage recorded by the volunteer rescue workers of the Syria Civil Defence (also known as the White Helmets) which, while revealing the horrors of the Syrian civil war (ongoing since 2011), inadvertently feeds the defamatory online campaign run by Russian trolls and supporters of President Bashar al-Assad's army (Solon 2017).[2]

The ethical protocol of taking a selfie, and of being recorded while taking a selfie, has been challenged recently by Giorgio Lambri's photograph of a man taking a selfie at the Piacenza train station on 26 May 2018. It shows a young man standing on a train platform and making a V-sign with his right hand while taking a selfie – immediately nearby, in the background is a first aid medical group attending to a gravely injured woman lying on the train tracks. Lambri's photograph was printed in *La Libertà* and then widely discussed across social media and online newspapers. Comments ranged from Lambri's own verdict on Facebook ('Houston, we have a problem! In fact, we have lost completely the ethical sense'[3]), disdain ('when selfies are eating your soul'[4]), ad-hoc reinterpretations of media ethics and media behavioural patterns ('[the man taking the selfie] is … an individual who gave up his soul and identity for the right to take a selfie' (Boralevi 2018)[5]). Finally, it was one of the Tweets on the BBC Twitter thread that highlighted the possible cultural and psychological profile of the social media *persona*: 'We live in a different society. If I don't get a picture, it didn't happen. If I don't check in, I didn't go. Record 1st, call for help after. Have to let everybody know what I do. Not saying it's right not saying it's wrong. Just saying it didn't effect [sic] me 1 way or the other.'[6] Therefore, people's visual engagement with a contextualised narrative, be it by means of taking selfies or by recording specific events, is an ongoing dialogue between gazes, in situ or on media.

The act of looking as a means of perception as well as a social interaction has its functional and interpretative baseline anchored in the double act of reflection and projection of identity and its contextualised cultural and ethical protocols (Berger 1972, 1980; Sontag 1978; Barthes 1981). For instance, Victoria Finlay recounts in her book, about the use of colour as an expression of human nature and imagination, the apocryphal story of the Buddha who when still living in Bihar. A young man was sent to make his portrait, despite the fact that painting had yet to be invented.

> [When the young man] arrived at the place where the Buddha was in meditation, [the artist] realised that he had a problem: he was so overwhelmed by his subject's enlightened glow that he could not look at him. But then the Buddha made a suggestion: 'We will go down to the bank of a clear and limpid pool,' he said helpfully. 'And you will look at me in the reflection of the water.' They found an appropriately limpid pool, and the [artist] happily painted the reflection.
>
> *(Finlay 2002, 228)*

It could then be argued that there might be a strong and credible link between, for instance, this story, the Korowai people's tradition in West Papua, Indonesia, about conventions of social visibility and invisibility (Stasch 2017),[7] the *Digital Narcissus* image published by *The Economist* (see front cover) and, perhaps most importantly, the validation of one of the earliest definitions of the self – the one proposed by William James in 1890. In James's opinion: 'A man has as many social selves as there are individuals who recognise him and carry an image of him in their mind' (James 1890, 294). This argument is later identified in the theories proposed by Christopher Peacocke and Kendall Walton. For instance, Peacocke argued that to imagine is fundamentally a simultaneous act of self-awareness and self-centring within a narrative (Peacocke 1985). In turn, Walton further argued that an individual's imaginings are always in part about oneself, even when daydreaming about third parties, and that, if not central to the story, the self is still present in its capacity as observer or narrator (Walton 1990). Therefore, elaborating on these hypotheses allows media scholars to explore visual narratives (experience, projected, imagined) as stories about the self. In what ways then can such theoretical approaches be relevant to the understanding of recent forms of new/amateur media and particularly to the ethics of political activism? One possibility is to borrow (again) from Mary Ann Doane's discussion of how identities, historic times and events have been recorded, distributed and consumed in the early years of the cinematographic experience (especially that of watching *actualités* (newsreels) – the first steps taken in the direction of a global audience and visual culture. The core theoretical framework proposed by Doane refers to the inherent tensions between instantaneity and archival aspirations, and the problematic of representability of the ephemeral and the archivability of presence (Doane 2002). These theoretical angles correspond with Patricia Zimmermann's definition of the new amateurised media context seen as a 'tsunami of user-generated, fan-produced, blogger-written, Twitter-feed practices' (Zimmermann 2013). What Zimmermann calls 'blurring, and more thorny ethical/legal problems' (ibid.) prompted by the new media can also be identified in earlier, older amateur films too (see analysis below, as well as Chapters 3 and 5), thus confirming the ongoing process of (self-) representability across most amateur media.

Anthropological and amateur media ethics: empire and war

A pertinent example of analogue media posing similar ethical issues is found in a one-minute sequence from a British colonial amateur film made in 1935 by Gerald Pakenham Stewart, a colonial officer stationed in Manipur, India.[8] When watching this sequence, the audience must pay close attention to the ways in which Stewart framed several Kuki men while they were performing a dance imitating primates having intercourse.[9] The viewers also need to be alert at those brief moments when the Kuki men interact with the filmmaker during their performance and, finally, to assess the ways in which this material is an example of (unethical) imperial visual ethnography due to visual constructions of the Others' selves (and implicitly of the filmmaker's self too). In his autobiography, *The Rough and the Smooth: an Autobiography* (1947), Gerald Stewart noted that he paid the Kuki men to perform for him, for the camera, and in full daylight (Figure 4.1):

> [Film] taken in a village in the Hill Tracts of Manipur State, Assam. It was a Kuki village. The Kukis normally would do this dance when drunk at night during some feast. The Chief obliged me by arranging it to be done or demonstrated by day so that I could film it. I think I gave him about 20 rupees buksheesh. In the dance, the Kuki tribesmen imitate monkeys so that it is somewhat lewd and suggestive in parts.

Of note, the ethical issues raised by the intrinsic visual syntax used by Stewart has been (involuntarily, perhaps) sanitised by the explanatory caption used on the British Film Institute webpage where this film is offered free-access. The tone of address and the detailed albeit misleading information included in the caption command credibility and therefore the core moral concern experienced by the audience at *prima facie* – i.e. reading the body language of the Kuki men when interacting with the filmmaker/camera – is blurred if not cancelled:

> A young troupe of dancers from Manipur, north-eastern India, rehearse monkey-like movements and the steps of a dance. They are highly skilled, in

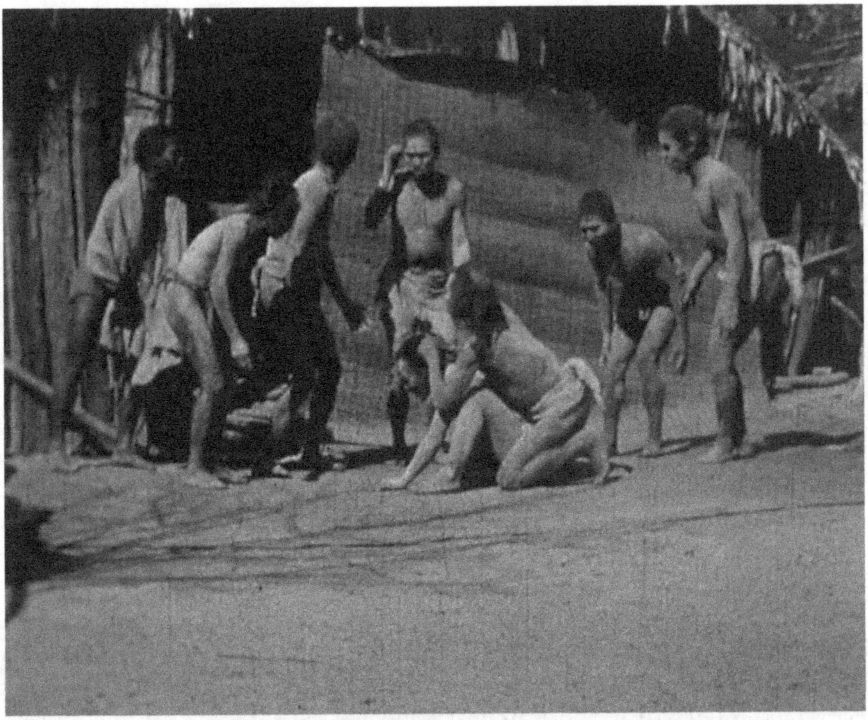

FIGURE 4.1 Stewart Collection, c. 1935. Courtesy of the Centre of South Asian Studies, Cambridge.

> costume and working on a performance mat. The tight frame almost excludes the drummer, until one of the dancers involves him. A brilliant contrasting shot at the end shows the performers lined up after their rehearsal, the monkeys banished to the forest. The drum is not the *pung*, a kind of drum for which Manipur is famous, which is more elongated and played by hand. Here the drum is played with a stick and is the same width at both ends. The performance space is demarcated by bamboo matting. The film was one of shot by amateur filmmaker Gerald P. Stewart, who seems to have taken an interest in the culture of India's northeast region.[10]

At first glance, and from many theoretical perspective, this short (colonial) amateur film offers a rich interpretative platform for discussing issues of ethics and visual constructions of the Other, and importantly, issues of ethics and visual constructions of the self (i.e. the filmmaker) through Stewart's use of visual language when deciding how to film the Kuki men.[11] For instance, if borrowing from Assenka Oksiloff's hypothesis that the primitive body defines the duality of (colonial) self and (colonised) other (Oksiloff 2001), then it is possible to argue that the 'primitive body' drives the visual rhetoric common to colonial/ethnographic travelogues. And, in the case of Stewart's film, more so than in most colonial amateur films, the re-enactment of an indigenous ritual subjects the audience to a slight arousing effect similar to the one usually provoked by peep shows. Finally, it could also be explored in what ways Stewart's request that the Kuki's ritual dance be performed for the camera exemplifies social Darwinism, a paradigm with latent as well as manifest racism, both of which posited the Other as inherently different, separate, unequal and inferior to European colonisers. Thus, from this perspective, their indigeneity was further stereotyped, ridiculed, infantilised and reduced to the level of subhuman (Naficy 2016).

Ethical issues of (self)-representations could successfully be addressed when elaborating on Walton's hypothesis concerning individuals' imaginings of self, whether as social agents or, more broadly and through mirrored narratives of one's role within specific contexts, of regional, racial, gender or national communities, whether across personal amateur media or by reworking such material. As such, issues of ethics and visual constructions of the self remain a point of contention as well as of revelation among scholars and key post-colonial visual artists working with colonial amateur footage. In particular, the ongoing consequences of imperial ideologies on contemporary understandings of national and gender identities is found in works by, for instance, Erika Tan (*Persistent Visions*, 2005), Yervant Gianikian and Angela Ricci Lucchi (*Dal Polo all'Equatore*, 1986; *Diario africano*, 1994; *Images d'Orient: Tourisme vandal*, 2001; *Frammenti elettrici no° 4 and 5 – Asia, Africa*, 2005; and *Imperium*, 2013), Péter Forgács (*Looming Fire. Stories from the Dutch East Indies 1900–1940*, 2013), and Rajkamal Kahlon (*Double Take*, 2010; and *People of the Earth*, 2017). In comparison, popular TV productions such as *The British Empire in Colour* (Carlton Television, TWI, 2002), while respectful of the wealth of historical data found in archival (and found) footage, often derail a post-colonial perspective by unwittingly endorsing the British (colonial) interests within imperial contexts. One such example is found in a sequence from the episode about the Partition of India. It shows vast landscapes filled with suffering, emaciated, wounded and dying South Asian refugees, all attempting to cross the border in either direction between India and the newly created state of Pakistan. The sequence is emotionally taxing – for most of its duration the audience is made to acknowledge details of the universal human tragedy brought by forced migration. Unpredictably, these images are given a bewildering image-sound addendum. The sequence ends with a medium shot of Edwina Mountbatten, the last Vicereine of India, shown while visiting a refugee camp. Simultaneously, the soundtrack shifts from sombre tones to a more nostalgic note. Moreover, the voiceover commentary announces rhetorically that 'after two hundred and fifty years in India, [Louis] Mountbatten [the last Viceroy of India, 12 February–15 August 1947] has given the British only seventy-three days to leave'.[12] As if it were an exercise of emotional priming, the audience is therefore left to ponder on this 'additional' trauma faced by British colonials, rather than on the horrors experienced by over 15 million displaced Hindus and Muslims at the end of the British rule in India.

The ubiquitous online network of shared visual documentation,[13] from allegedly monotonous scenes of domestic life – whether mid-twentieth-century British colonial amateur films and American home movies, or early twenty-first-century vlogs uploaded by victims of the civil war in Syria – require a thorough enquiry into existing hierarchies of private as well as official access to acts of remembrance about globally relevant historic events and repurposed national identities.[14] Moreover, it is often the case that archival data and artistic interpretations of specific collective traumas and of their respective collective memory narratives complement rather than determine ongoing exploratory processes. A valid example is found in the recent work of a Bavarian state crime office digital-imaging expert, Ralf Breker, who has designed a virtual reality programme that allows a pitch-perfect 3D reconstruction of the Auschwitz concentration camp. In Breker's opinion:

> [T]here is no more exact model of Auschwitz [...] It is much, much more precise than Google Earth [...] The advantage the model offers is that [it gives] a better overview of the camp and can recreate the perspective of a suspect, for example in a watchtower.
>
> *(Breker 2017)*[15]

Consequently, those equipped with a VR set, such as prosecutors, judges and co-plaintiffs 'can have the chilling experience of moving about 1940s-era Auschwitz at will. Even the trees stand where they once were, to determine whether they could have blocked the view from a certain vantage point.'[16] This example of forensic historical and criminal investigation, which combines the make-believe of VR with cartographic,[17] photographic and oral history crucial details,[18] becomes a valid counterpoint when addressing another media channel of investigation and distribution – Shahak Shapira's *Yolocaust*. Shapira, an Israeli-German blogger, has created this website-manifest by incorporating and reinterpreting twelve self-aggrandising or comical selfies taken by various visitors at the Berlin Holocaust memorial. His aim was to highlight the need for a universal, deferential acknowledgement of this particular historical trauma. It might be the case that, due to careless (or by default) use of online activist protocols, Shapira's message derailed into an equally unethical approach by trading intimidation for what was initially meant to be a lesson in historical awareness – his concluding message: '... selfie culture – be aware. I'm watching you!'[19]

Amateur 'phone media' and citizen journalism

Moral and civic crises prompted by ongoing interpretations of historic data are usually fought on the scaffolding of collective memories and of global cultural assumptions, which rely mostly on common (taught) perception protocols. Acting as a brief reminder of visual literacy and visual priming processes discussed in Chapter 3, and also as a preamble of the visual counter-histories explored in Chapter 5, is the 'subjective geographies' concept proposed by Mircea Eliade – renowned twentieth-century historian of religions and a philosopher – who remarked in his autobiography that '[f]irst happenings have an exceptional formative force. From a few such insignificant fragments [i.e. images, things, that 'struck us in the first moments', *ab initio*] we create our prodigious subjective geographies' (Eliade 1988, 18). These 'prodigious subjective geographies' shape our own, unique visual literacy, that will help us decipher as well as re-present/recount the world around us. Moreover, they act as foundation stones for our own visual priming – we build on them sets of visual narratives within (allegedly) coherent, immediate and private cultural contexts. Finally, Eliade's hypothesis about the formative role played by first happenings is particularly relevant in terms of visual and imaginative modes of experiencing and representations to which audiences are exposed and which they subsequently replicate through the two visual priming processes: the heuristic processing – shortcut decision-making rules leading to persuasive advocacy, and the cognitive systematic processing – the contemplative, analytic, and responsive model supporting a more argumentative quality of the message (Dillard and Peck 2000, 462) (see Chapter 3 and 5).[20] These processes are crucially important when discussing the media genres and social domains defined and defining the media behaviour of a specific net-community, the (now outdated term) netizens (Hauben 1995; Fung, 2012; Schiavenza 2013)[21] or more in line with what would be, in William Gibson's terms, the cyberpunks of amateur media.[22] In his analysis of the netizens' communities, Nick Couldry sketched several ideological activities such as sustained political mobilisation – i.e. live streaming and first-person media testimonials shared on YouTube during the Arab Spring (2010–mid-2012) are a suitable example. Such online communication channels have created a 'new media acting' space to ensure a constant remainder about a specific urgent topic, and to fight for the right to free speech, open access to information, and net neutrality. Importantly, the netizens are always 'vocal and co-ordinated' when challenging mainstream politics, and especially when access to media and social networks must be bypassed to reach the targeted audience (Couldry 2012, 129).[23]

Hierarchies of media tensions defined by the production, distribution and consumption of visual narratives across various cultures have also been researched by psychologists interested in charting the effects of media consumption. For instance, as discussed in Chapter 5 in relation to issues of memory, ethics and media counter-histories presented, it is useful to note here the Bushman et al. research on violent media effects on audiences. They concluded that there are (at least) three core effects at work when audiences are subjected to recurring examples of mediated violence. First, the aggressor effect where exposure to mediated violence leads to higher levels of aggression. Second, the fear of victimisation effect where mediated violence increases estimates of falling prey to violence. Finally, the conscience-numbing effect where exposure to violence leads to the desensitisation of natural negative emotional reactions (Bushman et al. 2009). In turn, Robert F. Potter and Paul D. Bolls (2012) highlighted the requirement to consider two approaches when studying (amateur, new) media used for online news channels and TV. There is the approach of 'uses and gratifications' which defines the audience's primary motive for news consumption to be their need for surveillance;

their intrinsic demand to always be aware of potential threats in what always appears to be an uncertain and precarious world (Rubin 2009) – see, for instance, recent terrorist attacks or mass shootings. Moreover, there is the 'agenda-setting' mode that highlights how context-driven selections of topics that are offered priority media coverage shape an audience's perception of what is or is being presented as (i.e. propaganda, fake news) relevant to a specific community of interests, whether regional or global (McLeod and Shah 2015). McLeod and Shah also argue that most often news content is external to audiences' direct experience; hence their hierarchies of priority topics seem to be based on introspection rather than automatic consumption of the news. This hypothesis could potentially challenge the long-held belief that manipulating public opinion is the result of the heuristic systematic processing (shortcut interpretation) rather than of the cognitive processing (contemplative, analytics and introspective interpretation). Another relevant perspective, alongside Potter and Bolls's theory, is Sarah Kember and Joanna Zylinska's understanding of how 'media ethics' works within the new media digital space. They claim that '[a]cross the increasing dynamic boundary of media production and consumption, there is a need to articulate what has become known as "media ethics" in terms of "an ethics of mediation"' (Kember and Zylinska 2012, 153). This ethics – in line with our expanded understanding of mediation as a vital process, a way of being and becoming in the technological world, or a way of emerging through time – can be categorised as 'an ethics of lifeness' (ibid.).

In this wide-angle theoretical context, there are several key questions that need to be considered (see also Chapter 5). For instance: what moral frameworks become available within the context of ongoing dynamic mediation (see, for example, the use of amateur footage in TV news), and who has ethical responsibility if we are all *media*?[24] Immediately relevant examples would include issues of internet privacy, media genres free from political or economic affiliations, and media journalism that uses the subject as a marketable prop for particular political agenda settings. Also worth evaluating and further developing are methodologies used in tracing *absence* as well as mapping how the visible is made invisible by using new digital media as an agent of political activism for global consumption. Finally, one of the goals relevant to media scholars, and within a cross-disciplinary framework, would be to assess how theoretical debates in visual anthropology can help address questions of historical authenticity across first-person (perspective) visual narratives – the equivalent of the first-person shooter in computer games. While the study of amateur media making allows us to explore new orders of historical, national and ethnic visibility, particular new media recordings, distribution and reception (see Chapter 1), such as videos or mobile phone films of war or terrorist attack casualties, reveal agonising instances of a mutable, open-ended collective memory – the new social media grand narrative of a plural, synchronous storytelling that defines our recent history. It is possible to argue that, to some extent, all anthropologists employ visual research methods, whether by 'reading and writing' about images or by 'making' visual records themselves – such images become then the equivalent of the first-person written documents (field reports). Also, most amateur media usually subscribes to the aesthetics of snapshots – instantaneous records of life, of the immediate real. Consequently, amateur media functions or is expected most often to act as self-evident documentation, a perspective proposed by Marcus Banks and Jay Ruby when defining visual records taken by anthropologist in support of their field work or as primary sources *per se* (Banks 2007; Banks and Ruby 2011). Moreover, viewing amateur media as part of an anthropological research project involves a higher incidence of scopophilia than when working with other visual categories such as those relying on genre-specific narratives like fiction films, documentaries, newsreels, etc. On watching amateur and new media, the viewer's identification with the people filmed subscribes to and confirms what Jean Rouch (1975) identified as the visual ethnographic work of the 'cine-voyeur'. It then seems feasible to propose that, paraphrasing Dziga Vertov's theory of *Kino-Glaz*, the 'cine-eye' of the amateur film/media maker becomes the audience's 'eye' and that the first-person visual narrative extends from that of the amateur/media maker to the open-ended first-person visual narrative of global audiences. This is the framework in which evolves, and is constantly reshaped, the open-ended collective memory anchored in historically relevant amateur visual records. It could be argued further that it is perhaps possible to define such (and similar) footage as representative of David MacDougall's theory of 'participatory cinema' within visual anthropology practice and research – a practice that, contrary to the more traditional and allegedly non-invasive observational cinema, *removes* the alleged invisibility of the filmmaker and allows instead for a collaborative authorship between the filmmaker and his/her subjects (MacDougall 1995). Furthermore, the research methodology proposed by Elizabeth Edwards in relation to photographs defined as objects of memory and history helps visual theorists and cultural anthropologists working with amateur media of trauma, terror and war casualties to structure their media forensic analysis (Edwards 2009, 2012).This is a methodology that focuses on questions of evidence, power and agency and, it could be added, also on questions of narratorial authority.[25] Whether still or moving images, new and amateur media's functionality as 'objects of memory and history' is almost always dependent on their context of distribution and use (ibid.).[26] Moreover, amateur media, more so than commissioned media productions (reportages, news, documentaries) of mass killings, coups d'états, natural disasters and terrorist attacks, are always negotiated by those directly affected either as highly efficient records of and in support of particular social agendas or as almost unbearable reminders of trauma. For instance, when discussing the mass shooting in Sutherland Springs, Texas, that took place on 5 November 2017, Alan Blinder et al. concluded that '[g]risly videos and other images captured by live-streams, security cameras and cell phones are increasingly becoming part of a raw historical record of mass shootings, haunting pieces of evidence left behind along with bullet fragments and bloodstains' (Blinder et al. 2017). Importantly, most of the amateur/user-generated images used across all media to document recent terrorist attacks and mass killings have raised urgent questions about media ethics, especially since their intrinsic role is to simultaneously preserve and reshape collective memory and so to advance particular political and social activist agendas. Blinder et al. also noted that the 'video is almost too terrible to imagine, much less contemplate watching', which points in the direction of two theoretical frameworks. First, the one proposed by Walton in *Mimesis as Make-Believe*, and in which he credits the role of an individual's imagination in his/her identity and memory-building as being on a par with his/her access to visual data. Second, the perspective proposed by Nick Couldry when claiming that in today's global network of social media and amateur/user-generated news, issues of private versus collective or nation-state identity boundaries are becoming superfluous, this being 'digital media's consequences for new politics' (Couldry 2012, 131). Importantly, and as discussed below, the live-streaming or post factum distribution of shocking images of public shootings, of civilians being killed by military forces, of genocide or of brutal attacks on civil and human rights demonstrators constantly alert the viewers as well as media scholars to renewed issues of ethical protocols and of moral judgements within a global context – an urgent albeit often quixotic task, especially when applied to dictatorial political contexts.

Some recent examples of raw media, and the ensuing issues of ethics of live-witnessed trauma, are found in the amateur footage recorded, for example, by Emad Burnat, Ahed Tamimi and Muhammad Najem in the West Bank and in Syria, respectively. Such images offer incontestable eye-witness accounts of raw histories defining specific, local conflicts that, once shared globally, become stories of human rights and endeavour.

A weekly protest in the Palestinian village Nabi Saleh, West Bank, against Israel's land confiscation for new settlements, made front page news across the world in the summer of 2015. In particular, a snapshot showing two Palestinian women and a young girl struggling to pull away an Israeli soldier who held trapped in a headlock, under his knees, Mohammed – an 11-year-old Palestinian boy; and their relative.[27] Everybody's face in this image expresses anger, fear and steely determination. Understandably, the image prompted several questions about the ethics of representation including, importantly, whether it may be dismissed as fake (media) activism? For instance, British journalist Peter Beaumont noted for *The Guardian* that

> [S]een in different ways by different commentators with different agendas, the only thing they could agree on was that the images represented an outline vivid summation of some idea of the brutality of the occupation, of the weakness of the soldier involved, of the need to use more or less violence on demonstrators, of the use by Palestinians of children as a propaganda tool.
>
> *(Beaumont 2015)*

The Palestinian women, girl and boy appearing in this image are members of the Tamimi family – Palestinian activists acclaimed by most (Western) international opinion and press, with the *New York Times Magazine* (Ehrenreich 2013) and *The Guardian* (Sherwood 2018) often covering stories about them. In 2012, three years before being photographed trying to release her younger brother from the tight grip of the Israeli soldier, the girl in the photo, Ahed Tamimi, received the bravery award from the Turkish government in praise of her courage while standing up to Israeli soldiers.[28] Echoing Beaumont's opinion, these images highlight the 'asymmetry of the conflict', an asymmetry buttressed by the 'leverage of social media', which can rank local conflicts as of immediate global relevance and with a high moral impact of new media usage and production (Lyon 2008; Beaumont 2015). Importantly, since late 2009, when the weekly protests in Nabi Saleh began, the video testimonials made in situ by the villagers have presented and promoted the Tamimi children – Ahed, Muhammed and Janna Ayyad – as leaders of the demonstrations. Also around that time was launched the Tamimi Press, a locally run private news agency supplied daily with user-generated amateur media documenting the Palestinian villagers' pleas and marches.[29] In this context, local, private and historically specific identities evident across examples of participatory citizen journalists' ephemeral media are thus reclaimed within wider ethical registers and modes of distribution. At the same time, the amateur media makers' identity gains political agency and so negotiates media tensions such as those between stasis and mobility (i.e. local crisis vs. global awareness) (Santone and Straw 2009; Straw 2010; Straw et al. 2011).

Similar interpretative issues intrinsic to the ethical and political implications of the Tamimi 'case' are also raised when discussing amateur media recorded and distributed by Emad Burnat and Muhammad Najem. For instance, Burnat's amateur videos showing Palestinian villagers demonstrating regularly in Bil'in and other villages against the gradual, undeterred development of Israeli settlements in the West Bank offers a complex example of amateur media making as citizen journalism, participatory culture, media therapy, visual anthropological fieldwork, and as an exercise in memory-building. His amateur video footage represents the core material used in the award-winning documentary *5 Broken Cameras*. [30] Having bought his fist video camera in early 2005, Burnat quickly altered his home-video practice, which he undertook to 'rediscover the world through his [fourth son's] eyes', into community-based art – 'I become the Bil'ins' cameraman' – filming events at the request of his co-villagers, such as touring acrobatic troupes or weddings. Gradually, his amateur media records transgressed even further, although never completely devoid of domestic scenes, from home-mode visual narratives into citizen journalism,[31] Soon, Burnat started filming his co-villagers' non-violent demonstrations against the Israel government's decision to build a barrier across Bil'in villagers' farmland with a view to protect recently built Jewish settlements – overall, he secured in this way more than 700 hours of footage (Goldman 2013). His new media activist practice subjected him to the risk of being arrested or even killed – '[m]y third camera might have saved my life; the bullet is lodged in it'.[32] However, throughout his filming, his practice remains located at the border between home-movie making and political activism, a status best exemplified in the short scene of his arrest when, in the voiceover commentary he announces: 'I take the camera to protect myself', and to defy Israeli soldiers, 'I am a journalist and

I can film in my own home.'[33] If most times his camera is both a campaigning tool and a physical shield, during the time he spent away from his family as part of his home arrest, it becomes part of his media therapy – 'I have nothing to do, so I film'. Moreover, he fine tuned his *ars poetica* as a means to evaluate the plight of the Palestinian people since 1948 within a wider, global political context:

> [H]ealing is the victim's sole obligation. By healing, you resist oppression. But when I'm hurt over and over again, I forget the wounds that rule my life. Forgotten wounds can't be healed. So, I film to heal [...] it helps me confront life and survive.[34]

Incidentally, Burnat's next development stage in his amateur media practice sees him employing one of the visual anthropologist's common methodologies – screening films about a particular community to its own members while simultaneously recording their reception of, and reaction to the respective images. As a result, Burnat's video tapes soon confirm his expectations for renewed solidarity and a greater, concerted effort in political activism among his own community and neighbouring villagers – '[B]y 2008, many villages in the West bank adopt the Bil'in demonstrations as a model of new kind of resistance.'[35] His amateur films also prove his unrelenting work as a human rights campaigner, in particular his video scenes showing Israeli soldiers arresting Palestinian boys in the middle of the night, when most villagers were asleep, or the shooting at point-blank range of a Palestinian man after having detained by Israeli soldiers during one of the protests in the Bil'in village. Such amateur media document undisputable instances of arbitrary deportation and torture – these are geopolitically localised crimes against humanity that have been accidentally recorded by an amateur video maker for a global audience. As an example of activist and citizen journalism,[36] *5 Broken Cameras* proposes a detailed evaluation of amateur media's role in shaping international humanitarian activism, awareness about minorities' rights, and ethical criteria for defining and defending the identities of disposed and displaced communities within constantly renewed geopolitical hierarchies.

As is the case with most visual anthropological work, the research of mediated violence across most new, digital and amateur media genres requires a strong sense of humanity, unrelenting visual endurance – watching disturbing images is emotionally corrosive – and humility. Drawing on this principle, it is then possible to acquire, to some degree, both theoretical objectivity and plausible answers to key research questions such as anthropological evidence, visual agency and narratorial authority – in short, new media ethics, as in 'Who has the right to narrate visual collective histories?' and 'Who has the right to create collective registers of ethical judgement and behavioural protocols?'[37] While interpretative agency and authority used to be the prerogative of scholars and, sometimes, political and economic monopolies, in the context of today's globally shared user-generated media and free online access to it, it could be argued that this role, or responsibility, is often embraced by the amateur media makers – their work acting as a *memory agent.*

Beside addressing urgent issues of political activism and pleas for humanitarian aid by way of 'citizen camera-witnessing' (Andén-Papadopoulos 2014),[38] virtual reality projects (Rettberg et al. 2016) or amateur video recording (Motrescu-Mayes 2016), there are other immediate research questions about how best to assess the visual economy of the amateur media maker's ethical engagement and responsibility while recording and distributing eye-witness amateur iconography.[39] This ever-changing visual (digital) language, and its online networks of (almost simultaneous) use, present them with a suitable and feasible means of instant communication far beyond their immediate geopolitical constraints.[40] In lieu of conclusion, two interpretative perspectives are employed in the last section of this chapter while discussing issues of remembrance and memorialisation concerning to the dialogue between the multiple amateur media records of public and private histories and their distribution, preservation and online re-purposing. First, issues pertaining to democratised media policies, their impact on the relation between specific cultural contexts, such as live-witnessing trauma and first-line war scenes, and how they define amateur media distribution channels (Facebook, YouTube) as integral to acts of remembrance and of ideological cannibalism of a specific identity-defining historic event. Second, issues of online identities constructed via mobile phone videos uploaded, for instance, on Facebook or YouTube, and how they document pervasive visual literacies specific to in situ subjective geographies of war zones and post-conflict areas. A relevant example for both interpretative frameworks is found in the video-selfies (vlogs) posted by the Syrian teenager Muhammad Najem in early 2018, and in his use of social media as a reliable channel for live streaming the horror experienced by the civilians struggling in the besieged suburb of Eastern Ghouta, Syria (Figure 4.2).

Muhammad posted his first video-selfie on YouTube and Twitter on 7 December 2017. Draped in the Syrian flag and looking directly at the camera – implicitly expecting to address a global audience – he recites (or reads) a brief text:

> I am Muhammed Najem. I am fifteen years old. I live in the eastern Gouta. I will convey to you all the events which is being commited by the assad rigime in the Eastern Gouta through my own social media Facebook and Twitter. My Twitter account [...] My Facebook account [...] My account on Instagram [...].[41]

Unwittingly, his first exercise in citizen (amateur) media journalism recalls, for the untrained eye, the visual rhetoric of video declarations streamed on social media by suicide bombers just before undertaking their missions. On 15 January 2018, Muhammad posted another video-selfie, this time filmed on the top terrace of a building, during an aerial bombing of Eastern Ghouta. Once again, he appears to recite a short headlines-like text:

> We know that you got bored from our blood pictures. We know you have seen videos how they kill us. But We will continue appealing to you to feel guilty. We are killed by your silence. Bashar Al-assad, potin and khaminei killed our childhood. Save us before it is too late. What is the world, which can send machines to the martian and can't do anything to stop killing people.[42]

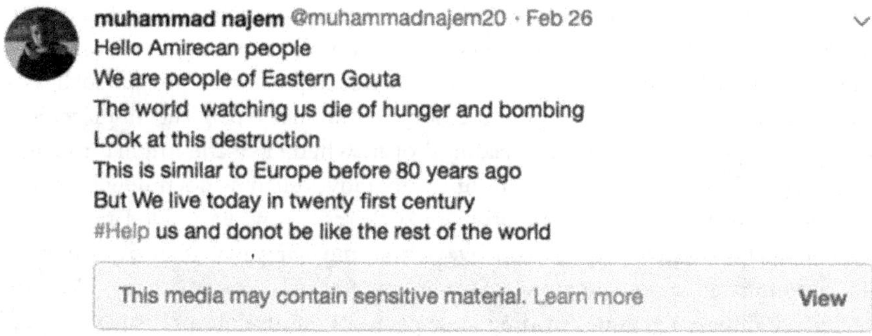

FIGURE 4.2 Muhammad Najem, Tweet posted on 26 February 2018. Screengrab via Twitter.

An alarming detail in this video-selfie is Muhammad's slight pause before quickly recomposing himself during the aerial bombing. His almost unflinching acknowledgement of the loud sound made by an approaching bomber, of the sharp whistle of the bomb dropping somewhere in his immediate vicinity, and of the thunderous blast heard when the bomb hit the houses nearby, confirms the boy's familiarity with the constant terror provoked by constant aerial bombings – his own and his community's state of being under siege. Muhammad's Twitter posts and uploads of phone amateur video and photographs in early 2018 often included horrendously disturbing images of Syrian babies and children whose bodies have been mutilated during the bombing of Ghouta.[43] Such images of undisputed agonising horror and pain almost instantaneously change the tone of his message from being a direct appeal for help to shocking his audience into emotional numbness. Moreover, the presence of such images on his Twitter account could easily raise questions of authorship. Without doubt, Muhammed's video-selfies give the viewers direct access to his message – even when he reads a text that he might or might not have written himself – and to the in situ context in which he filmed it. Hence, each of his video-selfies presents and preserves the immediacy and intimacy of the terror experienced by him. The same cannot be safely assumed when seeing the photographs of still-alive Syrian babies whose heads have been split open or backsides ripped apart – images that Muhammad used as visual vectors for his repeated plea for help; help he expected from his global online audience. The hypothesis that somebody else – say, a health worker or someone from a local or international media channel – has coached Muhammad to become a citizen journalist brands him as a propaganda *prop*, albeit it for the utmost humanitarian reasons and purposes. They can indeed invalidate his agency as an independent citizen journalist and social media agent.[44] Such images have therefore a possible dual documentary effect: they inform on the Syrian civilians' traumatic experiences during the civil war, while running the risk of discrediting the authorship of the amateur media maker and of his non-mediated access to front-line trauma.

These and other similar examples of amateur media, participatory culture and citizen journalism allow the hypothesis that it is perhaps the anonymity and the alleged ephemeral visual identity of the people shown in such images that preserves and perpetuates their visual testimonies of universal selves subjected to war and trauma. In conclusion, by recording and distributing amateur media such as the examples discussed here, the visual memory of trauma, terror and displacement is *saved* and perpetuated via future 'readings' of it, whether of the original footage or of its recycled meaning within more linear narratives such as documentaries or TV reportages. Furthermore, the reception of such scenes, while guided by the amateur media/filmmaker's first-person eye-witnessing narrative, is further multiplied and disseminated across regimes of open-ended collective memory. Audiences defined by different regimes of time and space constantly interpret such images by reconstructing the represented collective identities as re-imagined within a global, synchronous storytelling.

Notes

1 See *The White Helmets* (dir. Orlando von Einsiedel, UK, 2016) and *Last Men in Aleppo* (dir. Feras Fayyad, Germany, 2017).

2 For a discussion of the role played by amateur media, i.e. mobile phone video, in documenting as well as shaping the development of recent political crisis, see, for instance, *How Facebook Changed the World: The Arab Spring* (BBC, 2011) and *Winter on Fire: Ukraine's Fight for Freedom* (dir. Evgeny Afineevsky, 2015).

3 'HOUSTON, ABBIAMO UN PROBLEMA! Cioè abbiamo perso completamente il senso etico.' Italian in original. Available at www.facebook.com/giorgio.a.lambri [2 June 2018].

4 '[Q]uando il selfie ti mangia l'anima.' Italian in original (Boralevi 2018).

5 'È un automa della Rete. È una persona che ha spento la sua anima e la sua identità di persona per accendere il pulsante del selfie.' Italian in original (Boralevi 2018).

6 Available at https://twitter.com/MCondry80/status/1003783139158904832 [4 June 2018].

7 Rupert Stasch elaborates on this theme in his lectures for the 'Anthropology of Media & Visual Culture' paper at the Department of Social Anthropology, University of Cambridge (2015–present). Available at www.socanth.cam.ac.uk/current-students/ug-optional-papers/ug-san-eleven [1 January 2018].

8 Stewart joined the Indian Colonial Service in 1930 and, before being captured and imprisoned by the Japanese army in 1942, held posts in Assam and Manipur, in northeast India. Clip available at https://player.bfi.org.uk/free/film/watch-monkey-dance-1935-online [5 August 2017].

9 The Kukis, known as the Chin in the Chin state of Myanmar and as Mizo in the Indian state of Mizoram, are Tibeto-Burmese peoples living in northeast India.

10 Available at https://player.bfi.org.uk/free/film/watch-monkey-dance-1935-online [23 August 2017].

11 A similar scene, is found in the second episode, 'Surabaya, Java, 1929', of *Welt Spiegel Kino* (dir. Gustave Deutsch, 2005). However, on this occasion, the male dancers are clearly performing a comical masked drama for the camera – bare-chested, some with painted faces and all having attached to their costume something resembling a primate's tail. The scene belongs to a non-fiction film made by Tassilo Adame, *Mataram* (1927), and is introduced by the intertitle 'De Mismaakten' (The crippled) – information generously provided by Gustav Deutsch (email dated 1 June 2018).

12 Excerpt from voiceover commentary, *The British Empire in Colour.*

13 Material often reinterpreted and used by documentary filmmakers, political activists and artists.

14 The last decade saw two major (ongoing) enquiries into the alarming rise of online data privacy breaches, and the immediate repercussions on the construction and management of digital identities across social media networks, which rely on the use of amateur media. Edward Snowden's revelations made public since 2013 (available at https://edwardsnowden.com) about the US National Security Agency's mass surveillance programmes, and Christopher Wylie's testimonial about Cambridge Analytica – a British consulting firm and its misuse of more than 50 million Facebook profiles for targeted political advertisements during the 2016 presidential elections in the US (Greenfield 2018) – represent defining moments in the development and understanding of global social identities and new media [4 April 2018].

15 'Virtual reality helps Germany catch last Nazi war criminals', *The Guardian*, 2 October 2016.

16 Ibid.

17 Karim Ben Khelifa's VR and AR project *The Enemy* (2015) is a topical and revelatory inquiry into issues of identities challenged by ongoing armed conflict. Details about this project are available at www.doclab.org/2015/the-enemy [3 April 2018].

18 Another forensic visual analysis of collective trauma and collective memories defining Second World War European identities, could include, for instance, Harun Farocki's *Respite* (2007) video about the repurposed Dutch camp at Westerbork – first as a refugee camp for Jewish people (1939–1942) and then as a Nazi 'transit camp' (1942–1945); Claude Lanzmann's oral-history documentary *Shoah* (1985); and British documentary *German Concentration Camps Factual Survey* (IWM and BFI, 2017) which includes, as a DVD 'special feature', the few surviving filmed interviews recorded in 1945 with freed prisoners and SS soldiers at the Bergen-Belsen and Dachau concentration camps, as well as the filmed statements given by members of the British Army.

19 Available at https://yolocaust.de, https://www.youtube.com/watch?v=mjjV_X5re4g, and www.bbc.co.uk/news/world-europe-38675835. Access to Instagram profiles was censored by the BBC when covering the story online (www.bbc.co.uk/news/world-europe-38675835) by blurring the people's faces, while another British newspaper opted for full disclosure (Hartley-Parkinson 2017) [25 October 2017].

20 It is now common practice for higher education institutions to offer training to their academic staff and students about visual and cultural priming processes across recurrent of media *framing*; see, for instance, 'Ethics Unwrapped – Representation' training offered by the School for Business, University of Texas at Austin. Available at http://ethicsunwrapped.utexas.edu/video/representation [3 February 2018].

21 Michael F. Hauben (1995) is often credited with having coined this term.

22 Some of the popular cyberpunks since the mid-2010s are popular culture heroes from TV series such as *Mr Robot* (US, 2015–present), *Black Mirror* (UK, 2011–present), *Orphan Black* (Canada, 2013–2017) or *The OA* (US, 2016–present) – these are stories about activist new and amateur media makers and users, all mostly able to secure social executive influences and powers that, in the context of ongoing social media and new media technological developments, seem increasingly credible and feasible.

23 A case in point is the widespread use of virtual private network technologies and of Telegram Messenger to bypass governmental censorship in countries such as China and Iran respectively (Serendip 2016; Cordero 2018).

24 For instance, Paul Logan's vlog posted on 31 December 2017 and showing his discovery of a male body hanging from a tree in the Aokigahara forest (Japan), as well as his comment – 'I think this definitely marks a moment in Youtube history because I'm pretty sure this has never happened to anyone on Youtube ever' – have raised issues about the ethics of vlogging, with some of the viewers highlighting his lack of social and moral awareness – 'So dehumanising, utterly disgusted. Who in their right minds thinks this is okay? Using it in the thumbnail? Undefendable.' Having posted over 530 daily vlogs, with an audience of over 15 million subscribers, and being hailed as 'the fourth highest-paid YouTube star in 2016' (c. £9 million), Paul Logan's online presence offers a rich, albeit controversial research source for scholars of online behaviour and ethics.

Available at www.youtube.com/watch?v=WjNFGZLJLss, www.ballstatedaily.com/article/2018/01/logan-pauls-suicide-video-what-it-means-to-japan, www.bbc.com/news/technology-43950251 and www.bbc.com/news/world-asia-42644321 [2 May 2018].

25 Supporting a detailed discussion on this topic is amateur media, mobile phone films, crime scene photographs and CCTV footage made at the time of, for instance, the Columbine High School massacre (20 April 1999, Columbine, Colorado, US), Stade de France attack (14 November 2015, Paris), the Berlin truck attack (19 December 2016, Germany) the Pulse Nightclub shooting (12 June 2016, Orlando, Florida, US), the London Bridge attack (3 June 2017, London), the shooting at the Route 91 Harvest country music festival (1 October 2017, Las Vegas, Nevada, US), and the Stoneman Douglas High School shooting (14 February 2018, Parkland, Florida, US).

26 See Norio Imai's series *Time Clothing* (1978) and *Self-Portrait* (1985) for his use of Polaroid and video images as media tools in the perception of time and space.

27 Available at www.theguardian.com/world/2015/sep/01/nabi-saleh-images-illustrate-changing-asymmetry-of-israeli-palestinian-conflict [4 May 2016].

28 Nicknamed 'the Palestinian Rosa Parks', Ahed Tamimi became first known globally in 2012 when, as a 12-year-old, she was filmed and photographed during a demonstration in her village, Nabi Saleh, shouting and repeatedly raising her fist at armed Israeli soldiers in response to her older brother's arrest (Love 2018). Image available at https://en-gb.facebook.com/Ahed-Tamimi-311665059010028 [2 December 2017]. On 6 June 2018, Ahed Tamimi was sentence by an Israeli military court to eight months in prison for incitement and disturbance (Bob 2018).

29 Available at www.facebook.com/pg/Tamimipresspage/about/?tab=page_info [5 October 2017].

30 Trailer available at www.youtube.com/watch?v=cnaOxX49UhQ [4 April 2018]. Similar to Guy Davidi's use of Emad Burnat's home movies and amateur films, which he recorded with six consecutive video cameras, with the aim to establish an insider's perspective on issues of displacement and minority/diasporic communities, is Sandhya Suri's biographical documentary *I for India* (2005) about her father's home movie making practice. On this occasion, the amateur filmmaker, Yash Pal Suri, used two similar Super-8 cameras, two projectors, and two open-reel audiotape recordings. One set he used in the UK and the other he sent to his family in India. As a result, for almost 40 years (since 1965) he secured an ongoing amateur media dialogue with his family.

31 All quotes are from the voiceover commentary in *5 Broken Cameras* (dir. Emad Burnat, Guy Davidi, 2012).

32 Ibid.

33 Ibid.

34 Ibid.

35 Ibid. Of note, the amateur videos shown to the Bil'in villagers contained English subtitles, a detail attesting to Burnat having already secured international acknowledgement and distribution for his films. Also, excerpts from his amateur videos have been integrated in other documentaries such as Shai Carmeli Pollak's *Bil'in habibti* (*Bil'in My Love*, Israel, 2016).

36 Issues of authorship and political affiliations have been at the core of this film's distribution and reception given that it was co-directed by a Palestinian amateur filmmaker and an Israeli documentary filmmaker, both sharing similar political and civic principles (Winstanley 2013). Guy Davidi addressed similar issues in his previous documentary – *Interrupted Streams* (2010), co-directed with Alexandre Goetschmann. Available at https://sites.google.com/site/interruptedstreams10/About-The-Film [12 December 2017].

37 This theoretical framework will be considered again in Chapter 5 when discussing issues of new media and collective memory.

38 See, for instance, the killing of Nicaraguan journalist Ángel Gahona while live-streaming from his mobile phone on Facebook during the fourth day of the mass protests against President Daniel Ortega. Footage showing him being shot dead on 21 April 2018 was

recorded by another journalist who, after initially (instinctively) leaving the scene, returned almost immediately to record people approaching Gahona's dead body. The cries of anger, disbelief and pain heightened the viewers' reaction. Available at https://vimeo.com/266000627 [29 May 2018].

39 See also mobile phone camera footage showing Mamoudou Gassama, an undocumented Malian migrant in France, rescuing a 4-year-old boy who was hanging precariously on the balcony rails of his parents' apartment on the fourth floor of a block of flats. Gassama is seen climbing from one balcony to another with astonishing speed and saving the child in a record time. As in the case of the camera-witness footage of Gahona, this time, too, the immediately of shock and suspense is dictating re-evaluations of the ethical framework in which to discuss similar examples of amateur media: whether pertinent to validating crimes against humanity or supporting key changes in national immigration policies. Incidentally, the French President, Emmanuel Macron, met Mamoud Gassama and, alongside congratulating him for his bravery, indicated the prospect of him being granted a French residency card (Willsher 2018).

40 A notable example is *18 Days in Egypt*, an online collaborative and interactive documentary project based on the collection and distribution of mobile phone images (still or moving) recorded and uploaded by citizen journalists who have witnessed the Egyptian Revolution in 2011. Available at http://beta.18daysinegypt.com/#/ [1 March 2018]. Other relevant online collaborative, peer network-driven projects relying on uploaded amateur media (all sources and formats) are, for instance, *EngageMedia* (www.engagemedia.org/about-us/#) and *WITNESS* (https://witness.org/about) – both projects are discussed by Hunter et al. (2013) – and *MOSES* (the Mobile Story Exchange System; Smyth et al. 2010; Jacko 2012; Lannon and Halpin 2013).

41 Available atwww.youtube.com/watch?v=mka9iyFc4IM [1 March 2018]. Spelling as per transcription available on YouTube webpage.

42 It is highly possible that, as in the video posted on 7 December 2017, Muhammad read a pre-drafted text. Spelling as per transcription available on YouTube page. Available at www.youtube.com/watch?v=v5g6DPwD4B4 [5 May 2018].

43 A possible comparative analysis could further address the different ethical frameworks required by Muhammad Najem's phone-camera videos of fatally wounded Syrian babies, Paul Logan's vlogging about a Japanese man's corpse, and Emad Burnat's amateur video showing his friend being indiscriminately shot by an Israeli soldier. Each of these examples demands a nuanced perspective on the moral criteria used when assessing their impact on public opinion, online behaviour and on social media communication protocols.

44 Muhammad Najem's Twitter account includes several disturbing images – 'sensitive material', as defined in the disclaimer note accompanying several of his Tweets – particularly his early posts. Available at https://twitter.com/muhammadnajem20?lang=en [5 May 2018].

Selected bibliography

Andén-Papadopoulos, Kari. 2014. 'Citizen Camera-Witnessing: Embodied Political Dissent in the Age of "Mediated Mass Self-Communication"', *New Media & Society*, vol. 16, no. 5, 753–769. First published online 31 May 2013.

Banks, Marcus. 2007. *Using Visual Data in Qualitative Research*. London: Sage.

Banks, Marcus and Jay Ruby. 2011. *Made to be Seen*. Chicago: University of Chicago Press.

Barthes, Roland. 1981. *Camera Lucida: Reflections on Photography*. New York: Hill & Wang.

Beaumont, Peter. 2015. 'Nabi Saleh Images Illustrate Changing Asymmetry of Israeli-Palestinian Conflict', *The Guardian*, 1 September. Available at www.theguardian.com/world/2015/sep/01/nabi-saleh-images-illustrate-changing-asymmetry-of-israeli-palestinia n-conflict [3 October 2017].

Berger, John. 1972. *Ways of Seeing*. London: BBC and Penguin.

Berger, John. 1980. *About Looking*. London: Writers' & Readers' Publishing Co-op.

Blinder, Alan, David Montgomery and Jack Healy. 2017. 'Grisly Video of a Massacre Raises an Unsettling Question: Who Should See It?', *New York Times*, 9 November.

Bob, Yonah J. 2018. 'Ahed Tamimi Request for Early Prison Release Denied', *Jerusalem Post*, 6 June. Available at www.jpost.com/Arab-Israeli-Conflict/Ahed-Tamimi-request-for-early-prison-release-denied-559301 [6 June 2018].

Boralevi, Antonella. 2018. 'La Foto con il Ferito: Quando il Selfie ti Mangia l'Anima', *La Stampa*, 4 June. Available at www.lastampa.it/2018/06/04/societa/la-foto-con-il-ferito-quando-il-selfie-ti-mangia-lanima-BIELvqtuyVhmL7LXjTSjbI/pagina.html [4 June 2018].

Boxer, Paul, Huesmann, L. Rowell, Bushman, Brad J., O'Brien, Maureen. and Moceri, Dominic. 2009. 'The Role of Violent Media Preference in Cumulative Developmental Risk for Violence and General Aggression', *Journal of Youth and Adolescence*, vol. 38, no. 3, 417–428.

Brady, Tara. 2014. 'Selfskies from the Frontline: People of Crimea Pose up with the Masked Russian Invaders', Mail Online, 3 March. Available at www.dailymail.co.uk/news/article-2571799/Shocking-pictures-people-Crimea-taking-SELFIES-Russian-masked-gunmen-Ukraine-teeters-brink-war.html#ixzz4rec2hAcf [7 May 2016].

Bushman, Brad J., Huesmann, L.Rowell and Whitaker, Jodi L. 2009.'Violent Media Effects', in Robin L. Nabi and Mary Beth Oliver (eds), *Media Processes and Effects*. Thousand Oaks, CA: Sage, 2009, 361–376.

Cordero, Jacinto. 2018. 'How to Use VPNs in China without Breaking the Law. There Are Ways to Use Corporate VPNs in China to Protect Sensitive Data and not Run Afoul of China's Cybersecurity Laws', *TechWorld*, 26 January. Available at www.techworld.com.au/article/641631/box-ceo-aaron-levie-calls-global-data-protection-agreement [2 February 2018].

Couldry, Nick. 2012. *Media, Society, World, Social Theory and Digital Media Practice*. Cambridge: Polity Press.

Cubitt, Sean. 2007. 'Projection: Vanishing & Becoming', in Oliver Grau (ed.), *Media Art Histories*. Cambridge, MA: MIT Press, 407–422.

Dillard, James Price and Eugenia Peck. 2000. 'Affect and Persuasion: Emotional Responses to Public Service Announcements', *Communication Research*, vol. 27, no. 4, 461–495.

Doane, Mary Ann. 2002. *The Emergence of Cinematic Time: Modernity, Contingency, the Archive*. Cambridge, MA: Harvard University Press.

Edwards, Elizabeth. 2009. 'Photographs as Objects of Memory', in Fiona Candlin and Raiford Guins (eds), *The Object Reader*. London: Routledge.

Edwards, Elizabeth. 2012. *The Camera as Historian: Amateur Photographers and Historical Imagination, 1885–1918*. Durham, NC: Duke University Press.

Ehrenreich, Ben. 2013. 'Is This Where the Third Intifada Will Start?', *New York Times Magazine*, 15 March. Available at https://nyti.ms/ZAfgQJ [23 September 2017].

Eliade, Mircea. 1988. *Autobiography, Volume 2: 1937–1960, Exile's Odyssey*. Chicago: University of Chicago Press.

Finlay, Victoria. 2002. *Colour*. London: Sceptre.

Fung, Brian. 2012. '"Netizen": Why Is this Goofy-Sounding Word so Important in China?', *The Atlantic*, 11 October. Available at www.theatlantic.com/international/archive/2012/10/netizen-why-is-this-goofy-sounding-word-so-important-in-china/263245 [2 February 2018].

Goldman, Lisa. 2013. '5 Broken Cameras' Director: There Is no Room for Guilt – Only Taking Responsibility', *+972 Magazine*, 24 February. Available at https://972mag.com/

director-of-5-broken-cameras-there-is-no-room-for-guilt-only-taking-responsibility/66642/ [4 January 2018].

Greenfield, Patrick. 2018. 'The Cambridge Analytica Files: The Story so Far', *The Guardian*, 26 March. Available at www.theguardian.com/news/2018/mar/26/the-cambridge-analytica-files-the-story-so-far [5 April 2018].

Hammack, Phillip L. 2012. 'Narrative and the Cultural Psychology of Identity', in Kathleen D. Vohs and Roy F. Baumeister (eds), *Self and Identity. Volume IV. Aspects of the Self: Applications and Extensions*. Los Angeles andLondon: Sage, 133–181.

Hartley-Parkinson, Richard. 2017. 'Powerful Images that Show why Holocaust Memorial Selfies Are so Disrespectful', *Metro.co.uk*, Thursday 19 January.

Hauben, Michael F. 1995. 'The Netizens and Community Networks', paper presented at the Hypernetwork 1995 Beppu Bay Conference, 24 November.

Holley, Peter. 2016. 'These Protesters Wanted to Humiliate "Emperor" Trump. So They Took off His Clothes', *Washington Post*, 19 August. Available at www.washingtonpost.com/news/morning-mix/wp/2016/08/18/anarchists-unveil-naked-donald-trump-statues-in-several-u-s-cities/?noredirect=on&utm_term=.4f619cf97d60 [11 December 2017].

Hunter, Dan, Ramon Lobato, Megan Richardson and Julian Thomas (eds). 2012. *Amateur Media: Social, Cultural and Legal Perspectives*. London: Routledge.

Inextinguishable Fire, dir. Harun Farouki, Germany, 1969. Available at www.youtube.com/watch?v=aJXJRNB-5kk [25 May 2017].

Jacko, Julie A. 2012. *Human Computer Interaction Handbook: Fundamentals, Evolving Technologies, and Emerging Applications*, 3rd edn. Boca Raton, FL: CRC Press.

James, William. 1890. *The Principles of Psychology*, New York: Henry Holt & Co.

Kember, Sarah and Joanna Zylinska. 2012. *Life after New Media: Mediation as a Vital Process*. Cambridge, MA: MIT Press.

Kmec, Sonia and Vivian Thill (eds). 2012. *Tourists and Nomads: Amateur Images of Migration*. Magsburg: Jonas-Verlag.

Lannon, John and Edward Halpin. 2013. *Human Rights and Information Communication Technologies: Trends and Consequences of Use*. Hershey, PA: Information Science Reference.

'The Las Vegas Shootings', 1 October 2017. Available at www.youtube.com/watch?v=DZ5GDtObtwI [15 January 2018].

Lievrouw, Leah A. 2011. *Alternative & Activist New Media*. Cambridge: Polity Press.

Love, David A. 2018. 'Ahed Tamimi Is the Palestinian Rosa Parks', Al Jazeera, 15 January. Available at www.aljazeera.com/indepth/opinion/ahed-tamimi-palestinian-rosa-parks-180114114647043.html [1 June 2018].

Lyon, Alistair. 2008. 'Palestinians Shoot Back at Israelis – With Cameras', Reuters, 21 August. Available at www.reuters.com/article/us-palestinians-israel-cameras-idUSLK1628820080821 [12 July 2017].

MacDougall, David. 1995. 'Beyond Observational Cinema', in Paul Hockings (ed.), *Principles of Visual Anthropology*. Berlin: De Gruyter Mouton, 115–132.

McLeod, Douglas M. and Dhavan V. Shah. 2015. *News Frames and National Security: Covering Big Brother*. New York: Cambridge University Press.

Motrescu-Mayes, Annamaria. 2016. 'Ethnographies of Trauma and Migrant Emotions: South Asian Visual Narratives of War and Displacement', *Pakistan Journal of Historical Studies*, vol. 1, no. 1, 1–17.

Naficy, Hamid. 2016. 'Lured by the East: Ethnographic and Expedition Films about Nomadic Tribes – The Case of Grass (1924)', in Jonathan Kahana (ed.), *The Documentary Film Reader: History, Theory, Criticism*. New York: Oxford University Press, 93–109.

Oksiloff, Assenka. 2001. *Picturing the Primitive: Visual Culture, Ethnography, and Early German Cinema*. Basingstoke: Palgrave Macmillan.

Peacocke, Christopher. 1985. 'Imagination, Experience and Possibility: A Berkeleian View Defended', in John Foster and Howard Robinson (eds), *Essays on Berkeley: A Tercentennial Celebration*. Oxford: Clarendon Press.

Potter, Robert F. and Paul D. Bolls, 2012. *Psychophysiological Measurement and Meaning. Cognitive and Emotional Processing of Media*. London: Routledge.

Rettberg, Scott, Roderick Coover, Daria Tsoupikova and Arthur Nishimoto. 2016. 'Hearts and Minds: The Interrogations Project', developed for the UIC Electronic Visualization Laboratory (EVL) at the University of Illinois Chicago.

Rouch, Jean. 1975. 'The Camera and Man', in Paul Hockings (ed.), *Principles of Visual Anthropology*. The Hague: Mouton, 83–107.

Rubin, Alan M. 2009. 'Uses-and-Gratifications Perspectives on Media Effects', in Jennings Bryant and Mary Beth Oliver (eds), *Media Effects*. New York: Routledge, 165–184.

Santone, Jessica and Will Straw. 2009. 'Cultural Memory and Digital Preservation', *Convergence: The International Journal of Research into New Media Technologies*, vol. 15, no. 3, 259–262.

Schiavenza, Matt. 2013. 'Enough With the Word "Netizen"', *The Atlantic*, 25 September. Available at www.theatlantic.com/china/archive/2013/09/enough-with-the-word-netizen/279969 [4 June 2018].

Schulz, Martin. 2013. 'The Unmasking of Images: The Anacronism of TV-Faces', in Oliver Grau and Thomas Veigl (eds), *Imagery in the 21st Century*. Cambridge, MA: MIT Press, 37–55.

Serendip, Gus. 2016. 'Exploring the Real Iran, with Social Media as Your Guide', *The Guardian*, 19 April. Available at www.theguardian.com/travel/2016/apr/19/exploring-iran-travels-facebook-instagram-couchsurfing [2 February 2018].

Shapira, Shahak. *Yolocaust*. Available at https://yolocaust.de [22 May 2018].

Sherwood, Harriet. 2018. 'Palestinian 16-Year-Old Ahed Tamimi Is the Latest Child of Israel's Occupation', *The Guardian*, 2 January. Available at www.theguardian.com/commentisfree/2018/jan/02/ahed-tamimi-israel-occupation-palestinian-trauma [10 January 2018].

Smyth, Thomas, John Etherton and Michael L. Best. 2010. 'MOSES: Exploring New Ground in Media and Post-Conflict Reconciliation', in *Proceedings of the SIGCHI conference on Human Factors in Computing Systems*. New York: ACM, 1059–1068.

Solon, Olivia. 2017. 'How Syria's White Helmets Became Victims of an Online Propaganda Machine', *The Guardian*, 18 December. Available at www.theguardian.com/world/2017/dec/18/syria-white-helmets-conspiracy-theories [3 January 2018].

Sontag, Susan. 1978. *On Photography*. London: Penguin.

Stasch, Rupert. 2017. 'Primitivist Tourism and Anthropological Fieldwork: A Very Awkward Relation', visiting seminar, University of Helsinki, 3 March. Available at https://blogs.helsinki.fi/anthropology/2017/03/16/rupert-stasch-primitivist-tourism-and-anthropological-fieldwork-a-very-awkward-relation [8 March 2018].

Stewart, Gerald. 1947. *The Rough and the Smooth: An Autobiography*. 237pp. three boxes, 1870–1947. CSAS paper collections.

Straw, Will. 2010. 'The Circulatory Turn', in Barbara Crow, Michael Longford and Kim Sawchuk (eds), *The Wireless Spectrum: The Politics, Practices and Poetics of Mobile Media*. Toronto: University of Toronto Press.

Straw, Will, Sandra Gabriele and Ira Wagman. 2011. *Intersections of Media and Communications: Concepts and Critical Framework*. Toronto: Emond Montgomery Publications.

Sutherland, Richard. 2011. 'Regulating the Media', in Will Straw, Sandra Gabriele and Ira Wagman (eds), *Intersections of Media and Communications: Concepts and Critical Frameworks*. Toronto: Emond Montgomery Publications.

'Virtual Reality Helps Germany Catch Last Nazi War Criminals', *The Guardian*, 2 October 2016.

Walton, Kendall. 1990. *Mimesis as Make-Believe: On the Foundations of the Representational Arts*. Cambridge, MA: Harvard University Press.

Willsher, Kim. 2018. '"Spider-Man" of Paris to Get French Citizenship after Child Rescue', *The Guardian*, 29 May. Available at www.theguardian.com/world/2018/may/28/spider-man-of-paris-to-get-french-citizenship-after-rescuing-child [30 May 2018].

Winstanley, Asa. 2013. 'Is Oscar-nominated 5 Broken Cameras an Israeli or a Palestinian film?', *The Electronic Intifada*, 11 January. Available at https://electronicintifada.net/blogs/asa-winstanley/oscar-nominated-5-broken-cameras-israeli-or-palestinian-film [12 November 2017]

Zimmermann, Patricia. 2013. 'An Amateurized Media Universe', *Review of Amateur Media: Social, Cultural and Legal Perspectives*, ed. Dan Hunter, Ramon Lobato, Megan Richardson and Julian Thomas (London: Routledge, 2012), *Jump Cut. A Review of Contemporary Media*, vol. 55, Fall 2013.

5

MEMORY AND AMATEUR MEDIA'S VISUAL COUNTER-HISTORIES

A poster advertising Chase & Sanborn Coffee produced in the mid-1950s shows an action scene involving a heterosexual couple and a can of coffee beans. The man wears shiny black shoes, chequered socks, beige trousers with dark braces, and a light-coloured shirt. The woman wears black medium-high heels and a dark dress with a frothy-white petticoat. The can of coffee beans anchors the scene in the lower right-hand corner of the poster – this ensures a perfectly balanced framing. The couple's actions, however, shift the meaning of the advertisement between a low register of colloquial banter to that of crude aggressiveness. With his back at the viewers (audience/future buyers of the coffee beans), the man sits on a smokers bow armchair while precariously balancing the woman over his knees – her well-coiffured hair flowing mid-air. He is beating her, right hand raised for yet another blow over her backside. The slogan reads: 'If your husband ever finds out you're not "store-testing" for fresher coffee…'. To twenty-first century viewers, this visual narrative presents an acutely offensive visual narrative, which overwrites product placement with an example of commodified domestic abuse and gendered identities. Similar images representative of particular popular visual cultures and representations (memories) of abuse and trauma offer a feasible starting point for the discussion of re-imagined collective memories and of how old and new media presents (mis-)constructed and recyclable personal and global visual identities.

While twentieth-century home movies, and amateur film practice in general, usually centred on images of bucolic domesticity and leisure activities, their reassessment today highlights imbedded visual details informing private and/or collective counter-histories and memories of trauma and abuse. This rediscovery in hindsight of historical evidence of identity is an ongoing process that requires a reframing of critical perspective – a process that brings centre stage *that* detail that has always been present and yet never seen before because it was 'not looked for' (Elsaesser 2014). This self-centred amateur media forensic exercise has been the privilege of several documentary filmmakers such as Michelle Citron (*Daughter Rite*, USA, 1980), Andrew Jarecki (*Capturing the Friedmans*, USA, 2003), Jonathan Caouette (*Tarnation*, USA, 2003), Paul-Julien Robert (*Meine keine Familie*, Austria, 2012) and Sarah Polley (*Stories We Tell*, Canada, 2012). More recently, vlogs or YouTube short amateur films made in a similar self-(re-)documenting manner have become a popular (and more affordable) choice – see *Conversations with my ... old self*, discussed in Chapter 3 – albeit not necessarily (always) addressing issues of trauma. Furthermore, social media networks often allow for the occasional (and remarkable) rediscovery of lost identities as in the case of Samantha Futerman and Anaïs Bordier (*Twinsters*, USA, 2015), the South Korean-born identical twin sisters whose Facebook accounts made possible their reunion 25 years after having lived (unknowingly) apart as children adopted by an American and French family respectively. Whether recorded on Super-8mm, 16mm, VHS or as live Skype conversations, amateur media's intrinsic visual literacy continues thus to act as an agent of personal and/or collective counter-history. It illustrates specific cultural instances of memory-making and representations of personal and collective selves while allowing for renewed media mirrors – a constant reflection of contextualised modes of interpretations (i.e. age, moral codes, accrued information, and hindsight).

The ever-changing cultural and social networks of amateur film and amateur media help redefine key concepts of memory semantics, media ethics and visual rhetoric, particularly when studying images of (anonymous) suffering, pain and terror. As a sequel to some of the analyses from previous chapters, and in particular from Chapter 4, here are surveyed some of the theoretical perspectives informing the moral frameworks defined by watching footage of violence, crime and death in an attempt to define some of the ways in which amateur media footage of trauma shapes collective semantic memory, to borrow Endel Tulving's term (2000). The core argument in this chapter is that amateur footage and amateur (new) media bridge visual constructions of personal, intimate identities (usually shaped by episodic memory) with visual constructions of collective identities (usually shaped by semantic memory). With the risk of offering a doctrinaire perspective, but aiming to avoid the risk of reinventing a theoretical wheel, it is useful to recall key (and by now) rhetorical questions about the triad of morality – images – memory such as 'Is morality learnt or inborn?', 'What defines morality and moral judgement?' and 'Is morality reliant on thought or on emotion?' This remains an ongoing enquiry, one that perhaps started even before Aristotle's claim in the mid-300s BC that 'to the thinking soul images serve as present sensations: and when it affirms or denies good or evil, it avoids or pursues (this is why the soul never thinks without an image)' (Aristotle, trans. 1907, 141). Such philosophical and theoretical questions are also of immediate relevance to most contemporary visual theorists and anthropologists, among other scholars in the humanities and social sciences. It is in this context that the study of analogue and digital narratives produced with the aim to document historical identities could certify acts of first-person media-witnessing, remembering and memorialising trauma.

The case studies discussed in this chapter are particularly relevant when considering amateur media-witnessing as in *facing trauma* – whether as a subject of trauma (people filmed in war zones) or as a bearer of the look (audiences subjected to such images). Being part of or looking at images of people looking at the camera and re-presenting, symbolising for the viewer the experience of trauma create the space for dialogue – the viewers need to take a stance; they negotiate issues of authenticity, of cultural and ideological differences and of specific patterns in their respective visual priming processes. Witnessing as in 'observing trauma from behind' – this is the audience's prerogative when watching groups of people (the masses, the soldiers, the crowds, the anonymous makers of history) experiencing suffering and death. Often this mode of witnessing trauma is found in war reportages as well as in horror films – i.e. the scene in which the subjects (individuals or groups of people) are either unaware of their vulnerability (feature films) or desperately hopeful in spite of imminent danger. They are visually represented as *moving* targets, filmed from behind, in close-up or with a wide angle lens, as they advance towards a form or another of peril. On such occasions, there is no dialogue between the subject and the viewer. The visual monologue of the victims (or victims-to-be) is appropriated by the audience hence transforming the subject's amateur visual portrait of the then-and-there into audience's present-tense identity of re-experienced trauma. Moreover, this process of identification with trauma by proxy projects the audience – audience as *projectile*; audience as *superimposed* entity – into the anonymous subject's visual destiny (i.e. the unknown refugees, soldiers or casualties of terrorism). Thus, geographically or historically isolated, private traumas are relived publicly with a heightened intensity, one granted by the knowledge of its non-negotiable finality. Consequently, this (re)projected experience of trauma becomes briefly the viewers' self-awareness about their own role as generic and anonymous characters/subjects in the global master visual narratives of their historic times.

A possible theoretical buttress to this hypothesis about amateur media-witnessing of trauma is Endel Tulving's pertinent recommendation that scholars should adapt the term 'semantic' when referring to a system of memory that defines general meanings, events and facts shared by an individual with a specific community, whether geographical or virtual/online. For Tulving, this new analytical framework allows the researchers to delineate the semantic memory from the episodic one, also a relevant framework to amateur and new media studies when exploring an individual's (allegedly) unique personal experiences. The ongoing comparison of several examples of new media produced, distributed and consumed as markers of global identities, and defined by localised political crises, often offers credible answers to questions of how and whether amateur footage and amateur new media bridge visual constructions of personal, intimate identities. The aim remains therefore to assess how theoretical debates in visual, new media and digital anthropology can help address questions of memory-building and counter-historical authenticity across first-person visual narratives.

Amateur (raw) visual narratives of trauma

Minority and migrant communities defined by shared trauma function within specific domains of emotional contingency and historical agency. In 2001, Indian-born American artist Zarina Hashmi created the woodblock print 'Dividing Line'. In it, a thick, zigzagging black-ink line cuts through a handmade rectangular, beige-speckled piece of paper. The image does justice to the title: the line divides an even space into two irregular fragments. However, to those familiar with the historical and emotional geographies of India's Partition in August 1947, the shape of the line recalls that of the newly created border between India and Pakistan, and the emotional present continuous tense of painful ruptures within modern South Asian national and religious histories. This interpretation is not an exercise in superfluous art criticism: Hashmi's line appears identical to the contour of the contested frontier line and so the space that it divides could well function as the mental and emotional canvas for post-colonial interpretations, assumptions and visualisations of South Asian identities. Moreover, Hashmi's minimalist, abstract representation of the national identity fissures that defined the 1947 Partition visually summarises the South Asian national and diasporic consciousness of an ongoing identity rupture, a fluid state of self-(re)interpretation and historical adjustment to multi-racial, multi-ethnic and multicultural contexts.[1] From this perspective, 'Dividing Line' addresses an audience that can be simultaneously minority-specific – South Asian homeland and South Asian diaspora – and majority-relevant since it explores questions of displacement and borderline identities shaped by the trauma of never being *at home*, of always migrating across the dividing line between belonging, nostalgia and the myth of the return.[2]

While most historians are still cautious of changing the research protocol from the traditional, text-based methodology, to more flexible approaches that would incorporate images as primary sources rather than (just) as illustrations, cultural and media scholars have long proved that interdisciplinary and cross-cultural interpretations of images guarantee important counter-narrative discourses about specific events and cultures. This becomes possible and, importantly, credible as a research practice when visual records are explored by means of theories of perception, social psychology and visual anthropology. Whether used by the general public or by scholars, visual representations of events, identities and traumas are always anchored in a continuous information processing that combines emotional identification, identity-projection and narrative persuasion. At the core of this mental and intellectual modus operandi is the process of visual priming with its two types of cognitive processing: heuristic and systematic – the corner stone of most theories of persuasion (Dillard and Peck 2001; Block and Keller 1997). Moreover, it has been argued that people use two mental pathways when dealing with arguments and moral judgement – a central one based on logical perspectives and a peripheral one employing heuristic processing (Petty and Cacioppo 1986).[3] The difference highlighted by Dillard and Peck between the systematic process with its slow-paced analytic progression and the heuristic processing strategy in which images are understood and consumed almost instantaneously could often help explain why historiographic methodologies incorporating visual research methods are still infrequent, with most social scientists uncertain whether such protocols can be scientifically reliable in securing valid analytical and argumentative systems. In other words, those who include visual research methods in their historical studies are often suspected of being ruled by the emotional persuasiveness of visual records, or of being *idle* academics – scholars who might prefer the short-cut approach of heuristic processing, which allows one to take quicker interpretative decisions and, consequently, rely less on the analytical framework of the verbal/written sources. However, ex abrupto critical judgements based on the intrinsic emotional persuasive traits of an image are not sufficient to dismiss the image's merit as a valid primary research source – most visual narratives rely on multifaceted, interwoven narratives of personal and collective memories, identities and cultural histories. Moreover, when researching text-based primary sources, an individual relies on the formation of mental images and on his/her interpretation of those mental images. Importantly, the mental process at work when interpreting actual or mental images activates the same parts of the brain. Thus, it seems reasonable to argue that scholars employing traditional text-based historiographic methodologies, or experimenting with visual cross-disciplinary research models, employ a similar qualitative and cognitive processing with an almost equal degree of efficacy (Howard et al. 1997). In this context, relying on theories of perception and visual rhetoric while aiming to identify and develop new perspectives on historic events becomes an equally valid and applicable methodology as when working within a written-text rhetoric framework.

Understanding how the visual priming process operates and why audiences employ heuristics and systematic/contemplative cognitive processes when deciphering an image for the first time is also relevant to exploring media ethics. In particular, theories of perception are helpful in examining visual constructions of racial and ethnic minority identities and of (re-)imagined collective memories. Recent research in perception studies has highlighted that representations of traditional cultural themes are often processed using short-circuited routes of analysis (i.e. heuristic processing) whereas representations of new, exterior topics to a group's cultural and political identity are usually subjected to a lengthier and more meditative route, i.e. cognitive/systematic processing (Petty and Cacioppo, 1986) (see Chapter 4). The case studies discussed in this chapter are meant to illustrate how amateur visual records could be simultaneously an emotional prompter for remembering a particular collective trauma and an example of visual priming for global (diasporic) identities. Several examples of old and new amateur short films have thus been selected as reliable examples of historically valid records of trauma, terror and war casualties. The first set of scenes includes a short excerpt from a 16mm military amateur film made in August 1947 and an amateur new media (video/digital) sequence used as a first-person 'illustration' in the 2011 TV documentary *Sri Lanka's Killing Fields*. The former example proposes a faultless case of visually perpetuated memories of the Partition of India, while the second documents the horror of the recent civil war in Sri Lanka. Thus, while the first case study is discussed for its potential merit as a rare primary research source for collective memory and diaspora studies, the second is an ideal example of how media forensic analysis can raise questions of historical evidence, narratorial authority and the politics of ethical representation in amateur media.

Whether discussing a particular historic event or issues of historical and media studies in general, several key research questions anchor the discussion, such as 'Are traditional moral codes contingent to an audience's ethical responsibility towards the production, distribution and reception of particular media?' and 'How can certain first-person visual narratives of trauma be historically relevant across generations, faiths and political affiliations?' It is within this theoretical framework that a 25-second-long sequence from a military amateur film made by Captain Clifford H. Williams of the 11th Sikh Regiment while serving with the Punjab Boundary Force (PBF) in August 1947 provides a visual narrative specific to the historical context of the Partition of India and to the wider, contemporary issues faced by the South Asian diaspora (Figure 5.1).[4] The sequence shows a group of Indian refugees sitting exhausted by the edge of a country road. Very quickly it becomes clear that some of those lying on the ground are already dead.[5] At some point, an Indian

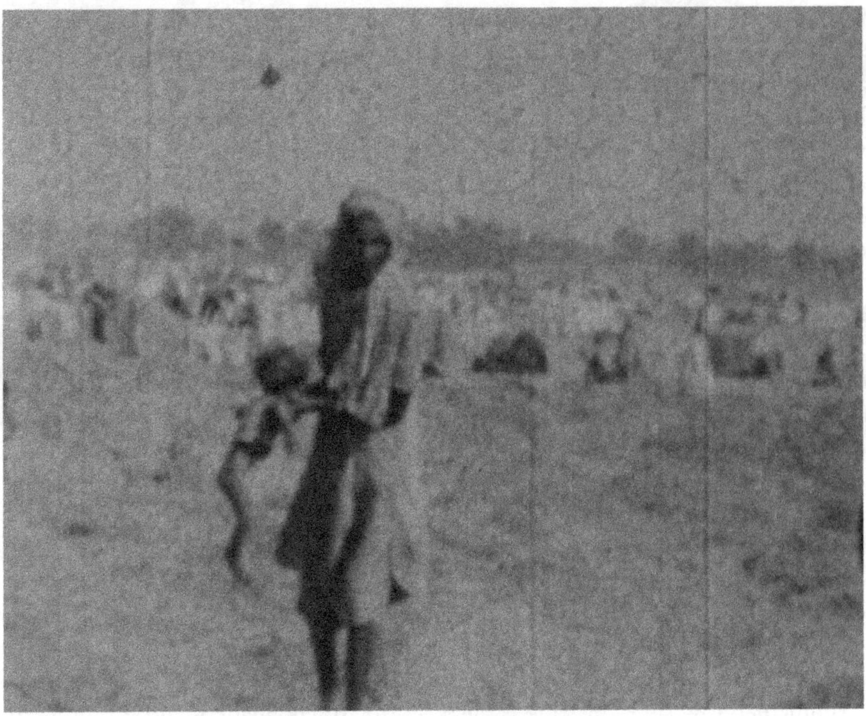

FIGURE 5.1 Still frame from Williams Collection, August 1947. Courtesy of the Centre of South Asian Studies, University of Cambridge.

soldier, possibly affiliated to the PBF, lifts a blanket-canvas to check what might be underneath it. He unveils a small child cuddled next to an inert body. At first, the child stares at the ground, seemingly playing with an object, silently and ignoring the soldier or those revealed *to* him once the blanket has been removed. The soldier walks away while making a hand gesture as if to disperse a wave of stench. The filming stops abruptly. The next scene shows the toddler looking straight at the camera. The filming stops again. The following scene shows a refugee man picking up the child and holding him/her up at arm's length – this makes it possible for the audience to assess that the child is, in fact, a baby.[6] The man carrying him/her starts walking away but then stops suddenly. He returns towards the camera. Held from underneath his/her small and frail shoulders, the baby's body swings in a wide curve during this to and from movement. The refugee man approaches the camera but a soldier nearby gestures to him to go away. The man obediently walks away with the baby's body suspended precariously in his hands. The sequence ends here.

Captain Williams' film of the baby's' accidental discovery acquires a particular metonymic merit within the wider framework of visual, textual and oral histories documenting and re-memorialising the Partition of India. A metaphoric criticism can help interpret the visual narrative of this silent sequence showing the to and fro steps taken by the refugee man holding the baby – his change of direction and pace dictated by the quick tempo of off-screen contradictory commands could thus epitomise the rushed political decisions that shaped the Partition of India. At the same time, the hasty swaying of the baby's body in a continuous arc of changed destinations is a valid, credible and functional *narateme* (narrative unit; Propp 1968) of a pervasive visual literacy relevant to nuanced understandings of visual records of South Asian collective trauma and, simultaneously, of the interrelated diasporic identities. Captain Williams' short amateur film sequence documents and simultaneously challenges the theme of post-Partition South Asian diasporic identities and of trans-visual narratives of South Asian collective trauma. It is the baby's body, held above the ground and moved from one side to another, that functions both as a metonym of the refugees' terrifying and unpredictable destiny and as a visual *narateme* with a strong connotation of displacement within post-colonial contexts. The images of the orphaned baby 'suspended' in between destinations evokes key questions of diasporic identity, split South Asian nationalities and fractured cultural affiliations. Most importantly, the emotional and visual merit of this sequence calls, within both heuristic and systematic processes of cognition and interpretation, for new perspectives on how irreversibly divided South Asian identities have become tropes of emotionally suppressed collective memories of trauma, displacement and death during the Partition of India. Finally, Captain Williams' accidental first-person (amateur) visual narrative documenting the discovery of the baby allows, within the online free-access context, global (online) audiences to simultaneously *borrow* his cine camera – primary cinematic identification – and so to develop a collaborative authorship regarding (re)memorialisation of war trauma and migration.

Whereas cultural and political changes can influence over time the system of beliefs and behaviour patterns of minority group members, it is usually the alterations in mass-media representations that influence the most the group's self-image and sense of self-worth and identity (Aronson 2012). Whereas numerous documentaries and feature films, alongside novels and oral history records, have explored and represented the trauma of migration, displacement and death brought by the Partition of India in the summer of 1947, Captain Williams' 25-second-long amateur film sequence is addressing such issues in a more direct manner, one independent of generational, faith and national perspectives. This sequence depicts the serendipity of a refugee, orphan baby being rescued from starvation and death while epitomising the in-between destiny faced by all the refugees crossing the newly established border between India and Pakistan. This sequence is also relevant when interpreting similar emotional legacies and visual constructions of global self-image identities shaped by equivalent historical traumas such as the current Syrian civil war and Europe's refugees crisis.[7] Most importantly, it is through the process of emotional contagion – the fast transfer of emotions and behaviour-related bias within a group or community – that the visual narrative found in Captain Williams' sequence is immediately relevant as a primary research source to contemporary South Asian studies. First, the mood-inducing and the cognitive content of the emotions provoked in the viewers while watching the baby's body being *placed* between two destinations – whether another family of refugees or a military/ medical rescue centre – sutures the visual priming process (James 1890). Also, the emotional impact shared by audience across time is often similar: shock and agonising pain at the horror of this double displacement – like most young refugees crossing the border between India and Pakistan in August 1947, the baby is both orphaned and stateless. Second, the perception and visual processes triggered by this short sequence are accompanied by two simultaneous cognitive constructs: the audience's mental availability to identify memories of that particular or similar trauma, and the audience's mental accessibility, readiness to construct a coherent narrative anchored in primary emotion-related memories. It is from these visual and cognitive perspectives that Zarina Hashmi's 'Dividing Line' and Captain Williams' amateur film sequence act as referential visual records in the cultural literacy of South Asian diasporic identities. Moreover, as discussed below, this theoretical framework proves valuable and with an immediate practical application when addressing questions of historical authenticity, political activism and visual constructions of other displaced identities across new media narratives.

The second example discussed from this perspective is a 56-second-long sequence belonging to an anonymous Tamil amateur video (mobile phone film?) made in response to the Sri Lankan government's military propaganda films produced during the recent civil war (July 1983–May 2009).[8] This example of new media is a strong indicator of how, within global online networks of media distribution and consumption, local-specific identities shaped by political crises and war can acquire, by a process of psychopathological mirroring, a transnational self-image. This short sequence has been integrated in the TV documentary *Sri Lanka's*

Killing Fields (dir. Callum Macrae. UK, 2011) – an award-winning, poignant and thoroughly documented journalistic investigation of the crucial events that took place in the final weeks of the civil war.[9] The sequence is analysed here from several perspectives borrowing from theories of media ethics, perception, memory studies and visual priming. The emotional impact of these anonymous, amateur images as well as that of the documentary as a whole require first to be considered in terms of the primary effects that media violence has on individuals. As mentioned in Chapter 4, it is now generally accepted that audiences exposed to images of sustained or even brief examples of violence experience at least one of the following three emotional and behavioural effects: the 'aggressor' effect that induces in the viewer (higher) levels of aggression, the 'fear of victimisation' effect that intensifies in the viewer the fear of becoming a victim him/herself, and the 'conscience-numbing' effect during which the individual (audience) is gradually desensitised of 'natural emotional reactions' provoked by the images of mediated violence (Potter and Bolls 2012). It is from this perspective that this amateur media forensic exercise relies on a visual research method organised in three investigative stages. Each stage addresses a particular visual, textual and aural narrative while considering the same set of research questions: 'What is the anthropological and historic evidence available in these images?', 'Is the visual agency shared or disputed by the filmmaker and the people filmed?', 'What are the specific visual constructions of collective identity and collective memory?' and 'What are the main questions of distribution and consumption raised by this sequence?'

The anonymous amateur video sequence has been filmed by someone holding a video recorder or a mobile phone – most possibly the former – while advancing at a fast pace towards a small group of people – men, women and young children – who just found shelter in a makeshift trench (Figure 5.2). The filmmaker approaches the group at close range – terrified, they all crouch in the ditch. Some women, crying with desperation, address the filmmaker. In turn, he/she continues to film without responding. Lasting less than a minute, the scene contains original sound and voiceover commentary. The first stage in the proposed forensic analysis of the scene is to examine it as a silent visual record, thus removing the original sound, English subtitles and commentary that provide introductory and concluding remarks. On this occasion, the images showing the small group of distressed people temporary sheltered from gunfire and death, (re)create the immediacy of a familiar, global and innate narrative of terror. Irrespective of the audience's cultural background, it can be argued that each individual viewing these images experiences, to some extent, a first-hand empathetic identification with the terror shown by the people filmed.

This example of first-person new media narrative recalls Alison Landsberg's theory of 'prosthetic memory' – a recent cultural construct facilitated by mass-media representational and almost ubiquitous trends, which allow everyone today to experience and share collective memories across radically different cultural, social and economic milieus (Landsberg 2004). When viewing this anonymous amateur video sequence as a visual record *per se*, this particular collective memory is

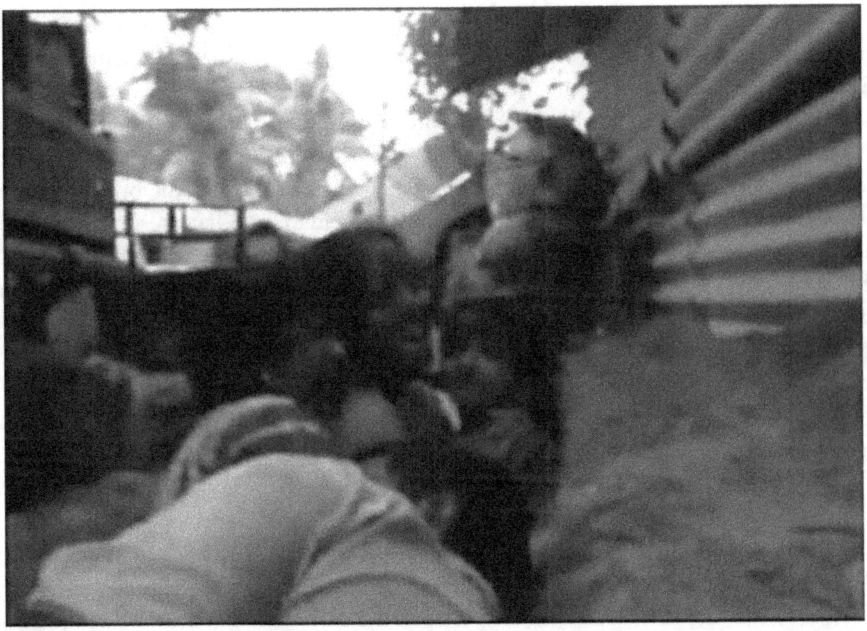

FIGURE 5.2 Still from *Sri Lanka's Killing Fields*, 3 June 2011, Channel 4. Screengrab via YouTube.

transferred, shared and reshaped by the online global audience. The small group's attempt to find shelter in the shallow trench is translated into an open-ended collective memory simultaneously lived *in* – the present tense of viewing the material – and lived *by proxy* – the construction and appropriation of the visual memory created by the amateur media. By removing the connotative input of original sound, voiceover commentary and English subtitles, these images merge the visual agency and narrative authority shared by the people filmed, the filmmaker and the audiences. As a result, the cine-voyeurism (Rouch 1975) of the filmmaker and of the multiple audiences is counteracted by the visual and emotional agency of the people filmed: their terror prompts an emotional contagion across all audiences in a repetitive lived *in* present tense prompted by the online viewing and re-viewing of these images. This is a valid interpretation especially if accepting the hypothesis that, within both anthropological and historical studies, there are infinite constructions of meaning and illustrations of events and identities – whether representational, anti-representational or non-representational. In spite of countless interpretative perspectives relevant to this short amateur sequence, the images showing the small group of desperate people who were most probably facing imminent death provides a strong example of how a specific visual construction of collective identity and memory is shared across online networks as a global prosthetic memory of trauma, displacement and war, whether experienced in situ or visually mediated online.

The second stage in the forensic visual research method considers the sound version of the same anonymous Tamil amateur video sequence, including the English subtitles added by the documentary filmmakers (Figure 5.3). Now, the people gathered in the small trench acquire a *voice* while the surrounding sounds provoke in the viewer a sense of urgency and danger. Crammed between other adults, a young mother holds her child tightly. Panicked, she and the other women cry and addresses the filmmaker: 'Don't take the video!', 'What are you going to do with the video?', 'They are killing everyone!', 'Can you hear us?'. At this point, the camera approaches the group as if to better *hear* the women's words. Viewed in its original version, original soundtrack included, this short amateur video/new media scene illustrates Gunnar Iversen and Jan Ketil Simonsen's theory about the role played by sound in representing reality and so in creating a palpable sense of historical authenticity (Iversen and Simonsen 2010). On this occasion, the images gain a stronger empathetic value due to the viewers' access to and experience of the Tamil people's screams and of the women's cry for help, one allegedly available from across all global media networks. Consequently, the emotional impact of the simultaneously implied and impending violence allows the audience to reinforce or challenge the meaning of the amateur video sequence. Since the original, complete version of this sequence offers an amplified sense of immediacy and intimacy with the terror experienced by the people filmed, it could be argued that the viewers would feel either the 'fear of victimisation' or the 'conscience-numbing' effects, as described by Potter and Bolls (2012).

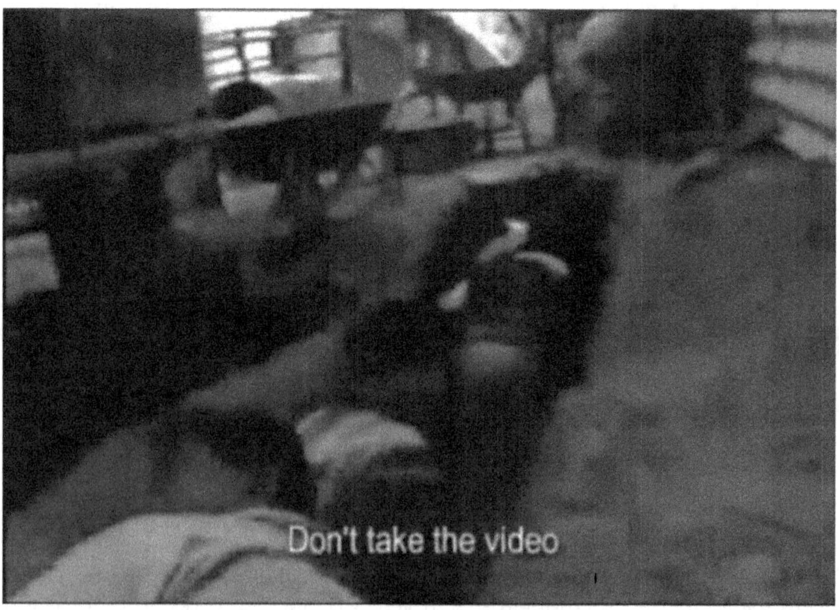

FIGURE 5.3 Still from *Sri Lanka's Killing Fields*, 3 June 2011, Channel 4. Screengrab via YouTube.

There is also a more nuanced emotional dialogue between the Tamil people shown in this sequence, the amateur media/filmmaker and the diverse global audiences. The filmmaker's choice not to respond to the women grants their words a rhetorical merit – consequently, they are addressing a wider, global audience and not just someone recording their experience of being doubly trapped – in a ditch and by a horrific civil war. The amateur media maker's authorial choice also prompts the audience to regroup in the analytical mode to estimate, emotionally and historically, the 'dialogue' between the filmmaker and the group of people. In this case, the visual agency is structured around the in situ participatory engagement between the filmmaker and the group of South Asian people, as well as around the atemporal and ubiquitous, online network that allows global audiences to create parallel and personalised first-person visual narratives of a shared collective memory of war and trauma. Moreover, the narrative authority and the scopophilic effect experienced by the audience, as well as by the historian or the anthropologist researching this scene, are guided by the women's words – her entrapment in a permanent state of terror governs the viewer's acute sense of ethical and moral panic, guilt and hopelessness. The documentary evidence of the horror is experienced now within a continuous present tense. It relies on previous instances of unachieved social and humanitarian responsibility and it also informs and primes future reception and consumption patterns of similar images. Thus, while the language spoken by the women indicates a specific geographic and ethnic identity, the visual collective memory shared in situ or by proxy integrates the historical relevance of the event recorded in this amateur video into a solipsistic trajectory of visual meaning-making across global audiences.

Finally, the third and final stage in the proposed forensic visual analysis explores the historical and anthropological merit of the anonymous Tamil amateur video based on the manner in which it has been integrated in the TV documentary *Sri Lanka's Killing Fields*. This time the visual, ethnic and historical identity of the people filmed is granted and emphasised by the voiceover commentary. The introductory note announces: 'On the ground, the Tamils were filming too. We don't know who shot this. It may have been a [Tamil] Tiger cameraman or it may have been a civilian. Whoever it was, they clearly thought it important to keep a record.' Towards the end of the clip, superimposed on the women's cries, the voiceover narration concludes: 'Families dug shallow trenches which provided limited protection, but nothing could protect their children.' The audience benefits on this occasion from a much easier-to-follow interpretative guidance: viewers are told about the possible authorial agency of the filmmaker and why he/she might have filmed the scene – 'they thought it important to keep a record' – and also about how to interpret these images. Also, due to a double rhetoric employed in the concluding statement – 'But nothing could protect the children against the fear' – a statement contiguous to the Tamil woman's prayer, 'Please God save all of these children', the global, online audiences are emotionally primed to strongly empathise with the immediacy of terror and trauma (Figure 5.4).

This narrative strategy replaces the expected heuristic processing, which an audience might experience when viewing the amateur video sequence – either without sound or accompanied only by its original soundtrack – with the systematic processing that allows for a more contemplative mode of reception and interpretation. This is particularly important when discussing the visual construction of collective identity and memory across this sequence. In particular, when assessing how the first interpretations of, and emotional responses to these images shift the empathetic attachment and relationship between the audience and the people filmed from a virtually universal, instinct-driven 'prosthetic memory' to that of an exclusive, localised historical and collective identity – the Sri Lankan civil war. Paraphrasing Maurice Halbwachs' claim that each individual belongs to simultaneously different social frameworks of memory, it could be argued that, since this Tamil amateur footage has been contextualised by the voiceover commentary within a certain historic time and space, the audience is primed to renounce its innate tendency to recognise the ubiquitously compassion-based memory framework (Halbwachs 1991).

As a result, the audience *de-identifies* itself from this specific case of collective memory of trauma and war so as to regain its role within the spectatorship dynamic; to re-acquire its role as a cine-voyeur. From this position, the audience then confirms the Tamil people's trauma based on their particular historical context rather than responding to it within a global emotional and visual agency. Finally, this particular narrative authority based on mixing two film genres (amateur and documentary) proposes a valuable example of recycled (South Asian) collective memory, of re-appropriated and re-attributed trauma across political and social crisis.[10]

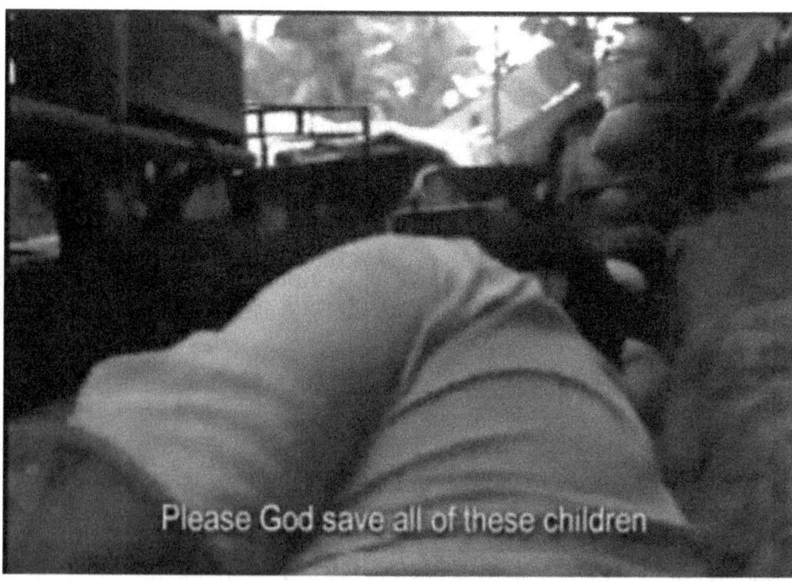

FIGURE 5.4 Still from *Sri Lanka's Killing Fields*, 3 June 2011, Channel 4. Screengrab via YouTube.

Before concluding, it is worth highlighting an additional theoretical approach in support of the identification and construction of visual and emotional collective memory, especially relevant to these two case studies. Julia Kristeva's theory of the Abject, and in particular her definition of it as the eruption of the real into the mundane, can be integrated in the discussion about how visual priming can influence audience interpretation of historical events and identities. Kristeva argues that the Abject could be seen as the danger of meaning breaking down, and that it constitutes our reaction to such a collapse: a re-establishment of our primal repression (Kristeva 1982). The Abject interpreted as such is relevant to those interpretative contexts that dislocate and challenge existing identity and cultural orders. Pertinent to the amateur footage discussed here, the Abject is then what negotiates the construction of a South Asian collective visual and emotional memory, one fastened on to the attraction towards the innate, repulsed familiarity with trauma. It seems then possible to propose that, while viewing Captain Williams' amateur film scene of the orphan baby and the anonymous Tamil amateur video, audiences are repetitively drawn to the Abject as if to experience the catharsis of negotiating abrupt changes in perception, emotions and moral breakdowns, and to reassess aesthetic and political boundaries. This visual and emotional framework indicates a new stage of visual priming by forcing the audiences to reconsider the visual and cultural tropes defining South Asia today. Importantly, there is a strong voyeuristic dichotomy experienced by the audiences when fighting their desire as well as their simultaneous refusal to watch gruesome scenes of pain, fear and death recorded during the Partition of India and/or the Sri Lankan civil war. This gripping, paralysing entrapment in visual trauma exemplifies Kristeva's theory of the Abject while also highlighting issues of media ethics. As a result, images similar to those filmed by Captain Williams and by the anonymous Tamil amateur video/filmmaker, once recycled within historical discourses of displacement and trauma, or as primary 'illustrations' in documentary films, could indicate critical differences in domains of moral contingency and moral judgement (Tamborini 2013). On such occasions, the intrinsic visual legacy of amateur media of war and trauma becomes integral to what could be defined an ongoing hyper-reality to which each new audience contributes interpretations of a particular historic past as a new form of emotional construction (Bennett et al. 2011). This adds 'Who has the right to interpret representations of collective memory of trauma?' to the set of research questions usually considered by historians and media scholars.[11] Moreover, issues of distribution and consumption of similar amateur (new) media have to be defined within a prescribed, visually primed and global broadcast framework. This is a setting in which images of our immediate past have been 'preselected and predetermined … not so much by accident as by people who were consciously or unconsciously imbued with a particular view and thought the facts which supported that view were worth preserving' (Carr 1990, 13) – a perspective plausibly presented in *Sri Lanka's Killing Fields*. A corollary to this theory is that cultural and visual priming often matches the *a priori* validation of 'history [as] a process of preselection and predetermination' (Bennett et al. 2011, 135) – an interpretative endorsement free of fact-based observations and arbitrations used in propaganda and promotional campaigns.

The analysis of these unique examples of amateur media filmed in 1947 and in the late 2000s allows for new interpretative perspectives on how and why visual records can mediate between different constructions of social reality, as well as of individual and national identities. The use of visual research methods, occasionally supported by theories of visual anthropology, perception and social psychology, permit the recognition of amateur visual records as effective and complementing research sources available to historians as well as to other social scientists. It is also possible to conclude at this stage that, by using visual narratives when re-assessing particular historical events and identities, the images in themselves are not, to use recurrent disparaging definitions, 'windows on the past' or 'vehicles for false history'. Instead, particular visual records often play a crucial role in challenging what could be defined as the limiting methodology of traditional text-based historiographical research. The efficient applicability of theories of visual rhetoric, and the inclusion of visual research methods in recent explorations of history are gradually revealing new modes of interpretation. Finally, it could be argued that the ongoing interpretative recycling of amateur video/media records allows the visual memory-maker of trauma, terror and displacement to be 'saved' and simultaneously perpetuated across future 'readings' of the material.

Collective memories of an anonymous, global 'I'

Assuming that today's new and amateur media world is producing ongoing instances of hyper-realities in which history is consumed solely as an emotional construction (Bennett et al. 2011) – a world that Patricia Zimmermann identified as ridden with 'more blurring, and more thorny ethical/legal problems' than the previous global media contexts (Zimmermann 2013) – then one possible enquiry should centre on examples of recycled collective memory across free-access social media networks. For instance, amateur film/video/new media records showing events that took place in the recent past offer rich research resources for establishing the ways in which old and new amateur media helped produce visual hyper-realities of specific collective memories. While the previous case studies selected from the Wilson Collection and *Sri Lanka's Killing Fields* indicated as well as illustrated the experience of ongoing trauma and terror, the next examples of amateur media reveal a passive rather than an action-documented history – they indicate established social and cultural protocols of representation around issues of ongoing or pending trauma. They also offer plausible examples of old (analogue) and new (digital) amateur media counter-histories and of specific visual taxidermies of re-imagined collective memories of trauma – an immersive new visual grammar about the ongoing negotiation of a global 'I'. Once again, the proposed analysis builds on the hypothesis that it is the anonymity and the alleged ephemeral visual identity of the peoples shown in these amateur images, that preserves and perpetuates their visual testimonies of the 'I' – of universal selves within particular constructions of identity, whether regional, historical or as examples of particular memory frameworks. As mentioned, through the act of witnessing trauma by proxy, audiences identify with anonymous victims more so than with specific, heroic or recurrent examples of victimhood. Since often there is a minimal need to negotiate cultural, social or even political differences, anonymity prompts higher levels of identification.[12] The relationship between those visually represented in horrific contexts and those seeing (witnessing by looking at) such representations creates an interpretative *tabula rasa* on which the sole possible interpretative criterion relies on mutual survival instinct. Moreover, witnessing disciplinary measures often subjects the viewers to repeated negotiations of the Abject – a process of self-assessment at the border between the individuals' mundane identity and their reaction to visual aggression. Images of death are then the cornerstone of such challenging social and emotional instances. Amateur photographic, cinematographic and, more recently, new media practice offer abundant illustrations of this topic, from Felice Beato's late nineteenth-century photographs of the British retaliation strategies employed during the Indian Mutiny (India's First War of Independence, 1857), to contemporary Islamic State of Iraq and the Levant's (ISIL) amateur videos of captured soldiers being beheaded – images live-streamed on various social media networks. For the purpose of the following brief discussion we have selected two visual representations of executions – a photograph made in the early 1930s in Burma (Myanmar) and a short clip from an illicit amateur film made in Malaya in the 1950s.

Decapitation and the display of human heads as visual and punitive markers was a practice successfully employed by the British military as late as the 1950s during the Malayan Emergency. However, while the British public decried the use of such images as illustrations in newspaper reports, amateur photographers and filmmakers continued to record and show them within a close distribution network formed by colleagues, family members and friends. Captain L.E. MacGregor's personal photographic albums contain several such examples. A keen amateur photographer, he documented most of his tour of duty as the officer commanding military police during the Upper Chindwin Expedition in the Naga Hill (27 December 1929–26 April 1930) – a British expedition that aimed to curb the slave trade for human sacrifice – and the Tarrawady Rebellion, District of (Lower) Burma in the early 1930s. At that time, the international economic crash and the fall of the price of rice in Burma prompted the Burmese farmers and villagers to demand fair representation and the implementation of their rights. It was in this context that Saya San – a physician and a monk, and self-declared king – led large numbers of villagers in several successful attacks against British government police posts. MacGregor's overview-statement included at the beginning of his photographic album with images of the uprising – highlights that '[t]wo battalions of British Infantry were called to help the Military Police [to] supress the rebellion – by 1932, 10,000 rebels had been killed, 9,000 captured and given prison sentences, and Saya San and other leaders hanged' (MacGregor, undated). It is in this historical context, that one of his photographs raises several interpretative perspectives and ethical issues (Figure 5.5). **The authors would like to bring to attention the graphic nature of the following image depicting a severed head.**

First, it reveals the visual rhetoric of disciplinary hypocrisy in the context of the British colonial presence in Burma in the early twentieth century. It shows that, while trying to eradicate the custom of human sacrifice, the British freely employed similar vindictive practices such as decapitation and the display of human heads. Second, it requires an exercise in archival research and visual taxidermy. While its intrinsic visual narrative centres on five anonymous male bodies (one in absentia), only the *non-being*, the head – in Barthes' terms, this would be the *punctum* of this image (Barthes 1981) – is given a name and an identity. The head thus becomes a historic prop used by the four men, alive and with executive disciplinary power, to confirm their own identities. As a key item in a specialised archival collection, this amateur photograph functions today as an official document about conjoined memories – simultaneously private and collective; simultaneously colonial and colonised memories of the Tarrawady Rebellion. In this case, as in in the following example analysed below, trauma is experienced within the immediacy of

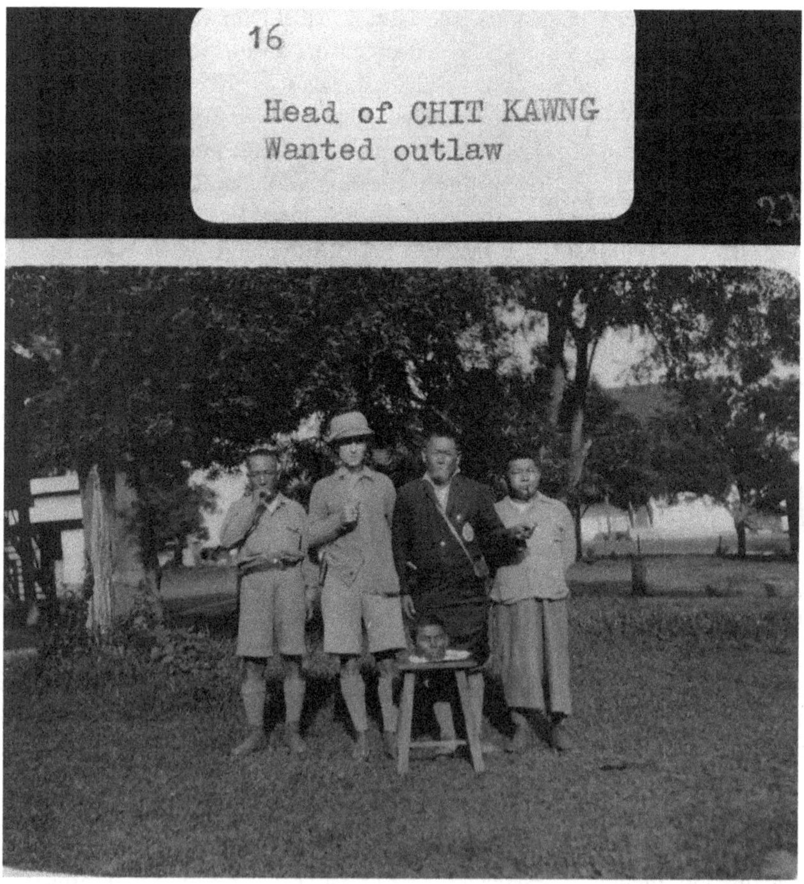

FIGURE 5.5 Photograph from MacGregor Photographic Collection, c. early 1930s. Courtesy of the Centre of South Asian Studies, University of Cambridge.

eye-witnessing as well as of media-witnessing the outcome of a retaliatory mission, from *inside* the event as well as *for* the camera.

More than two decades after MacGregor's amateur visual documentation of the Burmese uprisings, the British military implemented a new protocol to help with the identification (and disposal) of insurgents: plastic bags. This was in response to the British public opinion denouncing both the decapitation of communist insurgents and the British propaganda's use of images of beheaded people as a visual trope endorsing various armed interventions in South-East Asia in the mid-twentieth century. Decapitating captured enemies was at first a common practice during the Malayan Emergency (1948–1960) alongside other horrific punitive measures. For instance, on 6 November 1948, five months after the start of the Emergency, the Menteri Besar (Head of Government) of Kedah suggested to the British High Commissioner in Malaya, Sir Henry Gurney, that the police and military should follow the example of British counter-insurgent strategies employed in Palestine and so burn the Chinese squatters' villages 'leaving them to work out their own salvation'(Short 1975, 180). For the next 12 years, most Chinese communities located on the fringes of the jungle became a dual target. First, communist guerrilla forces asked them to provide food supplies and manpower. Second, representatives of the British and Malay governments coerced them into counter-insurgent actions. The Menteri Besar of Kedah's opinion, as well as that of many Malays and Europeans, echoed that of the Commissioner-General for the United Kingdom in Southeast Asia, Rt. Hon. Malcolm MacDonald, who declared in late 1948 that 'if it were possible to get rid of 25,000–50,000 Chinese within the next six or twelve months, the racial problem in the Federation would be erased' (Short 1975, 178). Throughout the 1950s – a time when British and Commonwealth forces fought the communist insurgents at a cost of £100 million a year – the Malayan Film Unit, newsreel companies and several amateur filmmakers from the military produced records with various degrees of historical and ethnographic merit (Stockwell 2001, 486). The Malayan Film Unit produced documentaries, newsreels and instructional films aligned to the government's radical policy concerning jungle warfare and anti-communist urban and rural military operations. Its productions were distributed on 16mm copies via mobile film units and were meant to appeal to rural, mostly illiterate Chinese, Malay and Indian communities on a larger scale than leaflet distribution or radio and newspaper campaigns. In their turn, British amateur filmmakers, mostly military personnel and doctors, while choosing topics and themes common to anti-communist propaganda, also filmed unwitting records of jungle warfare and British, Gurkha, Malay, Orang Asli and Chinese portraits, subjects that would rarely, if ever, be included in official broadcasts. Captain Roy Edgerton Wilson, during his tour of duty as a senior pilot with the Royal Navy 848 Helicopter Squadron from the mid-1950s to early 1960s, made seven colour 8mm films about British military operations in the Malayan jungle – images often interspersed with scenes of his family's leisure activities.[13] 'Operations in Malaya', the longest film reel in his collection lasts about 22 minutes and shows the 848 Squadron's Sikorsky S-55 helicopter operations alongside the 22 Special Air

Service regiment, Orang Asli tribes and the parachuting of troops and supplies into the jungle. His choice of colour film stock allows the viewers greater access to minute military and ethnographic details. Wilson edited his films in the camera (i.e. stopped and started filming whenever he considered a topic worth of his expensive film stock). Importantly, his filming technique often relied on steady hand shots and accurate framing. Jungle warfare operations were widely covered in British Pathé Newsreels which mostly showed British soldiers advancing slowly through thick jungle vegetation or in chest-deep swamps – images regularly interspersed with scenes of helicopter rescue operations, or of Chinese communists' jungle camps filmed post-ambush. Captain Wilson's 'Operations in Malaya' would seem at first to follow an identical narrative based on his scenes of helicopter manoeuvres, medical and food supply drop missions, troops parachuting into the jungle, casualties rescued by helicopter, and of soldiers stationed at jungle forts. His unedited film contains, however, a few sequences showing lesser-known and rarely publicised instances of jungle warfare. For instance, a sequence rapidly edited in the camera includes medium and close-up shots of a group of British soldiers busy at their jungle camp. Brief scenes show them preparing lunch in tin cups, checking their weapons, smiling at the camera and lifting up a plastic bag containing the corpse of a Chinese insurgent. Consequently, this sequence becomes a relevant visual *manuscript* since it reveals unsettling details of the normality, of the mundane *modus operandi* of British anti-guerrilla jungle warfare. Moreover, this is just one example of the ways in which Captain Wilson's amateur films document rarely seen instances of the terror experienced by British, Malay and Chinese people during the Malayan Emergency. Thus, his amateur film practice has a dual documentary merit. First, it confirms the risks he took when filming scenes which broke military confidentiality protocols. Second, it allows long-term access (i.e. archived, digitised, online streamed collection) to lesser-known features of the British military history during the Malayan Emergency and, consequently, often challenges the visual narrative of illustrations included in history textbooks.

The cases studies discussed in this chapter are meant to function within and beyond a fixed historical and cultural indexical framework. They are fluid, interchangeable trans-cultural amateur visual records able to support the thesis that, when assessed as primary research sources, they allow for nuanced and new perspectives on modern history. Within cross-disciplinary explorations, such images contribute to parallel, complementing or often counter-narrative histories of specific global events and cultural traditions. It is in this theoretical setting that the visual and cultural priming at work defines ongoing and often well-preserved historical narratives of war, migration and death – a compelling and complex exercise in producing visual ethnographies of collective memories and emotional legacies. In light of this, a preliminary conclusion would be that old and new amateur media records such as those discussed in this chapter, and throughout the book, present across different media forensic analyses credible examples of collective memories of trauma, terror and displacement, which have been conserved though a process of visual taxidermy. On such occasions, what appears at first to be brief and possibly inconsequential, ephemeral images (visual constructions) of other people's trauma, become in time an ongoing exercise in shaping and challenging visual identities of the global 'I'– an 'I' unified by the power of shared anonymity. A possible outcome, if pursuing this hypothesis, is that the alleged ephemerality of amateur/new media detritus – the visual footnotes to the popular master narratives in any given cultural context, as discussed in Chapter 3 – often define ongoing, non-ephemeral and consequently historically anchored constructions of media identities, whether in front or behind a recording device.[14] Future interpretations of these and similar images, whether viewed in their original version or as visual 'quotes' in genre-specific narratives such as documentaries or TV reportages, secure that their intrinsic emotional legacy is constantly recycled across various cultural and historical contexts (Schmieder 2015). Moreover, the amateur media voyeurism, and the visual and emotional construction and reinterpretation of particular identities, is thus re-imagined across an ongoing global, synchronous storytelling. Within this media consumption framework, it is then possible to predict a higher degree of reconciled political and moral consciousness, academic objectivity, and implicit self-disclosures of trauma and ongoing conflicts.

Issues of new media ethics, usually centred on questions such as, for instance, 'Who has the right to narrate visual collective histories and to re-present and re-imagine collective memories?', used to be the prerogative of scholars. Now, in the context of a globally shared network of user-generated media, and of free online access to it – whether digitised archival footage or new smartphone film uploads – addressing such questions has become the responsibility of both amateur media makers and amateur media consumers. Therefore, further studies could explore the ways in which amateur (new) media and issues of amateur cine-/media voyeurism define new regimes of citizen memory – a self-reflective representational process in which amateur media functions as ubiquitous, global memory-making agents, as well as private and collective meta-surveillance.

Notes

1 In an interview given in 2013, Zarina Hashmi explained: 'My story is one of all those people who leave their homeland … I was able to tell their story, the story of all exiles' (Patel 2013).
2 See, for instance, *Partition* (dir. Vic Sarin. Canada, South Africa, UK, 2008), *My Beautiful Launderette* (dir. Stephen Frears. UK, 1985), *Bollywood/Hollywood* (dir. Deepa Mehta. Canada, 2002) *and I for India* (dir. Sandhya Suri. India, 2005).
3 Understanding this cognitive framework is particularly relevant to educationalists and scholars designing pedagogical programmes for individuals with various cognitive disabilities, as well as to those teaching young children how to develop a more complex vocabulary and adaptive social skills. For instance, in *My Name is Khan* (dir. Karan Johar. India, 2010) a young boy is taught by means of simple drawings how to negotiate the dichotomy of good and evil and the risk of inter-ethnic hatred in a South Asian context.
4 For previous draft analyses of the scenes from the Williams Collection and *Sri Lanka's Killing Fields* documentary, see Motrescu-Mayes, A. 'Ethnographies of Trauma and Migrant Emotions' (2016).

5 A copy of the film is available at the Imperial War Museum, London and also available online at www.s-asian.cam.ac.uk/archive/films/collection/williams-collection [14 December 2017].
6 The badly deteriorated 16mm filmstrip makes it impossible to identify the baby's gender.
7 The Syrian Civil War began in 2011 as part of the Arab Spring protests. It is an ongoing conflict (June 2018).
8 The civil war was fought between the Sri Lankan government military forces and the Liberation Tigers of Tamil Eelam (LTTE, also known as the Tamil Tigers), a militant organisation that aimed to create an independent Tamil state in the north and north-east of Sri Lanka. Casualties recorded in the final weeks of the war have been estimated at over 40,000 people.
9 Available online at www.channel4.com/programmes/sri-lankas-killing-fields/on-demand [19 December 2017].
10 See, for instance, M.I.A., the British rap/pop artist of Sri Lankan descent who produced in 2015 'Borders' – a music video about the Middle Eastern refugees' perilous and often fatal journey to Europe. 'MIA's Borders: Artist Braves Boats and Barbed Wire in Video Crusade for Refugees', *The Guardian*, 27 November 2015. www.theguardian.com/music/2015/nov/27/mia-borders-video-refugee-crisis-europe [accessed 3 December 2015]. See also *MATANGI / MAYA / M.I.A.* (dir. Steve Loveridge, 2018), a biographical documentary, includes excerpts from her family home movies made in Sri Lanka and England.
11 This is particularly relevant when considering the ways in which new media records and social media networks have recently documented examples of collective memory of trauma and death – see, for instance, the Syrian refugees' exodus to Europe since 2012, and the terrorist attacks in Paris on the night of 13 November 2015.
12 For instance, amateur footage of mothers, children and elederly people walking or shopping on streets damaged by the armed conflict during the 'Troubles' in Belfast filmed on Super 8mm by Gordon McKnight (available at https://digitalfilmarchive.net/media/super-8-stories-extra-footage-troubles-575 [16 February 2018]), or recorded on 16mm by film historian Kevin Brownlow (private collection) in 1969, also in Belfast, highlight the ways in which the reality of terror became part of mundane activities. On such occassions, the audience's identification with trauma is prompted by the absence of images showing the conflict itself. Moreover, it is the people's portrayal as being accustomed to ongoing fear and to living in a state of emergency, as well as their anonymity in these amateur films, that allows online, global audiences today to witness and relate to this seminal event in European history.
13 For a previous discussion of this case study, see Motrescu-Mayes, A. 'Uncensored Imperial Politics' (2014).
14 Numerous other examples of amateur media can be interpreted from this perspective, such as children making mobile phone films of their enactments of street combat or war scenes seen in popular computer games, or soldiers' amateur media posted on either free access or closed-circuit social networks, and of live-streamed amateur recordings of terrorist attacks, national revolutions or urban guerrilla fighting.

Selected bibliography

Aristotle [trans. 1907]. *De Anima*. Translation, introduction and notes by R.D. Hicks. Cambridge: Cambridge University Press.

Aronson, Elliot. 2012. *The Social Animal*. New York: Worth Publishers.

Barthes, Roland. 1981. *Camera Lucida: Reflections on Photography*. New York: Hill & Wang.

Bennett, Peter, Alex Kendall and Julian McDougal (eds). 2011. *After the Media, Culture and Identity in 21st Century*. London: Routledge.

Block, Lauren and Punam Keller. 1997. 'Effects of Self-Efficacy and Vividness on the Persuasiveness of Health Communications', *Journal of Consumer Psychology*, vol. 6, no. 1, 31–54.

Brown, Judith and Wm. Roger Louis (eds). 1999. *The Oxford History of the British Empire, The Twentieth Century*. Oxford: Oxford University Press.

Bushman, Brad J., Huesmann, L.Rowell and Jodi L. Whitaker. 2009. 'Violent Media Effects', in Robin L. Nabi and Mary Beth Oliver (eds), *Media Processes and Effects*. Thousand Oaks, CA: Sage, 361–376.

Carr, Edward Hallett. 1990. *What Is History?*London: Penguin.

Dillard, James Price and Eugenia Peck. 2001. 'Persuasion and the Structure of Affect: Dual Systems and Discrete Emotions as Complementary Models', *Journal of Human Communication Research*, vol. 27, no. 1, January, 38–68.

Elsaesser, Thomas. 2014. *Harun Faroki Diagrams*. Conversation with Alexander Alberro, 8 September. Available at www.youtube.com/watch?v=oISkbMq99TU [9 May 2018].

Gibsone, Harriet. 2015. 'MIA's Borders: Artist Braves Boats and Barbed Wire in Video Crusade for Refugees'. *The Guardian*, 27 November. Available at www.theguardian.com/music/2015/nov/27/mia-borders-video-refugee-crisis-europe [3 December 2015].

Haidt, Jonathan, Jesse Graham and Joseph Craig. 2009. 'Above and Below Left-Right: Ideological Narratives and Culturally Variable Virtues'. *Daedalus*: Special Issue on Human Nature, vol. 133, no. 4, 55–66.

Halbwachs, Maurice. 1992. *On Collective Memory*. Chicago: University of Chicago Press.

Hoffman, Wilhelm and Anna Baumert. 2010. 'Immediate Affect as a Basis for Moral Judgement: An Adaptation for the Effect Misattribution Procedure', *Cognition & Emotion*, vol. 24, 522–535.

Howard, Robertet al. 1997. 'Seeing Visual Hallucinations with Functional Magnetic Resonance Imaging', *Dementia and Geriatric Cognitive Disorders*, vol. 8, no. 2, 73–77.

Iversen, Gunnar and Jan Ketil Simonsen. 2010. *Beyond the Visual: Sound and Image in Ethnographic and Documentary Film*. London: Routledge.

James, William. 1890. *The Principles of Psychology*. New York: Holt.

Kember, Sarah and Joanna Zylinska. 2012. *Life after New Media: Mediation as a Vital Process*. Cambridge, MA: MIT Press.

Kristeva, Julia. 1982. *Powers of Horror: An Essay on Abjection*. New York: Columbia University Press.

Landsberg, Alison. 2004. *Prosthetic Memory. The Transformation of American Remembrance in the Age of Mass Culture*. Columbia, OH: Columbia University Press.

MacGregor, L.E. *Photographic Collection*. 1924–1932. *Burma. Kashmir*. Photographs, two volumes. Centre of South Asian Studies, University of Cambridge.

Motrescu-Mayes, Annamaria. 2014. 'Uncensored Imperial Politics in British Home Movies from 1920s–1950s', in Laura Rascaroli, Gwenda Young, with Barry Monahan (eds), *Amateur Filmmaking: The Home Movie, the Archive, the Web*. London and New York: Bloomsbury Academic, 95–107.

Motrescu-Mayes, Annamaria. 2016. 'Ethnographies of Trauma and Migrant Emotions: South Asian Visual Narratives of War and Displacement', *Pakistan Journal of Historical Studies*, vol. 1, no. 1, 1–17.

Patel, Vibhuti. 2013. 'Dividing Lines and the Art of the Exile', *The Wall Street Journal*, 24 January (11:06pm ET).

Petty, Richard E. and John T. Cacioppo. 1986. *Communication and Persuasion: Central and Peripheral Routes to Attitude Change*. New York: Springer-Verlag.

Potter, RobertF. and Paul D. Bolls. 2012. *Psychophysiological Measurement and Meaning. Cognitive and Emotional Processing of Media*. London: Routledge.

Propp, Vladimir. 1968. *Morphology of the Folktale*, 2nd edn. Austin: University of Texas Press.

Rouch, Jean. 1975. 'The Camera and Man', in Paul Hockings (ed.). *Principles of Visual Anthropology*. The Hague: Mouton, 83–107.

Rubin, Alan M. 2009. 'Uses and Gratifications Perspectives on Media Effects', in Jennings Bryant and Mary Beth Oliver (eds), *Media Effects: Advances in Theory and Research*. New York: Routledge.

Schmieder, Kathrin. 2015. 'Amateur Photographs as Visual Quotes. Does the Rise of Amateur Photography Lead to Fundamental Changes in the News Media?', *Journal of Journalism Practice*, vol. 9, no. 4, 580–596.

Short, Anthony. 1975*The Communist Insurrection in Malaya, 1948–1960*. London: Frederick Muller.

Stockwell, Anthony J. 2001. 'Imperialism and Nationalism in South-East Asia', in Judith Brown and Wm. Roger Louis (eds), *The Oxford History of the British Empire: The Twentieth Century*. Oxford: Oxford University Press, 465–489.

Tamborini, Ron. 2013. *Media and the Moral Mind*. London: Routledge.

Tulving, Endel. 2000. 'Memory: Overview', in Alan E. Kazdin (ed.), *Encyclopedia of Psychology, Vol. 5*. New York: American Psychological Association and Oxford University Press, 161–162.

Tulving, Endel. 2005. 'Concepts of Memory', in Endel Tulving and Fergus I.M. Craik (eds), *The Oxford Handbook of Memory*. New York: Oxford University Press, 33–43.

Vertov, Dziga. 1928. 'Man with a Movie Camera', *Pravda*.

Vertov, Dziga. 1929. 'Man with Movie Camera: Absolute Kinography and Radio Eye'. *Nova Generatsiya*, vol. 3, no. 1.

Vohs, KathleenD. and Roy F. Baumeister (eds). 2012. *Self and Identity, Vol. I: Self-Concept and Self-Esteem*. London: Sage.

Zimmermann, Patricia. 2013. 'An Amateurized Media Universe', Review of *Amateur Media: Social, Cultural and Legal Perspectives*, ed. Dan Hunter, Ramon Lobato, Megan Richardson and Julian Thomas (London: Routledge, 2012), *Jump Cut. A Review of Contemporary Media*, vol. 55, Fall 2013.

6

LOST AND FOUND

Amateur media in the archive

Throughout this book, we have encountered multiple examples of mundane as well as spectacular amateur media texts. We can find some of them in archives and local memory institutions, whereas others are stored in private attics or on social media platforms and video-sharing websites. This chapter discusses the pressing issue of whether we will be able to revisit these amateur media expressions in the near future or if they are doomed to disappear. Many fear that this might be the fate of born-digital records in particular. In 2015, Vint Cerf, an Internet pioneer and Google's vice-president, warned the world about the possibility that our times might go on to become a 'digital dark age'. Cerf is convinced that the majority of digital content will either disappear or become unreadable by machines owing to a lack of backward compatibility. According to him, the situation in question is urgent and requires immediate action by convincing governments, cultural institutions and citizens to embrace a shared 'multi-governance' approach towards the Internet.[1]

Cerf is certainly not the first or the only one to draw attention towards the vulnerability of many of today's digital cultural expressions. According to historian Abby Smith Rumsey we have dramatically expanded our capacity to record, but at the same time, we have failed to expand our backup systems at the same pace: '[W]e outsmart ourselves, and we have to scramble to catch up with our inventions' (Smith Rumsey 2016, 3). There is indeed a serious threat that we might lose our 'cultural reference memory' as described by Aleida Assmann. In her influential text 'The Canon and the Archive', Assmann (2008) addresses this growing threat that is nearly an 'uncontrollable process'. However, she also made it clear that this anxiety has surfaced continuously throughout history. She refers to George Simmel, who described this anxiety in the early twentieth century as 'the tragedy of culture' and even cites notions presented by Plato, who mourned the impact of writing on oral culture and memory (Assmann 2008, 104).

This chapter focuses on the relationship between the shifts in memory-recording and memory-archiving practices (see Chapter 5). As a memory-recording practice, home-movie and video making blossomed throughout the twentieth century, but it took some time before such type of private documentation was valued as archival documents. Only by the end of the twentieth century did home movies enter public archives, as it gradually became an accepted practice for several cultural heritage institutions to collect this type of material. In conjunction with this shift in archival appreciation, legal issues of ownership and copyright, ethical questions on reuse of personal archival footage and problems of obsolescence also arose. Moreover, the rapid and overwhelming growth of digital content, such as the daily mass production of YouTube videos, demands a new set of archival considerations with regard to the status of such records.

We need to rethink what constitutes a record, as a historical document, and what signifies an archive. A classical definition of a document was proposed by Suzanne Briet in her famous study from 1956, stating that a document can only be interpreted to be one if it is intended as evidence and is framed as such. Briet used the example of the antelope: the moment this animal is captured and exposed in a zoo, it is transformed into a document (Briet 2006). However, as concluded by Lisa Gitelman in her study on paper documents, the meaning of a document is not stable, but depends on the context of use and on the specific technologies used for producing and duplicating documents (Gitelman 2014). In addition, she also observed that the emergence of photocopiers changed perceptions pertaining to the status of the document: it transformed the concept of copying as just a technical form of reproduction into a more creative notion of cultural production, thereby instigating a 'cultural logic of the copy' (ibid., 109). According to Gitelman, the genre of the document has widened over time as new types of format and carrier, such as pdf (digital), videotape (video), online videos or live streams invite us to reconsider these as 'living' sites that can be both fluid (different versions) and fixed (ibid., 110).

Digital media expressions, especially when they are shared online, are even more difficult to define as objects or documents, owing to their lack of material substance, which encourages the perception that they are extremely ephemeral. As discussed, new generations of amateur media makers opt for ephemeral media recordings in some cases by choosing apps that enable time-restricted distributions (see Chapter 3). These types of digital material resemble oral culture better than the more stable regimes of print or film cultures (Uricchio 2009). Moreover, online materials can be subjected to regular updates and synchronisation, paradoxically 'making the ephemeral endure' (Chun 2016, 78). In addition, online materials are not always easily defined in terms of authorship or location, as they can be 'networked collaborative forms of cultural production that are multiply voiced, collective and ongoing' (Uricchio 2009, 137). Furthermore, they can be interconnected, remixed or even just fragmented pieces that lack a clear origin in terms of their location or date. With the traditional idea of a record destabilised, so has the concept of the classical archive evaporated. Several users embrace social media platforms as their 'default archive', which, as pointed out by Rick Prelinger (2009) disrupts the exclusiveness of scholarly access and transforms everyday conceptions of institutional archives. Lastly, digital recording and storage technologies caused a repositioning of the archive and everyday life (Featherstone 2006). The archive, once thought of as a stable state-oriented institution, has somehow become detached from its foundation and turned into a slippery concept accompanied by a discourse that characterises archives as immaterial, unstable, fluid, non-hierarchical and pluralistic constellations. Within this new context, new archival models have emerged or are being proposed, such as tactical media archives, global media archives, popular archives, fluid archives, rogue archives, emotional archives, ego archives, personal archives or just databases. The central position of user-generated content in these new concepts concerning archives has provided citizens with a new agency and a new voice, or, as the Canadian archivist Terry Cook observed: '[T]hey leave through digital social media all kinds of new and potentially exciting, and potentially archival, traces of human life' (Cook 2012, 5).

This chapter explores the issues raised by analogue and digital amateur media archives. Furthermore, it offers an overview of the challenges that institutional, popular, amateur and personal archives face in keeping our memories safe. In addition, it considers concrete strategies, policies and user tactics adopted to overcome the potential difficulties. Since so many people almost constantly document and share their daily lives digitally these days, the emphasis has to be on born-digital videos. Despite such videos being a pervasive element in everyday media culture, most people lack awareness with regard to safely storing these ephemeral and everyday expressions. Hence, what are the institutional, technical, commercial or political and social possibilities and constraints that influence a secure way of keeping our present and past safe for the future? How do we deal with current non-official 'popular archives' such as YouTube, with their own set of affordances that are both technically and commercially driven? Moreover, what about the personal archives stored in a desktop computer, smartphone, memory stick or a cloud service? What are the associated possibilities and risks of digital technology and commercial services in relation to amateur media? Subsequently, how can we ensure that not only the moving image text but also its historical context is being preserved? Under the header of personal digital archiving and/or web archiving, librarians, archivists and information scientists are currently struggling to develop new policy practices and technologies alongside deploying strategies for reaching out to the public so as to prevent 'a digital dark age'. The chapter presents an overview of the current issues and concludes with a discussion about the challenges surrounding the abundance of user-generated content: should we save it all?

Institutional archives

The acknowledgment of the importance both of popular culture and of documents representing everyday life is intertwined with how archives, in the twentieth century, took up the task to start collecting and preserving home movies. Somewhere during the twentieth century the idea shifted that archives should only represent the state, or official events, but rather could be, as the Dutch archivist Eric Ketelaar once stated, more democratic and become archives 'of the people, for the people, even by the people' (cited in Cook 2001, 18). Terry Cook (2001) emphasised how changing perceptions in society stimulated the emergence of new archival paradigms, which ultimately infused more dynamic concepts of what an archive could or should be: responsible for the safekeeping of our culture and identity, on both a personal and collective level. Eventually, this paradigm shift gave a strong impetus towards a more positive archival appraisal of modern visual media culture, although it was not until the 1980s that the importance of audio-visual media was fully recognised and deemed worthy of preservation. The 1980 UNESCO report *Recommendation for the Safeguarding and Preservation of Moving Images* was an important document in this respect. The report proposed to take moving images seriously as 'an expression of the cultural identity of peoples, and because of their educational, cultural, artistic, scientific and historical value, form an integral part of a nation's cultural heritage'. Finally, moving images were acknowledged as 'important and often unique testimonies' in the archives (UNESCO 1980).

In the wake of this new appraisal, home movies became an accepted part of our cultural heritage. In both Europe and the United States, local and regional archives first took the initiative to collect amateur material (Aasman 2014). The mid-1990s especially represented a watershed moment, for both archivists and scholars recognised the importance of amateur footage as cultural heritage. Eventually, home movies came out of the attics (Horak 1998). Since 1986, several initiatives by regional archives in the United States, such as the Northeast Historic Film Archive, have supported the collection and preservation of amateur and other non-theatrical films. The foundation of the 'Small Gauge Task Force' in 1999, by the Association of Moving Image Archivists, was also important. Other initiatives and projects were geared towards raising public awareness. One such project is the yearly 'Home Movie Day', organised by the Center for Home Movies, which, as stated by its organisers, aims 'to transform the way people think about home movies by providing the means to discover, celebrate, and preserve them as cultural heritage'.[2] This event started out as a national event in the United States, and it soon became a worldwide phenomenon. The biennial Orphan Film Symposium, organised by film historian Dan Streible since 1999, was an equally important force. From the start, this influential symposium has drawn attention to all types of neglected moving images, including those made by amateurs. Furthermore, the 'Prelinger Archives', a collection of what its founder Rick Prelinger labelled 'ephemeral' films, including home movies, has received much attention by scholars, artists and archivists.[3] In 2002, Prelinger donated his collection of 60,000 ephemeral films to the Library of Congress, while a subset of this archive became available online via the Internet Archive.

In Europe, from the 1990s onwards, equally important steps were taken on regional, national and even transnational levels. In 1991, the European Amateur Film Association Inédits was established in Paris. The association was constituted by filmmakers, archivists, producers and scholars and aimed to stimulate the collection, preservation, study and valorisation of amateur films in Europe. Over the years, publicly funded policies emerged in several European countries, including Sweden, Italy, Belgium, Austria, France, Scotland, Luxembourg and Ireland. A special case is the Dutch Small-Gauge Museum (Smalfilmmuseum) founded by Henk Verheul (1948–2007) in 1985. Verheul passionately pleaded for the recognition of the cultural history of amateur filmmaking by collecting and preserving almost everything related to it. By the time the Netherlands Institute for Sound and Vision adopted the museum's collection in 2006, it consisted of thousands of amateur films (e.g. the Peereboom collection; see Chapter 1), national and international amateur film magazines and how-to guides, minutes of amateur cine-clubs and a vast collection of objects, including amateur film cameras and projectors.[4]

It is important to reflect on why home movies were so readily accepted and embraced as rich sources. Museums, documentary filmmakers, scholars and a wide audience all embraced this type of moving image because of its capacity to evoke a sense of the past. Artists appreciated the aesthetic and multiple layers of those texts; audiences often felt affected by nostalgia of images of a past long gone or adored the spontaneity and non-conformity of this tradition; and historians and anthropologists appreciated them as a way to gain an insight into other, non-official perspectives on everyday life. However, the same level of appreciation has been lacking for home videos. Analogue videotapes, like VHS, are particularly neglected. The cultural and social value of amateur video is still not acknowledged to be on the same level as home movies, also because the average duration of a videotape makes the whole archival process of selection, description and cataloguing a much more tedious activity. Another reason relates to the complex technical issues and the fact that there are many formats that circulated often during a short time span. This is a serious threat; video is more vulnerable and less durable than celluloid because it can suffer from both magnetic (the signal on the tape) and chemical (the tape carrier and/or the video machines) decay (Figure 6.1). Luckily, there are more and more archival initiatives that try to develop special strategies to collect and preserve video. Large archival institutions such as the Library of Congress, but also

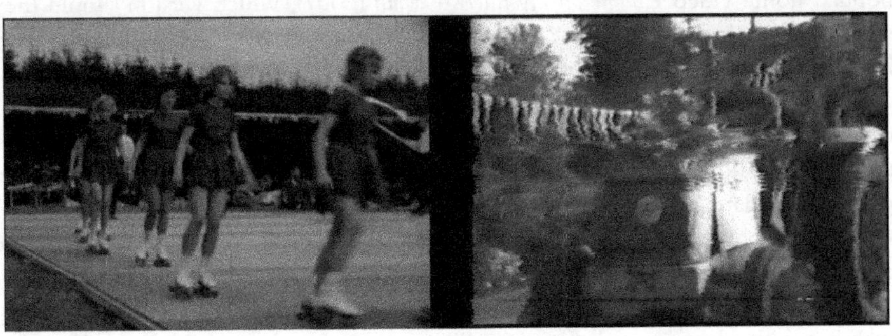

FIGURE 6.1 Still frame from *Film and Video Comparison*. 2017. Courtesy of the Groninger Archieven.

local audio-visual archives, deal with this urgent problem and thereby try to prevent a gap in our more recent audio-visual cultural heritage.

The same issues are faced when discussing contemporary digital amateur media. Already by 2003 UNESCO had underlined the general threat to digital cultural heritage, as can be read in their Charter: 'Digital heritage is made up of computer-based materials of enduring value that should be kept for future generations.' The ephemeral nature of digital materials triggered UNESCO to make explicit the immediate need for purposeful preservation actions. Even more pressing, according to UNESCO, are the multilingual and multi-script uses of the Internet, which causes disadvantages to non-English documents because of the predominant use of English on the Internet. That is why UNESCO wanted to make sure that digital heritage becomes and remains a global issue relevant to all countries and communities. Since then, web archiving has become an important topic on the agenda of libraries and archives, with the Internet Archive (since 1996) but one well-known example, although there many more now. The International Internet Preservation Consortium (IIPC), founded in 2003, stimulated international collaboration and helped to raise awareness of the fact that much of our present-day culture takes place online.

Most publicly funded archival institutions are aware of their responsibilities in regard to our digital audio-visual culture. However, there are many challenges to deal with when it comes to long-term digital storage. For one, the selection and collection of digital material is not an easy task: the materials are often recent, abundantly available and fragile due to rapid obsolescence. The evolution of different media formats occured more quickly than the archives have been able to keep up with: in many archives and libraries digital formats such as CD-ROMs and DVDs and other carriers have become antiquated. Archives also struggle with the issue of how to make the transition from archiving materials that are physical objects (film or tape), to more collaborative and ephemeral digital artefacts. In addition, some of the key elements of the archiving process, such as provenance (the origin of the record) and authority (who decides to select and preserve), do work differently in the YouTube era. For example, if an archive wants keep the popular home video *Charlie bit my finger – again* (2007), which version should they select: the original upload on YouTube, by Howard Davies-Carr, or should they, in order to illustrate the impact of the original video, also include the multiple, globally produced remakes and remixes – in some cases without clear authorship or ownership? And what kind of archive should preserve the videos: a national (British), local (London) or transnational/global (but where?) online archive? Would a proper candidate be the British Film Institute (collecting film and television), the UK Web Archive, hosted by the British Library (collecting web material) or maybe even the BBC Television Archive (collecting broadcasts)? More generally speaking, who should take responsibility for storing the daily uploads on video-sharing websites with such a global outreach? Will it be the users themselves or the companies that host the videos? Should online material be connected to one specific national identity or, rather, should the Internet Archive, a non-state and private institution, based in the US but with a more global outreach, and already hosting home movies and videos, preserve this type of amateur material?

Popular archives

Paradoxically, the question about what type of institution should take responsibility for YouTube uploads has become less relevant since YouTube has become the 'default' moving-image archive for the average user. Ask students to find audio-visual sources related to some recent historical event and YouTube will often be their first destination. YouTube is, however, not an archive in the traditional sense, because archives are often publicly funded institutions in which various archival specialists are responsible for the long-term preservation of historically, socially or culturally significant materials. Nevertheless, 'YouTube might well be an archive; that in the public mind it is not simply an archive but an ideal form of archive' (Prelinger 2009, 268). Prelinger uses several arguments to substantiate his claim: YouTube's vast collections offers the illusion of comprehensiveness; the mix of commercial and personal expressions makes it a very attractive place to find audio-visual materials; the platform offers easy access, even to people who would never visit an official archive; and lastly, the social-network features makes sharing easy (Prelinger 2009, 270–272). These aspects quickly made YouTube a truly global 'popular archive'.[5] Additional, easy-to use features that strengthen its use are curation, playlist creation, and tagging and commenting on videos. Those who enter the platform step into a parallel universe where babies are born or take their first steps; where children go to school, make friends, have fights, get bullied; where people fall in love and marry and chronicle their growing family. It is the place where you watch heated political debates, participate in social action or become a witness of horrible attacks, of people doing pranks and sick jokes. YouTube can also be a place to learn about mathematics, cars, new makeup styles, healthy recipes or new smartphones. It even has become a place where people announce their plans to commit suicide or where they ask for help to prevent themselves from doing so. Long before YouTube, Manual Castells had already predicted the capacity of the Internet:

> Every cultural expression, from the worst to the best, from the elitist to the most popular, comes together in this digital universe that links up a giant, historical supertext, past, present and future manifestations of the communicative mind. By doing so, they construct a new symbolic environment. They make virtually our reality.
>
> *(Castells 1996, 375)*

Being this huge database of millions and millions of mediated human traces, of happy and unhappy moments, makes YouTube a 'digital Wunderkammer' (Gehl 2009, 45), or, as Burgess and Green argued, 'a heterogeneous, but for the most part accidental and disordered public archive' (Burgess and Green 2009, 88). The combination of audio-visual content and the responses by viewers, including commenting, liking, hating, suggesting, supporting, etc., constitutes YouTube as a particularly valuable place for future historical research as it brings together the whole chain of production, distribution and reception. If preserved properly and durably, future historians might be able to understand the whole process of meaning making in digital audio-visual culture. However, there are several reasons to be cautious if one decides to regard YouTube as an archive. First, YouTube and its users are under no obligation to safeguard data, which means that the typical archival protocols and routines are absent with regard to acquisition, appraisal, description and preservation. Second, YouTube is resorting more and more to censorship by deploying algorithms that actively seek out 'unwanted' content, meaning uploads that could 'harm' the viewer or, more importantly, the advertiser. Ever since YouTube's infrastructure changed towards a business model based on monetising content via advertisements and by deals with major copyright holders from the entertainment industries, the company has become increasingly cautious about users' content. As such, the platform gradually prioritised the interests of the advertisers, who, in turn, want to avoid controversies at any cost. As a consequence, YouTube puts more effort in following the community guidelines that include regulations about, for instance, sexual explicit content, graphic violence, disturbing video footage, copyrighted material and hate speech.[6] More than ever, YouTube acts as an advertising platform rather than a video-sharing platform catering for a community of both large and small content creators. This means that it behaves not like an archive at all. Detecting infringements of their guidelines has led to millions of videos being blocked on YouTube. Under growing public pressure, in 2017 YouTube deleted millions of videos for content violation and in the first quarter of 2018, the platform removed 8 million videos.[7]

Another reason to be critical about the idea that YouTube could function as an archive is the fact that it is impossible to have precise knowledge about the exact parameters of this collection. The YouTube video repository is extremely dynamic. As stated before, YouTube's growth appears to be beyond control and almost 400 hours of content are uploaded every minute. In addition, there is also a continuous process of deletion, although it is unclear how much is deleted and by whom. Users with an account can delete the content they have uploaded. Once a user deletes a video, it is removed permanently from YouTube, without any possibility of recovery. This means that what remains on, or disappears from, YouTube is the responsibility of the user, because the platform is, indeed, not a traditional archive.

Lastly, there is another reason why YouTube should not be regarded as an archive: it doesn't like its own history. The search algorithms favour recent and popular uploads, rather than assisting users to find historical or unique material that has rarely been viewed before. In addition, the YouTube search filters only allow the user go back one year. Because of these constraints it is almost impossible to go back and trace user-generated content from many years ago. If a user abandons a channel, the footage becomes orphaned and eventually becomes untraceable.

To conclude, if we acknowledge that YouTube somehow has the potential of being an extremely rich audio-visual repository of our culture, then how do we keep safe this heritage for the future? How can we prevent videos from disappearing? Who owns this cultural treasure trove that provides free content, but that is also ruled by commercial companies who do not aim for long-term policies to protect our collective memory (Smith Rumsey 2016). The last decade demonstrated that it is more than likely that popular sites will eventually disappear or discontinue their services. The Internet has proved to be very transient since its inception: think of the social networking site Friendster.[8] This website had a vast number of users but then it suddenly disappeared, leaving the Internet without a trace. An exemption is the former app Vine, founded in 2012 and acquired by Twitter in 2016. The app service enabled the creation of six-second-long videos and had over 200 million active monthly users and more than 1.5 billion views. In January 2017 the video platform stopped working. It warned its users to download and archive their material to prevent their short videos from being deleted. Eventually, that did not happen; instead, Twitter supported an online Vine Archive (vine.go) that enables users to view four years' worth of six-second video loops.[9]

Do-it-yourself archives

In 2009 Yahoo discontinued its popular website GeoCities. Its disappearance marked the end of a 15-year-old history and around 38 million user-built pages. The Archive Team, a self-proclaimed rescue team for doomed Internet content, founded by Jason Scott in that same year, set out on a mission to safeguard parts of the website in an attempt to prevent Yahoo! from destroying 'the most amount of history in the shortest amount of time, certainly on purpose, in known memory. Millions of files, user accounts, all gone.'[10] From the Archive Team's perspective, GeoCities represents early Internet history when a strong rise of online amateur DIY cultures became visible with millions of everyday users turning into active producers of web content. The rescue operation mirrored this DIY culture, as the Archive Team called on volunteers to collaborate in downloading parts of the digital heritage on to local computers. Similarly, the Archive Team also entices volunteers to save relevant data from other early social networking sites such as Friendster and Hyves. Once a rescue is complete, locally stored data are then uploaded to the servers of the Internet Archive. By means of do-it-yourself or amateur-based tactics, coupled with communal and collaborative efforts, volunteers thus aim to prevent a 'data massacre'.[11]

According to Abigail de Kosnik, taking care of endangered digital culture and not waiting for publicly funded archives to step in indicates that 'memory has fallen into the hand of rogues' (De Kosnik 2016, 1). De Kosnik argues that there is a growing movement of amateur archivists – fans, pirates, social and political activists, volunteers and artists – who collect, share and redistribute media culture through so-called 'rogue archives'. These counter-initiatives represent an entirely new model of online archiving; one that entails collecting data in an idiosyncratic manner. An example would be amateur fan creations that reuse traces of audio-visual footage that was lost and that reappear in the public domain once uploaded on websites such as YouTube. This type of fan-based circulation of, at times, rare and elusive material has become a common practice in the age of the Internet (Greenberg 2008; Hilderbrand 2009). However, some scholars argued that in a networked culture sharing could be seen as a new kind of storage model (Snickars 2010, 304). Every file available online will at least be shared with someone, enhancing its chances of survival. It is a model that clearly differs from the institutional archives that collect unique documents rather than residual copies. In addition, rogue archives ignore the idea that experts should be responsible for what should or not be selected. Consequently, these self-designated archives might ignore notions of canon. On the contrary, according to De Kosnik, in this ecosystem each individual builds his or her own canon. As a result, a multitude of personal cultural canons – 'canons-of-one' – stimulate a kind of democratic archival turn (De Kosnik 2016, 74).

These types of non-canonical amateur archive are not a new phenomenon, as Lucas Hilderbrand also discovered when he reconstructed how, in the 1980s and 1990s, fans embraced the new affordances of the VCR and began to preserve on video tape enthusiastically whatever TV programmes or films they wanted to keep, thus likewise building personal non-canonical 'archives' (Hilderbrand 2009). This insight aligns with Gitelman's notion of the 'cultural logic of the copy' (Gitelman 2014, 109). To illustrate this, the video collection of 1980s TV programmes made by Paul Petrovsky, also known as Weird Paul, is a case in point. In Chapter 1, Weird Paul's home videos were discussed in order to show how television influenced his style and choice of topics. We learned that a year before the video camera came to his home in 1984, Paul's family already owned a VCR to tape TV shows, commercials and music videos. Compared with the other members of his family, Paul eventually became the most enthusiastic user of the VCR. Much later, he converted his original video tapes of television recordings and his home videos into digital files and uploaded them to his YouTube channel. On this channel, Paul adopted the vlog format to go back to the early days of his youth, not just by uploading the original VHS footage, but also by re-editing some footage into new videos and adding spoken commentary.[12] In his vlog *My First Videotape 1982*, Weird Paul explored all the aspects that were formative in his youth, including the many TV shows he taped on video when he was little. This particular video demonstrates what De Kosnik terms the 'canons-of-one', namely as a cherished aggregation of television programmes from the early 1980s, which does not so much represent any 'official' canon of great TV moments in US history, but rather shows a strictly personal one.

Another interesting point is that Weird Paul did not just share items from his video archive; he also discussed the challenges of reconstructing and retracing all of his old VHS tapes. After he noticed that some of his videotapes got lost, he goes to his parents' house, rummages through the attic and eventually retraces a missing

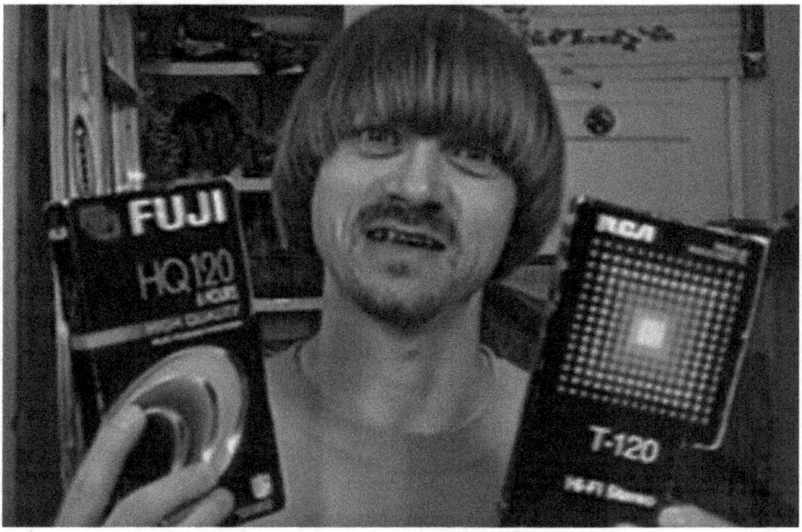

FIGURE 6.2 *Lost home movies VHS.* 1985. Screengrab via YouTube.

videotape, sharing the good news with his subscribers in *Lost home movies* (Figure 6.2). In this vlog, Paul starts by explaining to his viewers that the only evidence of his television recordings he owns is a handwritten list detailing the scenes and topics recorded on a six-hour-long VHS tape. However, to his great surprise, he then discovers that some of the scenes and fragments of that missing tape had been transferred to other tapes many years ago. Sadly, as it turned out, these snippets of 1980s' personal memories and pop culture were heavily damaged because Paul probably reproduced those clips one time too many.

Weird Paul can perhaps best be described as an 'new archivist', a term that Prelinger uses to describe someone who engages in a rather hybrid practice of archiving books, video and audiotapes, but also enjoys keeping digital content, thereby creating a highly personal and idiosyncratic archive (Prelinger 2010). This particular nature of Weird Paul's practices most clearly emerges in *A Conversation with my … old self* (2014) (see also Chapter 3). Weird Paul juxtaposed footage of his current 'vlogging' self with the digitised video footage of his younger, 'archived self' so as to create the illusion of a conversation taking place between the past and the present. It is uncanny, nostalgic and funny, but also proves to be an interesting experiment that goes beyond the idea of the archive as a storage space as it does create new types of reuse of the archive, adding new forms of temporality and performativity, while challenging the idea of an archival document as a fixed object but rather seeing the archive as an experimental encounter.

In sum, these 'rogue' archivists demonstrate a sense of shared responsibility towards our cultural heritage, which is often personal and collective at the same time. Richard J. Cox (2008) already suggested that archival professionals need the help of such individual allies to take care of our culture. Their archival efforts do not necessarily have to revolve around cultural expressions of everyday life, but could also focus on social and political activism. In the last decade, a multitude of activism-oriented archives started to document various organised socio-political struggles during the protests in Egypt and the war in Syria, but also of marginalised groups like the LGBTQ community or social movements such as 'Black Lives Matter' in the US. Some of these websites emerged during or shortly after major events. The archive Iamjan25.com, for example, went online shortly after 25 January 2011 when hundreds of thousands of Egyptians gathered on the streets to successfully protest against the Mubarak government. Many eyewitnesses captured the events during and also after the days of protest. The website collected more than 7,000 videos and pictures; as did the interactive database 18DaysInEgypt.com, after the website invited protesters to upload their content: 'You witnessed it, you recorded it. Now, let's write our country's history' (see Chapter 4).[13] Traditional archives have been collecting eyewitness accounts for much longer than these websites, but never before did the active content collection and distribution of amateur media have such immediacy or be related so closely to important events and participants.

Personal archives

According to archivist Richard Cox (2008, 3–4), collecting is a basic human instinct and is part of a basic human impulse to resist oblivion. Moreover, as Leah Dilworth noticed, a well-kept personal archive can be interpreted as 'a narrative activity' (Dilworth 2003, 7).[14] For quite some time, it was mostly affluent families that kept family archives – often standing in a long tradition of honouring the various artefacts and traces of their ancestry. Societal changes and new consumer technologies eventually enabled a democratisation of family archiving. During the twentieth century more and more people could potentially record their own personal or family history and turn their homes into mini-archives. As the British historian Raphael Samuel (1994) already observed in his famous book *Theatres of Memory* everyone could be an archivist and a historian. The history of amateur media technologies runs parallel to these changing dynamics. As we saw in Chapter 1, film became early on in the twentieth century a prime instrument for making and cherishing family memories; home-movie making developed into a new obligation for parents to create family archives. This development deeply influenced our sense of being part of history. Even with today's more ephemeral interactions on the Internet, such as those on Snapchat and WhatsApp, or on social media platforms like Facebook and Twitter, users continue to welcome the possibility of storing their daily online interactions. There is a paradox at work that, on the one hand, technology pushes users to produce countless volumes of multiple audiovisual expressions enabling their traces to pile up endlessly, while, on the other, the overload of files make people feel overwhelmed. They even may lose the emotional connection due to the amount of stored data. As a result, some users give up, leaving their digital files orphaned, in the sense of being uncategorised, untraceable and even unreadable because of obsolete formats and software.

Personal digital archiving has now become both a personal and a societal challenge. Since the 2000s, librarians, archivists, scholars and the industry itself have started looking for solutions. In the US, the Library of Congress opened a website that includes many 'how-to' tips and tricks and a preservation guideline.[15] In the UK, the Digital Preservation Coalition (DPC) was established in 2001with the goal of developing a digital preservation agenda.[16] In addition, there is the annual 'Personal Digital Archiving' conference in the US. And there is the input of companies, specialising in hard- and software or online cloud services; Microsoft and Apple, and also Google, are all interested in supporting the archival desires of their users. Research group Microsoft Research Cambridge (UK) especially conducted interesting research into what it describes as 'socio-digital system', exploring the relationship between technology and human memory.[17] In one of its reports, it explained how archiving can be understood as a stage that encapsulates complex considerations of what constitutes remembering and how this might help envision the future of domestic archiving systems (Banks et al. 2012). Conceptual design as a means to gain deeper knowledge is one of their methods, as shown by the experimental device 'Backup Box' (ibid.). This device is a wooden box that stores and displays the Tweets of a loved one who has passed away: by combining the digital with a more material quality of traces, people might feel stimulated to reminisce digital materials in new ways.

Most of the time, people employ different although not always archival-safe strategies: they store their images on to a computer, moving files around from one machine to the other; they send files from a laptop to a cloud storage services or use their email, sending video clips as attachments to which they can go back and view later in life (Marshall 2008). Others upload their mediated memories to social networks or they make hard copies at home using a printer or burn them to a CD or DVD. Some people retain their old computers plus compatible software as a means of archiving their precious files. Even more worrisome is the fact that many users keep their images on the device itself, without making a backup.[18] Each of these choices has its potential benefits and risks. Although we often think that our mediated memories are safely stored in folders on our desktop computer, in the cloud or on any other storage medium, we should not rely on assumptions of everlasting durability. For instance, technical solutions for the storage of family archives, such as cloud storage, are often also commercial solutions. Using the cloud to store private data has several drawbacks. Various tragic examples tell stories of lost digital memories due to forgotten passwords, closed accounts after the owner died, failed subscription fees or companies going out of business. In 2013, for instance, the website Ancestry.com acquired 1000memories.com, after which the users of the latter were given 30 days to retrieve their files. When they tried after the 30-day deadline, their data had already been deleted. The same happened to customers of the Kodak Gallery, an early online digital photo-storage service that, ironically, used the slogan: 'Keep Me, Protect Me, Share Me and I Will Live Forever'. After the service became inactive in 2012, thousands of private collections were deleted and lost forever.

Not only commercial failures but also regular technological changes may disrupt the roles and routines in memory and archiving practices of a household. For instance, in a research project that focused on archival strategies by everyday users, it became clear how changes in habits could easily disrupt the family archive.[19] In one family, the mother was in charge of making analogue photographs and putting them in the family albums, while the father created digital videos and photos and curated the digital family archive, using a private server and a website. As the mother explained, the world of digital memory-making belonged to her spouse and was therefore not part of her routine (Figures 6.3 and 6.4). So, when the mother eventually did replace her analogue camera with a smartphone, she forgot to take pictures of the family on several special occasions. As she explained, she could not connect the new device to her old custom of taking pictures at Christmas. It shows what happens when new ones replace old machines without being fully integrated into established habits and routines. Another outcome of the research showed how the father, who was confident he had created a highly durable and secure digital archive, realised that only he had access to the password-protected server on which the family files were stored.[20]

The example demonstrates clearly that family archiving is not only a technological but also a social and cultural practice, with families having their own set of protocols (Garde-Hansen et al. 2009). Family members, for instance, quite often adopt different roles (as to who is in charge of making, editing, storing, distributing and screening the video), depending on their age, expertise and gender. Skills, roles and know-how about these different stages that are part of audio-visual memory practices can be distributed between individuals and generations. Still, the fast pace of technological change may outpace the in-house skills of different family members. Once people realise the risks, they feel overwhelmed by the many issues related to keeping, managing, sharing and sustaining a personal archive. The former Microsoft computer expert Catherine Marshall concluded the following in her user research studies on personal digital archiving: 'While institutional archiving efforts are making great strides forward, consumers are unintentionally flirting with digital brinkmanship' (Marshall 2008, 2).

Lost and found

In the British science fiction TV series *Black Mirror*, there is an episode called 'The Entire History of You' (UK, Channel 4, season 1, episode 3, 18 December 2011). It portrays an imaginable but dystopian future where humanity is doomed to remember everything because almost everyone has a chip implanted in their brain (see Chapter 3). This chip indiscriminately records and stores everything you do, hear and see. Instant playback is another feature, which enables one to replay the scenes of one's life as though it is a movie. As the narrative progresses, it becomes clear that such a feature makes people deeply unhappy, and the protagonist eventually destroys this automated recording and storage device by forcefully removing it from his body. The episode is an interesting allegory of the contradictory desires

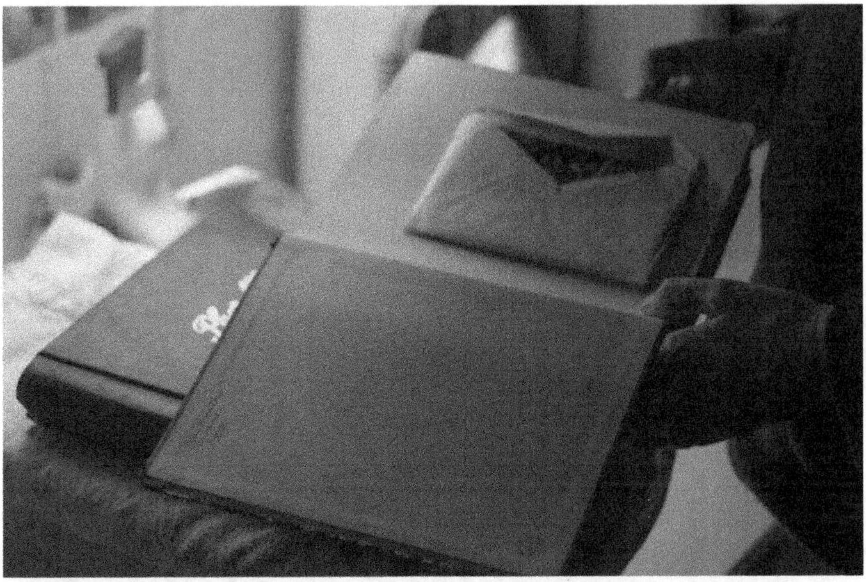

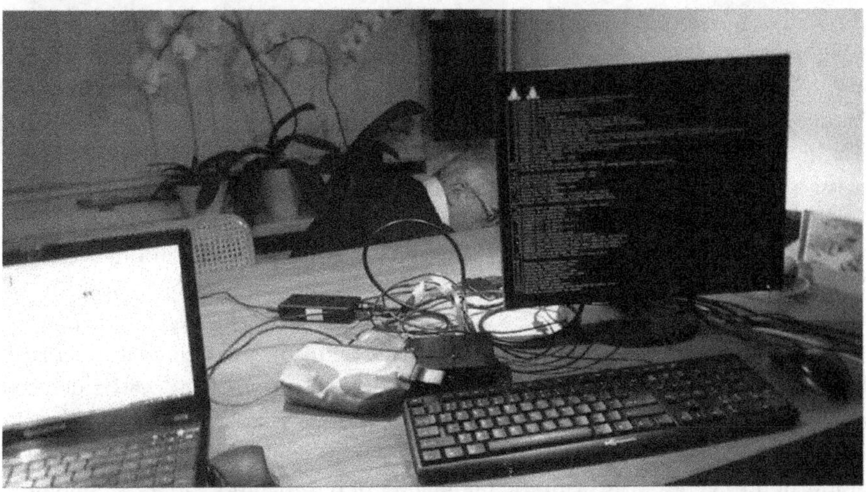

FIGURE 6.3 and **FIGURE 6.4** Stills from interview with family Jongsma. 2015. Courtesy of Lieuwe Jongsma.

to keep all our memories safe and nearby, while at the same time being overwhelmed by the oppressive force of memory overload. The episode shows our eagerness to embrace solutions from the tech industries to store whatever we can.

Such solutions offer also scientific opportunities, as Catherine Marshall proposed in her plea to collect and store all personal digital content posted on Facebook in a single virtual store so that historians of the future can do research in this gigantic dataset (Marshall and Shipman 2014). Likewise, some archivists pleaded to store digital content as much as possible hoping that someday the data can be properly described, accessed and reused. Clifford Lynch, one of the advocates of this approach, stated that either we can seek perfection and store very little or we can be sloppy and preserve more, discarding what is simply intractable (DeRidder 2011). This strategy resembles what Jason Scott of the Archive Team summarised as 'save now, ask questions later' (Scott 2014).

On the other hand, we should not equate memory with storage and storage capacity. 'Rather when we recollect our past, we construct rather than access and "replay" our memories' (Sellen and Whittaker 2010; Banks et al. 2012). In other words, memory is just as much about forgetting, as Aleida Assmann once stated

> When thinking about memory, we must start with forgetting. The dynamics of individual memory consists in a perpetual interaction between remembering and forgetting. In order to remember some things, other things must be forgotten. Our memory is highly selective. And our memory capacity is limited.
> *(Assmann 2008, 103)*

This insight is one of the reasons some scholars and critical thinkers argue for a more active practice of forgetting. They would prefer to resist the ongoing technological push of devices that encroach on our daily life. For instance, Martin Dodge and Rob Kitchin perceive media devices as technologies that produce digital shadows, stating that 'the totality of an individual's experiences, captured multi-modally through digital sensors and stored permanently as a personal multimedia archive' (Dodge and Kitchin 2007, 431). To resist such a perfect archive, they propose a range of algorithmic strategies such as erasing, blurring or even injecting noise, in order to upset the life-long records. Viktor Mayer-Schönberger is another outspoken voice in the debate on digital remembering who aims to reset the balance between remembering and forgetting. He believes that forgetting should be made 'just a tiny bit easier again than remembering' (Mayer-Schönberger 2009, 169). If technology can be designed in a way that we, automatically and almost unaware of it, store our data, it can also help us to avoid certain unwanted situations by introducing 'an expiration date for information to confront us with the infiniteness of our memory' (ibid., 15). Some of the issues that Mayer-Schönberger addressed did receive political action, such as when the European regulation concerning 'the right to be forgotten' was installed.[21] This means that individuals can request Google to erase 'irrelevant' links to certain search results. Since then, Google has received requests to remove more than 2 million links from its search results.[22] However, some problems that users are currently facing cannot easily be avoided. How, for instance, can we protect ourselves against unwanted memories that emerge due to algorithms employed by social media services? How can we restrain Facebook from reminding us of important past events we would rather forget? As Joanna Garde-Hansen et al. explained, mediated memories can return 'as mediatised ghosts to haunt participants far beyond the life-stage of their online social networking' (Garde-Hansen et al. 2009, 60).

To conclude, archiving amateur media has become an expansive and rewarding goal but it simultaneously remains a real challenge, especially when it comes to born-digital artefacts. In today's amateur media culture, everyday amateur media producers prefer either permanent storage or short-lived ephemeral existence. New and amateur media appear and then suddenly disappear, either on purpose or because they are hard to collect and store. The different archival models (institutional, popular, amateur or personal) aim to aid in keeping amateur media safe, but they are not always suitable or up to date. Basically, the complexities and contradictions that characterise present-day amateur media culture are mirrored by, and reproduced in, the complexities and contradictions of archiving digital memories. There are neither simple solutions nor simple guidelines, as amateur media archives – whether personal or collective – have been caught up in ethical, emotional, commercial, political and juridical contested areas. No matter how many guidelines or policy standards continue to be published, these issues will remain unsolved.

Notes

1 Lauren Maffeo, 'Google's Vint Cerf on How to Prevent a Digital Dark Age' , *The Guardian*, 29 May 2015. Available at www.theguardian.com/media-network/2015/may/29/googles-vint-cerf-prevent-digital-dark-age [15 December 2017].
2 For more on the CHM, see www.centerforhomemovies.org/about.
3 For an overview of the Prelinger Archives, see www.prelinger.com.
4 A large part of this film collection is now online: since the Amateur Film Platform was established in 2014 when the Netherlands Institute for Sound and Vision started collaborating with multiple regional archives in order to make their separate collections accessible in one portal: www.amateurfilmplatform.nl.
5 There are other video-sharing websites that host many videos as well: VIMEO, Daily Motion or Facebook. In China, Tudou (www.tudou.com) is one of the more popular websites.
6 www.youtube.com/yt/about/policies/#community-guidelines.
7 http://money.cnn.com/2018/04/23/technology/youtube-community-guidelines-report/index.html.
8 Friendster was founded as a social networking site in 2002 and gained over 100 million registered users. In 2011 it was relaunched as a social gaming site. In 2015 Friendster closed: www.friendster.com.
9 Archival policies are subject to change: see for the most recent guidelines on the vine Archive: https://help.twitter.com/en/using-twitter/vine-faqs.
10 Archive Team, www.archiveteam.org/index.php?title=GeoCities.
11 See the main page of Archive Team: https://archiveteam.org.
12 Weird Paul channel. www.youtube.com/channel/UChe9i_1QOu0izWI2l_CveKw.
13 For more information, see http://beta.18daysinegypt.com.
14 For a detailed discussion of archiving and collecting practices as features of the surviving instinct, see Annamaria Motrescu-Mayes, 'The Ascent of (Wo)man. Visual Priming in Early Photographs and Films of Ceylon, 1880s–1930s', in *Imagining the Isle Across. Vintage Photography from Ceylon*. Colombo: Alkazi Foundation for the Arts, 90–105.
15 For more information, see Library of Congress. http://digitalpreservation.gov/personalarchiving. See also *Perspectives on Personal Digital Archiving*, 2003. Available at www.digitalpreservation.gov/documents/ebookpdf_march18.pdf.
16 For a detailed report, see *Personal Digital Archiving*, 2015. Available at www.dpconline.org/docs/technology-watch-reports/1460-twr15-01/file.
17 See www.microsoft.com/en-us/research/research-area/human-computer-interaction.

18 See report: www.mintel.com/press-centre/technology-press-centre/sales-of-digital-cameras-decline-as-consumers-snap-up-smartphones.
19 This interview was part of a research seminar on 'The Living Archive' (Master History Today, University of Groningen) for which students interviewed peers or parents. For this interview, see the blog post by Lieuwe Jongsma: https://historage.wordpress.com/2015/01/05/analysis-interview-with-my-mother.
20 https://historage.wordpress.com/2014/11/27/case-1-my-fathers-archival-practice.
21 EU site 'Rights for citizens'. Available at https://ec.europa.eu/info/law/law-topic/data-protection/reform/rights-citizens_en.
22 For more on the issue, see Jamie Grierson, '"Right to be Forgotten" Claimant Wants to Rewrite History, says Google', *The Guardian*, 27 February 2018. Search engines can reject applications if they believe the public interest in accessing the information outweighs a right to privacy.

Selected bibliography

Aasman, Susan. 2014. 'Saving Private Reels: Archival Practices and Digital Memories (Formerly Known as Home Movies) in the Digital Age', in Laura Rascaroli, Gwenda Young and Barry Monahan (eds), *Amateur Filmmaking: The Home Movie, the Archive, the Web*. New York and London: Bloomsbury, 245–257.

Assmann, Aleida. 2008. 'The Canon and the Archive', in Astrid Erll and Ansgar Nünning (eds), *Cultural Memory Studies: An International and Interdisciplinary Handbook*. Berlin and New York: De Gruyter, 97–109.

Banks, Richard. 2011. *The Future of Looking Back*. Washington: Microsoft Press.

Banks, Richard, A. Sellen and A. Taylor. 2012. *Things We've Learned about Memory*, issue 2. Microsoft Research Cambridge (UK). Available at www.microsoft.com/en-us/research/wp-content/uploads/2016/02/thingswevelearnt-things_issue2_memory.pdf.

Briet, Suzanne. 2006. *What is Documentation? English Translation of the Classical French Text*. Lanham, MD: Scarecrow.

Burgess, Jean and Joshua Green. 2009. *YouTube: Online Video and Participatory Culture*. Cambridge: Polity Press.

Carrol, Evan and John Romano. 2011. *Your Digital Afterlife*. Berkeley, CA: New Riders.

Castells, Manuel. 1996. *The Rise of the Network Society, Vol. 1*. London: Blackwell.

Chun, Wendy. 2016. *Updating to Remain the Same: Habitual New Media*. Cambridge, MA: MIT Press.

Cook, Terry. 2001. 'Archival Science and Postmodernism: New Formulations for Old Concepts', *Archival Science*, vol. 1, no. 1, 3–24.

Cook, Terry. 2012. 'Evidence, Memory, Identity, and Community: Four Shifting Archival Paradigms', *Archival Science*, vols 2–3, no. 13, 95–120.

Cox, Richard J. 2008. *Personal Archives and New Archival Calling: Readings, Reflections and Ruminations*. Duluth, MN: Litwin Books.

De Kosnik, Abigail. 2016. *Rogue Archives: Digital Cultural Memory and Media Fandom*. Cambridge, MA: MIT Press.

DeRidder, Jody L. 2011. 'Benign Neglect: Developing Life Rafts for Digital Content', *Information Technologies and Libraries*, vol. 30, no. 2, 71–74.

Dodge, Martin and Rob Kitchin, 2007. 'Outlines of a World Coming into Existence: Pervasive Computing and the Ethics of Forgetting', *Environment and Planning B: Planning and Design*, vol. 34, no. 3, 431–445.

Edmondson, Ray. 2004. *Audiovisual Archiving: Philosophy and Principles*. Paris: United Nations Educational, Scientific and Cultural Organization. Document code: CI.2004/WS/2.

Featherstone, Mike. 2006. 'Archive', *Theory, Culture and Society*, vol. 23, no. 2–3, 591–596.

Garde-Hansen, Joanna, A. Hoskins and A. Reading (eds). 2009. *Save As … Digital Memories.* Basingstoke: Palgrave Macmillan.

Gehl, Robert. 2009. 'YouTube as Archive. Who Will Curate this Digital Wunderkammer?', *International Journal of Cultural Studies*, vol. 12, no. 1, 43–60.

Gitelman, Lisa. 2014. *Paper Knowledge: Toward a Media History of Documents.* Durham, NC, and London: Duke University Press.

Greenberg, Joshua. 2008. *From Betamax to Blockbuster: Video Stores and the Invention of Movies on Video.* Cambridge, MA: MIT Press.

Hawkins, Donald T. (ed.). 2015. *Personal Archiving: Preserving our Digital Heritage.* Trenton, NJ: Information Today Inc.

Hilderbrand, Lucas. 2009. *Inherent Vice: Bootleg Histories of Videotape and Copyright.* Durham, NC: Duke University Press.

Horak, Jan-Christopher. 1998. 'Out of the Attic: Archiving Amateur Film', *Journal of Film Preservation*, vol. 56, no. 6, 50–53.

Hoskins Andrew. 2011. 'Media, Memory, Metaphor: Remembering and the Connective Turn', *Parallax*, vol. 17, no. 4, 19–31.

Ishizuka, Karen L. and Patricia R. Zimmermann (eds). 2008. *Mining the Home Movie: Excavations in Histories and Memories.* Berkeley, CA: University of California Press.

Kula, Sam. 1983. *The Archival Appraisal of Moving Images: A RAMP Study with Guidelines.* Paris: United Nations Educational, Scientific and Cultural Organization. Document code: PGI-83/WS/18.

Kula, Sam. 1995. 'Film Archives at the Centenary of Film', *Archivaria*, vol. 40 (Fall), 210–224.

Marshall, Catherine C. 2008. 'Rethinking Personal Digital Archiving, Part 1', *D-Lib Magazine*, vol. 14, nos 3–4, 1–21.

Marshall, Catherine C. and F.M. Shipman. 2014. 'An Argument for Archiving Facebook as a Heterogeneous Personal store', in *Proceedings of the 14th ACM/IEEE-CS Joint Conference on Digital Libraries* (JCDL '14). Piscataway, NJ: IEEE Press, 11–20.

Mayer-Schönberger, Victor. 2009. *Delete.* Princeton, NJ: Princeton University Press.

Prelinger, Rick. 2009. 'The Appearance of Archives', in Pelle Snickars and Patrick Vonderau (eds), *The YouTube Reader.* Stockholm: National Library of Sweden, 268–275.

Prelinger, Rick. 2010. 'We Are New Archivists: Artisans, Activists, Cinephiles, Citizens', Reimagining the Archive, UCLA, November 2010. Available at www.slideshare.net/footage/reimagining-the-archive-keynote-presentation.

Samuel, Raphael. 1994. *Theatres of Memory: Past and Present in Contemporary Culture, Vol. 1.* London and New York: Verso.

Scott, Jason. 2014. 'From Colo to Yolo: Confession of the Angriest Archivist', speech at the Bacon Conference, London, 16–17 May 2014. Available at http://devslovebacon.com/conferences/bacon-2014/talks/from-colo-to-yolo-confessions-of-the-angriest-archivist.

Sellen, Abigail and S. Whittaker. 2010. 'Beyond Total Capture: A Constructive Critique of Lifelogging', *Communications of ACM*, vol. 53, no. 5, 70–77.

Sheldon, Karan. 2017. 'A Place for Moving Images: Thirty Years of Northeast Historic Film', in Martha J. McNamara and Karan Sheldon (eds), *Amateur Movie Making. Aesthetics of the Everyday in New England Film, 1915–1960.* Bloomington: Indiana University Press, 17–39.

Snickars, Pelle. 2010. 'Archival Transitions: Some Digital Propositions', in Kingsley Bolton and Jan Olsson (eds), *Media, Popular Culture and the American Century.* Stockholm and London: Jan Libbey, 302–329.

Smith Rumsey, Abby. 2016. *When We Are No More: How Digital Memory Is Shaping Our Future.* New York: Bloomsbury Press.

Streible, Dan. 2007. 'The Role of Orphan Films in the 21st Century Archive', *Cinema Journal*, vol. 46, no. 3, 124–128.

UNESCO. 1980. *Recommendation for the Safeguarding and Preservation of Moving Images*. Available at http://portal.unesco.org/en/ev.php-URL_ID=13139&URL_DO=DO_TOPIC&URL_SECTION=201.html.

UNESCO. 2003. *Charter on the Preservation of Digital Heritage*. Available at http://portal.unesco.org/en/ev.php-URL_ID=17721&URL_DO=DO_TOPIC&URL_SECTION=201.html.

Uricchio, William. 2009. 'Moving Beyond the Artifact: Lessons from Participatory Culture', in Marianne van den Boomen, Sybille Lammes, Ann-Sophie Lehmann and Joost Rae (eds), *Digital Material: Tracing New Media in Everyday Life and Technology*. Amsterdam: Amsterdam University Press, 135–147.

AFTERWORD

This book is meant as a preliminary exploration of various amateur media practices and examples dating from the early 1900s to the mid-2010s. It explores a variety of case studies, from stereotypical representations of domesticity to horrific images of trauma and war, from home movies showing mundane activities as a means of concealing the daily dangers of a military occupation, to children and adolescents' explorations of the 1980s video culture and YouTubers' reckless live-streaming in the early 2000s of scenes of sexual abuse and suicide. Also considered are accounts of amateur citizen journalism and of multiple counter-histories, whether of colonial fake ethnographies, of crimes against humanity or of compulsive vlogging. In particular, the book aims to address the shift in amateur media practice from the domestic to the public, both in terms of topics and themes, and of distribution and viewing practices – from the luxury of private (family) screenings in the early twentieth century to the twenty-first century online, live broadcast of monetised private and collective identities for the consumption of global audiences.

Working on this book project was an intense and rewarding journey through a long century of amateur media technologies, each appropriated by amateur media makers with diverse understandings and protocols for using visual narratives. The case studies discussed throughout the book have been interpreted through the lens of a media historian and of a visual anthropologist; hence multiple theories have been tested to encompass the survey of past and contemporary amateur media cultures – all viewed as expressions of specific social, cultural, political and psychological frameworks. The authors' interpretative dialogue provided different critical perspectives that traced technological, aesthetic, ideological and economic interactions and interrelations. One unplanned outcome was the mapping of several theoretical agendas defining the 'ephemerality' of amateur and new media as the feature of what was once outside official archiving protocols. The authors have also explored the process of visual priming evident across old and new amateur media practices, including the online daily streaming of videos, by way of re-interpreting potential counter-histories. Rather than being a textbook or a detailed introduction to amateur media, the book offers a kaleidoscopic yet detailed overview of key historic, theoretic and technological developments in this cross-disciplinary field of studies. Perhaps an appropriate concluding note would be to echo William Uricchio's opinion (see Foreword) that *amateur* is both a difficult concept to define and a highly contested, ever-changing key feature of contemporary media and digital culture.

MEDIA LIST

7ac2dc3. 2012. *Nana's birthday surprise*. YouTube video, 3.58 mins. Uploaded on 22 March 2012. www.youtube.com/watch?v=-0Qx75GsKI4.

Anner, Polly. 2017. *DaddyOfive explanation deleted video*. YouTube video, 12.00 mins. Uploaded on 22 April 2017. www.youtube.com/watch?v=pwcorpHu8WQ.

Atlanta Journal-Constitution. 2018. *What is a 'Finstagram?*, YouTube tutorial, 1.23 mins. Uploaded on 22 January 2018. www.youtube.com/watch?v=LkOwCutgsAY.

Blaze, Jennie. 2012. *mommy drunk*. YouTube video, 1.48 mins. Uploaded on 13 April 2012. www.youtube.com/watch?v=uyUsteVTV1g.

Content With Jeremiah. 2012. *A Conversation With My 12 Year Old Self: 20th Anniversary Edition*. YouTube video, 3.46 mins. Uploaded on 5 July 2012. www.youtube.com/watch?v=XFGAQrEUaeU.

Court TV News. 1992. *California v. Powell, et al.* TV episode, 1 hour and 51 mins. 29 April 1992. www.youtube.com/watch?v=rMESBBEQTV0&t=2467s.

DaddyOFive. 2017. *DaddyOFive Founders Issue Public Apology*. YouTube video, 2.51 mins. Uploaded on 28 June 2017. www.youtube.com/watch?v=yeraLEdNOBA.

Davidi, Guy and Emad Burnat. 2012. *5 Broken Cameras*. France/Israel, 94 mins.

Farocki, Harun. 1969. *Inextinguishable Fire*. Germany, 28 mins.

Farocki, Harun. 2007. *Respite*. Germany, 39.33 mins.

Festen, Theo. 1942–1943. *One day based on many days* [Een dag opgebouwd uit vele dagen]. 16 mm film, 19.07 mins. FLM14072. Eye Film Museum, Amsterdam.

Franco, Phillipede. 2017. *Wow… we need to talk about this*. YouTube video, 13.44 mins. Uploaded on 17 April 2017. www.youtube.com/watch?v=fvoLmsXKkYM.

Good Morning America. 2017. *Popular YouTube family speaks out about backlash from prank videos*. YouTube video, 5.01 mins. Uploaded on 28 April 2017. www.youtube.com/watch?v=t2hDM_I25mE.

Groninger Archieven. 2017. *Film and Video comparison*. Vimeo video, 1 hour and 7 mins. https://vimeo.com/207081928.

Harmukh News. 2018. *Reporter Angel Gahona shot dead during live broadcast in Nicaragua*. Vimeo video, 4.46 mins. Uploaded on 22 April 2018. https://vimeo.com/266000627.

HDCYT. 2007. *Charlie bit my finger-again!* YouTube video, 0.55 min. Uploaded on 22 May 2007. www.youtube.com/watch?v=_OBlgSz8sSM.

Holliday, George. 1991. *Rodney King Video Tape*. Video recording. First broadcast on KTLA, 3 March 1991.

Jongsma, Lieuwe. 2014. *Interview with my father about his archival practice*. YouTube video, 17.12 mins. Uploaded on 22 October 2014. www.youtube.com/watch?v=8N86TbT2KLo.

Jongsma, Lieuwe. 2015. *Interview with my mother about her archival practice*. YouTube video, 17.43 mins. Uploaded on 2 January 2015. www.youtube.com/watch?time_continue=11&v=A-iG-NfNc1U.

McCrudden, Michael. 2017. *YouTube show Poppy – Before they were famous*. YouTube video, 8.02 mins. Uploaded on 7 August 2017. www.youtube.com/watch?v=ByALPykLvDU.

McKnight, Gordon. 1969. *Super 8 Stories Extra Footage: Troubles Footage, August 1969*. 2.25 mins. Northern Ireland Digital Film Archive. https://digitalfilmarchive.net/media/super-8-stories-extra-footage-troubles-575.

Najem, Muhammad. 2017. *I am Muhammad Najem I am fifteen years old from the Eastern Ghouta*. YouTube video, 0.25 sec. Uploaded on 7 December 2017. www.youtube.com/watch?v=mka9iyFc4IM.

Najem, Muhammad. 2018. *Bashar Al-assad, potin and khaminei killed our childhood Save us before it is too late*. YouTube, 0.34 sec. Uploaded on 15 January 2018. www.youtube.com/watch?v=v5g6DPwD4B.

Neistat, Casey. 2017. *DEMONITIZED DEMONITIZED DEMONITIZED*. YouTube video, 15.22 mins. Uploaded on 17 October 2017. www.youtube.com/watch?v=HZakJFqdpRY&t=470s.

Peereboom, Max. 1937–1942. *Compilation family Bouman-Noach in Vlissingen* [Diverse opnamen familie Bouman-Noach in Vlissingen]. 8 mm film, 20.51 mins. The Netherlands Institute for Sound and Vision, Hilversum. www.amateurfilmplatform.nl/films/diverse-opnamen-van-familie-bouman-noach-in-vlissingen-amateuropname-max-peereboom.

Poppy. *I am Poppy*.2015. YouTube video, 10.01 mins. Uploaded on 6 January 2015. www.youtube.com/watch?v=fpCXxqiTjqE.

Poppy. 2015. *Everybody wants to be Poppy*. YouTube video, 2.23 min. Uploaded on 22 September 2015. www.youtube.com/watch?v=qjCSH2e-cOo.

POPPY – Before They Were Famous. YouTube video, 8.02 mins. Uploaded on 7 August 2017. www.youtube.com/watch?v=ByALPykLvDU.

Poppy, Delete Your Facebook. YouTube video, 3.02 mins. Uploaded on 23 January 2017. www.youtube.com/watch?v=k_Jq38JKN3A.

Rural Cork. 2013. *Let's Party on Skype! Ben in Australia - his family in Farran Co. Cork*, YouTube video, 7.31 mins. Uploaded on 5 May 2013. www.youtube.com/watch?v=ruXPvsPAlTA.

Shaytards. 2013. *Who are the Shaytards?* YouTube video, 0.43 mins. Uploaded on 1 October 2013. www.youtube.com/watch?v=XCNsQ-lLQV0.

Shaytards. 2015. *The kids are vlogging!* YouTube video, 11.49 mins. Uploaded on 1 July 2015. www.youtube.com/watch?v=DZFyIWnH9no.

Shaytards. 2018. *i did not edit this vlog*. YouTube video. 13.51 mins. Uploaded on 21 March 2018. www.youtube.com/watch?v=KWDUojLbxn4.

Shaytards. 2016. *#WhyIVlog*. YouTube video, 9 mins. Uploaded on 28 October 2016. www.youtube.com/watch? v=krYAuFTjLFc&feature=share

Shesnailie, 2013. *JenniCam's Jenni on Letterman's Late Show*. YouTube video, 7.20 mins. Uploaded on 27 October 2013. www.youtube.com/watch?v=0AmIntaD5VE&t=301s.

Sri Lanka's Killing Fields. 2011. Channel 4 on demand. 49 mins. www.channel4.com/programmes/sri-lankas-killing-fields/on-demand.

Trippy, Charles and Allie Wes. 2016. Internet Killed TV, S8, E2475, Why is this so funny?!? (5.17.16 – Day 2574). YouTube video, 11.38 mins. Uploaded 18 May 2016. https://www.youtube.com/watch?v=_2jM1aAlWyI.

unclenats. 2012. *Is YouTube Amateur Hour Over?* YouTube video, 1.46 mins. Uploaded on 5 October 2012. www.youtube.com/watch?v=d4C9146WKCg.

Van der Heijden, Tim 2014. *Staging the Amateur Dispositif*, Vimeo video, 16.43 mins. Uploaded on 14 May 2014. https://vimeo.com/95314562.

Weird Paul. *Weird Paul Channel Trailer! Original Vlogger 80s Nostalgia Retro Vintage 1980s.* YouTube video. 49 secs. Uploaded on 17 May 2015. www.youtube.com/watch?v=TV2kw8LszKY.

Weird Paul. 2012. *First night with the video camera 1984.* YouTube video, 1.49 mins. Uploaded on 29 February 2012. www.youtube.com/watch?v=v303z4cCIg0.

Weird Paul. 2012. *We're not gonna take it. Fan Video 1985 Twisted Sister music video -(Weird Paul) Bent Brother.* YouTube video, 4.08 mins. Uploaded on 18 June 2012. www.youtube.com/watch?v=hrjdjZUW2VE.

Weird Paul. 2014. *A Conversation With My 13 Year Old Self: 30th Anniversary Edition.* YouTube video, 3.11 mins. Uploaded on 22 September 2014. www.youtube.com/watch?v=E8LjvyMOvhg&t=1s.

Weird Paul. 2015. *Lost Home Movies VHS 1985 - (Weird Paul) 80s vhs camera footage memories.* YouTube video, 4.37 mins. Uploaded on 17 August 2015. www.youtube.com/watch?v=ZXCGc7Jmh7w.

Weird Paul. 2015. *My First Videotape 1982 VHS - (Weird Paul) old vintage VHS tape footage VCR nostalgia.* YouTube video, 3.46 mins. Uploaded on 26 January 2015. www.youtube.com/watch?v=uzBtA3i0hhw&t=38s.

Weird Paul. 2016. *Family Christmas Gifts 80s - (Weird Paul) Memories Video Presents Vlog Christmas Morning 2016.* YouTube video, 5.57 mins. Uploaded on 19 December 2016. www.youtube.com/watch?v=WrynowOZ7G8.

Welsh, Brian. 2011. 'The entire history of you', *Black Mirror*, series 1, episode 3, 49 mins. Aired on 18 December 2011 on Channel 4 (UK).

Williams Collection, Centre of South Asian Studies, University of Cambridge. www.s-asian.cam.ac.uk/archive/films/collection/williams-collection.

Wilson, Roy Edgerton. 1950s. *Operations in Malaya.* Malaya and UK. 8mm. Bristol City Council Archive, UK.

yo guys this is my twitter live and this is my sister playing with her toys lol so yea enjoy the live stream. Periscope, 11.21 mins. Uploaded in 2016. www.pscp.tv/w/1YqJDXMvEPQJV.

INDEX